The Viper on the Hearth

RELIGION IN AMERICA
Harry S. Stout, General Editor

Recent titles in the series:

The Viper on
the Hearth

Mormons, Myths, and the
Construction of Heresy

UPDATED EDITION

Terryl L. Givens

OXFORD
UNIVERSITY PRESS

OXFORD
UNIVERSITY PRESS

Oxford University Press is a department of the University of Oxford.
It furthers the University's objective of excellence in research, scholarship,
and education by publishing worldwide.

Oxford   New York
Auckland   Cape Town   Dar es Salaam   Hong Kong   Karachi
Kuala Lumpur   Madrid   Melbourne   Mexico City   Nairobi
New Delhi   Shanghai   Taipei   Toronto

With offices in
Argentina   Austria   Brazil   Chile   Czech Republic   France   Greece
Guatemala   Hungary   Italy   Japan   Poland   Portugal   Singapore
South Korea   Switzerland   Thailand   Turkey   Ukraine   Vietnam

Oxford is a registered trademark of Oxford University Press
in the UK and certain other countries.

Published in the United States of America by
Oxford University Press
198 Madison Avenue, New York, NY 10016

Library of Congress Cataloging-in-Publication Data

The viper on the hearth: Mormons, myths, and the construction of
heresy / Terryl L. Givens. — Updated ed.
p. cm.
Includes bibliographical references and index.
ISBN 978–0–19–993380–8 (pbk.: alk. paper)   1. Mormon Church—Controversial
literature--History and criticism.   2.   Church of Jesus Christ of Latter-Day
Saints—Controversial literature—History and criticism.   3. American
literature—19th century—History and criticism.   I. Title.
BX8645.5.G58 2013
289.3—dc23
2012025138

ISBN 978–0–19–993380–8

For Fiona

CONTENTS

ACKNOWLEDGMENTS

My love of history generally and the history of Mormon representations specifically was shaped by my father, who often urged me to take the elements of his anti-Mormon collection and study their patterns and significance. To him I also owe the initial idea for the project. His enthusiasm and advice carried me over many obstacles, and I treasure the many collaborative discussions we shared on the subject.

I am fortunate to have a number of professional friendships that were immensely important in this work's evolution. Louis Schwartz read drafts and tirelessly offered incisive, provocative criticism. He is a subtle thinker and approached my project with the same kind of energy and passion he devotes to his own work. Several years ago he volunteered me, in my absence, to make a faculty presentation on what was then a mere outline for a paper. His gesture was rash, presumptuous, and, it would seem, the catalyst I needed to begin the project in earnest. When I was further encouraged by the late professor Wayne C. Booth to turn drafts for two articles into a full-length treatment, the present book began to take shape. My good friend Anthony Russell vigorously debated numerous points with me, and made me a more careful thinker and writer.

W. D. Taylor, a scholar of American literature, was especially encouraging in early stages, reviewing drafts and insisting that this was a book I needed to write, while another good friend, Gardner Campbell, provided productive provocation of his own by hinting that perhaps this was a book I could not write. H. B. Cavalcanti offered rich insights and source material relating to matters of religious sociology. Generous support for my research has been provided by the University of Richmond, and Nancy Vick and Kit Davison at Interlibrary Loan successfully created the illusion that I was working in the midst of a major research library's collections. I here acknowledge the kind permission of SUNY Press to incorporate in chapter 8 material I published in *Mediation and Violence in Contemporary Culture* (eds. Ronald Bogue and Marcel Cornis-Pope, 1996). A portion of chapter 7 appeared previously in the journal *Nineteenth-Century Contexts* (winter 1994).

I have been ably assisted along the way by three research assistants: Carrie Woods, Lisa Devine, and Kelly Bruce. My special thanks go to William Slaughter, photo-archivist at the LDS archives in Salt Lake City, and to the LDS Historical Department generally, for their warm cooperation. Tom Wells and the staff at the Photographic Archives at the Harold B. Lee Library, Brigham Young University, were also helpful in securing photographs. Professor Clark Johnson provided useful historical criticism. As this second edition goes to press, I must make special mention of Cynthia Read, my editor at Oxford. Few people have done as much to further the project of a high-quality religious scholarship in America, freed from the clutter, noise, and manipulations that this book chronicles. I thank her for her faith and friendship. Finally, as ever, my loving gratitude goes to my wife, Fiona, partner in the joys of my life and collaborator in all my writing ventures.

The Viper on the Hearth

⌒⋎⌒

Introduction

Fictions can degenerate into myths whenever
they are not consciously held to be fictive.
                    Frank Kermode, *The Sense of an Ending*

In the heyday of the American humorous tradition, few subjects were off-limits. If Artemus Ward could swagger through a defeated Richmond gloating and joking about Confederate defeats before the blood had even stopped flowing, surely that American curiosity known as Mormonism could hardly hope to escape unscathed. Ward, in fact, would devote the second half of his *Travels* (1865) to that very subject. The section called "Among the Mormons" contains a short fiction entitled "A Mormon Romance—Reginald Gloverson." It is not really a story, and hardly—at only nine pages—a sketch. There is no plot to the piece, just a "young and thrifty Mormon, with an interesting family of twenty young and handsome wives," who dies and leaves his widows to argue about which one gets to put flowers on his grave. Then they are summarily "inherited" by the next eager-beaver polygamist who arrives on the scene and makes a collective proposal to the collective "Widow Gloverson." In attempting to draw a conclusion from this story, Ward writes, "Does not the moral of this romance show that—does it not, in fact, show that . . . —well, never mind what it *shows*. Only this writing Mormon romances is confusing to the intellect. You try it and see."[1]

Ward's difficulty in drawing morals from Mormon practices may be excused him. Certainly humor does not need to justify itself in terms other than the effect it produces, and Ward here, as elsewhere, is in fact very funny. Actually, however, his illustration "shows" a great deal as well. While distortion of one kind or another is an inevitable consequence of literary representation, caricature is especially revealing of social or political circumstances the author is motivated to represent. More specifically, caricature tends to illuminate what is valued and what is shunned by various social groups at different historical junctures. Edward Said has said that cultural "self-confirmation" in general is "based on a constantly practiced differentiation of itself from what it believes to be not itself. And this differentiation is frequently performed by setting the valorized culture over the Other."[2] Caricature represents one mode of exaggerating otherness that is both self-revealing and entertaining.

In the case of Ward, selecting the romance genre as a vehicle for his piece sets up a series of expectations that includes such elements as binary relationships, mutual love interests, and happy resolutions. In the world of Mormon polygamy, however, all such expectations are hopelessly dashed, and the narrative collapses in on itself as a result of the failure of genre conventions to negotiate the unfamiliar terrain of mass courtships, collective rivalries, and the hitherto unimagined complexities of plural widowhood and bereavement. This may all be "confusing to the intellect" indeed, although it makes for great farce.

Ward's intellectual discomfiture in the absence of applicable methods of tried-and-true literary closure may very well have been only half feigned. For the larger confusion of which his parody is but a shadow is the more serious discomfiture of an American public when faced with the many unprecedented threats to orthodoxy—religious, cultural, and social—Mormonism posed. Ward's difficulty in reducing Mormonism to moralistic romance, in other words, has its parallel in the resistance of Mormonism to societal modes of understanding and control. His comic sketch also shows that differences so extreme as to defy assimilation into familiar literary structures may require more innovative methods of representation if they are to be disarmed and contained. As we shall see, most creators of Mormon characters have tended to choose methods more alarmist in nature than comic.

Fictional depictions of Mormonism, then, may serve as more than barometers of hostility or contempt, or as examples of their cultural propagation. Fiction—popular fiction especially—may take us beyond the historical origins of anti-Mormonism to register not just the presence of conflict and contention, but the psychological and ideological causes and consequences of those tensions among the non-Mormon populace. In the context of nineteenth- and early twentieth-century America, popular depictions of Mormonism both revealed and exploited any number of anxieties and contradictions involving a vast readership's sense of self and of nation. At the same time, as I hope to show, writers of popular fiction made use of their craft to work toward resolutions of the dilemmas Mormonism posed to mainstream culture. The imaginatively rendered instances of "the Mormon problem" and the creative solutions to that problem that fiction made possible are documents that have a great deal to tell us about how identity can be threatened, manipulated, and constituted.

The list of authors who resorted to the Mormon caricature as a stock villain spans genres from mystery to western to popular romance, and it includes both American and English writers: from Arthur Conan Doyle's first Sherlock Holmes mystery to Zane Grey's *Riders of the Purple Sage*, from Robert Louis Stevenson's *Dynamiters* to Jack London's *Star Rover*, as well as scores of novels, short stories, and poems by lesser names. Such works of fiction can add a great deal to our understanding of the long and tumultuous relationship between Mormonism and American society.

Historical reasons for ridicule of and even hostility toward the Mormon religion vary with both the period and setting of the Mormon story. The earliest recorded complaints concerned the church's religious peculiarity based on ongoing revelation and additional scripture, and the threat its phenomenal missionary success posed to mainstream churches. In addition, Mormons preached an irksome doctrine of exclusivity and engaged in communalistic economic practices (and prosperously besides). Unlike the Shakers, who considered their unconventional way of life a higher order of existence but only for those who felt the call to so live, the Mormons claimed a monopoly on the path to salvation.

These irritants would later be exacerbated by polygamy, the most notorious of their religious practices. Although this doctrine was not publicly announced until 1852 and was not practiced by the majority of Mormons, from the later nineteenth century to the present Mormonism has been synonymous in the minds of many with plural marriage.[3] Add to this the Mormons' role in frontier politics and the theocratic inclinations of the early Mormon leaders and we begin to get a sense of the complex of factors that contributed to "the Mormon problem."

The relationship between the sociopolitical context of the period and the Mormon persecutions has traditionally been the province of the historian, and has been well excavated. Still, the situation described by historians of Mormonism Leonard J. Arrington and Jon Haupt has changed little since their 1970 pronouncement that "few scholars have sought to improve their understanding of Latter-day Saint or Mormon history through a systematic analysis of fictional works which treat the Mormons."⁴ The following study in no way constitutes such a historical overview of the extensive body of anti-Mormon literature. It attempts, rather, to suggest that certain representational patterns we find in some of these works may contribute to our understanding of such issues as anti-Mormon persecution, the construction of heresy, and the construction of collective identity.

When neither militia, armies, prohibitions, nor divestment could succeed in quelling the Mormon menace, popular fiction provided a new front. Consistently recurring patterns in these representations reveal a proclivity to depict the Mormons as a violent and peculiar people. Physical and psychological coercion define the action, and Oriental, exotic characteristics define the villains. These representations contributed effectively to the refashioning of Mormonism from a religious sect into a secular entity, whose unpalatable religious features could the more easily be made the objects of public ridicule and censure. For, although the political and cultural conflicts Mormonism provoked were real enough, the peculiar challenges the new faith posed to religious orthodoxy—and the legitimate mechanisms available to meet them—were especially difficult to negotiate in the context of the early Republic. Fiction made it possible to reconfigure this conflict in terms that were consistent with American conceptions about the nature and limits of religious pluralism—and America's premier role in that tradition.

This is, therefore, a book about fiction and its political uses. And one of those political uses may be to reconfigure in its own terms a debate that is rooted—or at least entangled—in fundamentally religious conflicts. Specifically, I intend to show how fiction has served, in the case of Mormonism, to obscure the theological aspects of a century and more of discord and confrontation between Mormonism and American society. These religious roots of the conflict preceded the first allegations of polygamy, permeated the Missouri War and Illinois expulsion, continued into the Utah period, and inform the marginalization of Mormonism in contemporary American society. In the process, I hope to illuminate both the peculiar nature of the Mormon "heresy" and the contortions by which that heresy was reconstructed into a target more amenable to social censure and political solutions.

The phrase "viper on the hearth," which *Cosmopolitan* used to characterize Mormonism in 1911, suggests the urgency of a threat that has invaded the domestic sphere. The metaphor compounds the outrage over an incursion that has already been successful with a reminder that this violation strikes at the very heart of one's private space. But the metaphor is also

a hopeful one. To discern the serpent is to have just cause and opportunity for its destruction. Mormonism was seen to fit the bill in the first
two particulars. Even before the formal organization of the church, the
Book of Mormon was published and circulated and missionaries began to
add converts to the Mormon fold. And radical Mormon doctrines regarding God, scripture, "gathering," and, later, marriage, directly challenged
those sacred spheres of church, family, and American society. In the final
analysis, however, Mormonism was not so accommodating to the image
of a palpable threat uncovered. This is because it was, paradoxically, very
hard to see. Mormons were, after all, usually ethnically identical to one's
neighbors and even one's family. In fact, the lack of discernible parameters to the Mormon community, the dread of its "invisible tentacles,"
would be the most exacerbating factor in the anti-Mormon paranoia of
the nineteenth century. This anxiety necessitated a reconstruction of this
new community into one that was more readily identifiable.

The view of modern sociologists and other observers that Mormonism
itself came ultimately to represent an "indigenously developed ethnic minority" (Thomas O'Dea and Dean May),[5] "subculture" (Armand
Mauss),[6] a "global tribe" (Joel Kotkin),[7] or simply "a religion that became
a people" (Harold Bloom and Martin Marty),[8] is powerful indication of
how successfully Mormonism has been constructed into a distinct people with a distinctive set of identifying characteristics.[9] Ironically, of
course, assimilation in the late twentieth century was so successful that
in contemporary culture, "Mormon" can occasionally serve as shorthand
for a certain vision of mainstream American values of healthy, patriotic,
family-centered living. Nevertheless, that the term "Mormon" still functions as a powerful indicator of peculiar difference, in a way blatantly
unlike, say, Protestant denominational tags, is evident in a perusal of any
week's news items. One finds the media reporting that an FBI mole apprehended some years back "was a Mormon,"[10] that one of Bill Clinton's inspi-
rational gurus was a "Utah Mormon and author,"[11] and that acclaimed
scholar Laurel Thatcher Ulrich may be a "diligent and skilled historian,
for sure. But the fact is,…she's a very devout Mormon,"[12] and so on. A
"Presbyterian CIA agent" or a "Methodist sociologist" would be an absurd
juxtaposition. The journalistic appeal of the Mormon label is itself evidence that the term exploits a range of inferences and stereotypes that
obviously involve more than denominational affiliation. As we will see, in
political reporting, identification as Mormon is guaranteed. We will deal
with this practice in depth, as it starkly reveals the limits on representing
Mormonism as an innocuous cultural entity, in the face of what some continue to see as its threatening theological enterprise.

This virtual ethnicity of Mormons, to which their cohesiveness as a body certainly contributed, is in large measure a product of deliberate strategies of representation—strategies that both Mormon and non-Mormon had vested interests in perpetuating. To explain the reasons and strategies behind this construction, and the role popular fiction played in it, is the central project of this book.

I will begin by outlining the problem nineteenth-century writers and critics of Mormonism faced in reconciling a rhetoric of vituperation and a practice of exclusion with an ideology of Jeffersonian religious toleration and pluralism. One of the challenges Mormonism—like other heterodoxies—presented to its detractors, in other words, was that its religious radicalism was an opportunity for toleration at the same time it was an occasion for outrage. At those times when outrage carried the day, the pressures of pluralism made it desirable to cast the objectionability of Mormonism in nonreligious terms.

In chapter 2, I provide an overview of the history of the nineteenth-century "Mormon problem" with its attendant violence and conflict from the perspective of one of its participants, Warren Foote. I turn to examine the sources of that conflict in chapter 3. Nowhere will I suggest that social, economic, or political factors were irrelevant to the clash of religion and society. But I will maintain that none of these can be put forward as the central—or even a constant—factor in the long history of Mormon persecution. On the other hand, even when the theological dimensions of conflict are not decisive, they are inescapable and present a constant feature in anti-Mormon antagonisms.

In chapter 4, I situate Mormonism relative to contemporaneous heterodoxies to further illuminate what was distinctive and what was common about public hostility to this particular nineteenth-century religious innovation. The unique nature of the Mormon heresy I then explore in detail in chapter 5. Taking as my point of departure the claim of Rudolf Otto that the idea of the holy is the precondition for all religious experience, I suggest that Mormonism presents a reconceptualizing of the sacred that is not amenable to Christian orthodoxy. Its thoroughgoing demystification of the numinous, its radical historicizing of Christian origins, constitute a profanation of religion as traditionally conceived and practiced in the West. Mormonism, in other words, is heretical not by virtue of the articles of faith to which it demands adherence, but rather by virtue of the kind of faith it can be said to disable.

Having ventured to assert the ubiquity of the religious factor throughout Mormonism's history of conflict, and having defined the peculiar nature of the religious heresy Mormonism represented, I then turn in part 2 to examine how the study of fiction can corroborate these claims. One problem with traditional approaches to religious intolerance is the seemingly reasonable assumption that such animosities are essentially comprehended by a focus on the sources of friction. So, while I argue that the Mormon image prevalent throughout most of the nineteenth century was largely a response to a perceived Mormon heresy, in chapter 6 I suggest that tensions can be compounded, facilitated, and exaggerated by prevailing norms and mechanisms of rhetorical practice. Construction of the Mormon image was profoundly affected by revolutions in publishing, literacy, and literary form that conditioned an entire generation of literature hostile to religious heterodoxy.

The particular strategies popular-fiction writers inherited and adapted to Mormon subject matter are analyzed in chapter 7. Pervasive patterns of representation in a host of examples emerge as a means by which Mormon ethnicity and character are constructed in such a way as to alleviate the dread of contagion posed by this "viper on the hearth." At the same time, these representations, by recasting a religious conflict in terms of political struggle and ideological self-preservation, reveal the ideological conflicts present when a secular, pluralistic democracy engages the heretical.

Finally, I turn to recent developments in the representation of Mormons in popular culture. It is a cliché in Mormon studies that Mormonism successfully adapted itself to mainstream culture by the mid-twentieth century. I don't challenge this claim, but argue in chapter 8 that just as developments in rhetorical practice facilitated a public campaign against the religion in the nineteenth century, so have more recent developments conspired to restrain and domesticate literature of the hostile imagination in general. Still, the Mormon image in popular fiction was too versatile a tool to abandon once moral indignation became unmasked as bigotry. Recurrent uses to which Mormon characters have been put, in theater, television, and popular fiction, suggest the script may have changed considerably, but the resilient Mormon caricature has found new roles to play.

PART ONE

Mormonism, Politics, and History

CHAPTER 1

"Out of the Sphere of Religion": The Sacred, the Profane, and the Mormons

It is said that an altar of sacrifice was actually built...in the temple block, upon which human sacrifices were to be made.

Senator Aaron Harrison Cragin, on the U.S. Senate floor, May 18, 1870

Writers have characterized Mormonism as everything from "the American Religion" to the "Great Modern Abomination." For some, the story is simply told: Moved by a religious awakening in the area surrounding his home in upstate New York, a fourteen-year-old Joseph Smith went into a woods in the spring of 1820 in search of spiritual guidance. There, God the Father and God the Son appeared to him, initiating a series of heavenly communications that paved the way for the restoration of Christianity to the earth, which had dwindled into apostasy in the centuries after Christ's death. As prophet of the new dispensation, the young Joseph was led to a buried sacred record of the ancient inhabitants of America, which he translated "by the gift and power of God" and presented to the world as a scriptural companion to the Bible.[1] He preached the restored gospel to friends and relatives, and dozens and then hundreds and thousands flocked to the church he founded. But the forces of religious prejudice, intolerance, and jealousies stirred up a storm of opposition that drove the "Latter-day Saints" from New York to Ohio to Missouri to Illinois to the Salt Lake Valley. They made the Utah desert blossom as a rose, flourished as a people, and became the kingdom of God on earth.

For others, it is the story of a charlatan or a misguided mystic and his earnest but deluded followers. The tale involves literary forgeries, theological monstrosities, and moral outrages. Political misjudgments, bad timing, and a rhetoric of antirepublican theocratic ambitions combine to create a tragedy of errors. After expulsion by the state militia, later intervention by a federal army, and the crushing weight of legislative sanctions, deviance is finally domesticated, and confrontation becomes assimilation.

A prominent scholar of Mormonism has remarked that "the 'facts' of LDS history do not necessarily speak for themselves."[2] In part, this is because the sources of social conflict and religious strife are usually fraught with images, impressions, anxieties, and fears, none of them easily reducible to historical "facts." In plumbing the reasons behind the Mormon conflict—or behind any historical phenomenon—we find that perceptions were to a large extent the "realities" that did shape events.

Whether the Latter-day Saints in 1830s Missouri, for example, were abolitionists or neutrals in the slavery debate is still disputed. And whether the Utah Mormons offered human sacrifices in the Salt Lake Temple is not even a viable question for most respectable scholars. Nevertheless, that they were *perceived* as abolitionists was a decisive factor in their expulsion from the state of Missouri in 1838. And for a U.S. senator to cite allegations of human sacrifice in congressional debate was to render rumor an active ingredient in the federal legislative process where the fate of the Mormons was at that moment being shaped.

Images of entire peoples do not take shape unhindered and unfiltered, like the forms in reflecting pools. They are constructions that result from impassioned political rhetoric and from media portrayals, by pulpit bombast and by travelers' narratives. And in the last two centuries, they have been influenced by one of the most pervasive and powerful media of modern history—popular fiction. The story of Mormonism that fiction tells is distorted by a number of factors. Novels have their own conventions, novelists have axes to grind, and publishers have audiences to please and profit to make. But in spite of these competing factors, patterns of depiction in popular fiction may nevertheless illuminate some of the fears, anxieties, and animosities behind the Mormon conflict and may reveal something about the ways in which fiction constructs identity—of self and Other—in response to ideological and psychological needs. When *Cosmopolitan* published a series of vitriolic attacks on Mormonism under the heading "The Viper on the Hearth" (1911), the author invoked an image that captures a thematic core of over a century of representations of Mormonism, an image that I will attempt to explicate in detail.

COLONIALIST DISCOURSE AND MARGINALITY

Certainly more than the ordinary creative and political imperatives were at work in representations of the Mormons. Recent studies in colonialism, self-fashioning, and the construction of the Other have done much to illuminate the complex ways in which hegemonic discourse can operate.[3] Subordinate peoples or groups (women, African Americans, "natives") have typically been represented in ways that justify the inequality of power relations, and serve to rationalize or reinforce the identity, interests, or agenda of those in positions of dominance. Such processes have long been at work, from the first imposition of "barbarian" categories upon non-Greeks, through centuries of anti-Semitism, slavery, and colonialism, and down to a host of contemporary examples of political demonization and literary caricaturing of the unempowered Other. But sometimes, complications can arise in this strategy, as suggested by Peter Hulme's account of colonial reactions to cannibals: "Human beings who eat other human beings have always been placed on the very borders of humanity. They are not regarded as *in*human because if they were animals their behaviour would be natural and could not cause the outrage and fear that 'cannibalism' has always provoked."[4]

Hulme's idea that we are more disturbed by transgressive behavior displayed by our close counterparts than by utterly foreign entities is surely correct. More doubtful—and confused—is his claim that we do not "place" cannibals outside the human category because that would leave us without an explanation for the psychic trauma they cause (and, as he suggests elsewhere, because their placement outside the pale would be an unacceptable violation of observable facts). In reality, colonial discourse has found it relatively easy to dehumanize human populations (as in the case of an 1857 Supreme Court decision to declare African Americans a species of property). So pronounced was this colonial tendency by 1537 that Pope Paul III in that year found it necessary to declare in three bulls that Native Americans were in fact rational creatures and therefore were "human beings."[5]

Constructions to the contrary were in large part feasible because most colonizers enjoyed the signal benefit of encountering the Other across vast stretches of distance. Such encounters were therefore relatively unproblematic from the colonizers' points of view. Not only was military power often available to impose counterintuitive categories and construct identities with unhindered license, but there was also, in most colonialist encounters, a sufficient space to inscribe comforting and self-affirming distance. The vast oceans that separated cultures, the seeming lack of linguistic contiguity, the disparateness of skin color—all served as very literal spaces in which ideology and imagination had free rein to rationalize and reify difference in self-serving ways. The space suggested by radical difference is both the precondition and the great facilitator of that colonialist discourse that freely fashions identity.

The study of such encounters may emphasize the one-sidedness of colonial discourse as an act of imperialist aggression, as Edward Said does. Typically, Said writes, colonizers use language as a means of erasure, whereby alien identity is completely subordinated to the demands of imperialism and exploitation.[6] Mary Louise Pratt stresses the dialectic, or "transculturation" of colonizer and colonized, shifting emphasis from "separateness or apartheid" to "co-presence, interaction," in what she labels the "contact zone."[7] In this model, a foreign invader still controls the terms by which the identity of the host shall be constructed, but that invader is not himself unaffected by the process. For both authors, however, it is clear that the study of colonial discourse generally presumes that a preexisting disjuncture of history, geography, language, and culture is the material out of which self and Other construction are (relatively freely) built.

The situation becomes somewhat more complicated, however, when these constructions operate in the *absence* of great distances. Writers and chroniclers in such circumstances—whatever their political power—face serious difficulties of representation. Cannibalism encountered by a European an ocean away may be repugnant, but it would hardly be as distressing—or as challenging to domesticating discourse—as cannibalism discovered in one's neighborhood or family tree. These kinds of marginal categories especially test the limits of ideological construction; they are where the imagination, in its efforts to create complete alterity, meets empirical limitations, the constraints of observed and felt commonalities. These liminal realms, which include the heretic—and the fetus—host some of the most agonized and fractious conflicts of history.

This marginal status of Mormons has been noted by the distinguished sociologist Thomas O'Dea, who calls them "the clearest example to be found in our national history of the evolution of a native and indigenously developed ethnic minority."[8] Even if O'Dea exaggerates their status as ethnic group, Mormons clearly provide an excellent opportunity for the study of a marginal category rife with inconsistencies, discord, and clever rhetorical strategies, where familiar patterns of colonial discourse adjust to the difficulties imposed by empirical constraints.

To this day, debate continues as to whether Mormons are best understood in terms of their deviance and marginalized past, or as the quintessentially American religion—or even, perversely, as both at the same time[9]

Leo Tolstoy's reputed opinion that Mormonism was the quintessentially American religion is cited at second hand in a number of Mormon sources, as well as by Harold Bloom, who claims "there is something of Joseph Smith's spirit in every manifestation of American religion." Indeed, he adds, "what matters most about Joseph Smith is how American both the man and his religion have proved to be."[10] At the same time, of course, Mormonism was perceived—and often continues to be seen—as so far out of touch with mainstream American Christianity as to be "the Great Modern Abomination," a blasphemous parody of Christianity.

There is little question as to how the public by and large regarded the Mormons, at least in the early years of their existence. Persecution and ostracism may have their socially and religiously fortifying consequences, but Mormonism had no need to exaggerate its deviance or beleaguered status. Indeed, this persecution took place despite the fact that when Joseph Smith presented Mormonism's "Articles of Faith" to the world, he emphasized what Mormons shared with Christians in general. Mormonism's most inflammatory doctrines were revealed late in Smith's career (his teaching on the plurality of gods came only months before his death in 1844) or were in fact disavowed until the Saints were presumably safe in their Utah exile (where polygamy would first be publicly acknowledged in 1852).

In fact, from the date of their first unsuccessful bid for statehood, Mormons engaged in a quite conscientious "campaign of superior virtue," by which means they intended to convince their compatriots that they were *not* deviants, but rather more American than apple pie.[11] And, more to the point, detractors and hack writers were willing enough to exaggerate their deviance for them, as we shall see.

The public campaign against Mormonism, therefore, would seem to have been an easy affair on the face of it, since as Joseph Smith complained, its enemies ran the presses. Nevertheless, the contradictions and paradox of Mormonism's position do, in fact, present considerable challenges to its portrayers. Anti-Mormon fiction of the nineteenth century especially is rife with distinctive and surprising patterns that both respond to and condition Mormonism's peculiar place in American society. These patterns, I will argue, suggest a psychological motivation that only Mormonism's liminal status as an artificial ethnic group can explain.

MORMONISM AND ETHNICITY

The decisive factor in the way Mormonism is perceived and depicted concerns its indigenous origins and subsequent development into a community with cultural autonomy. This community, O'Dea writes, has "its own history, its own traditions, its conviction of peculiarity, and even its native territory or homeland."[12] He neglects to add that after finding refuge in the Salt Lake Valley, the Mormons would develop their own "Deseret Alphabet." Schoolchildren were taught the phonetic system, and a number of books were published in the artificial sound-based alphabet. Although the endeavor was short-lived, it is perhaps the best example ever of the reification of their cultural distinctness. O'Dea is far from alone in imputing such distinctive cultural status to Mormons. Writing more recently, Joel Kotkin prefers the term "global tribe" to characterize Mormons. Like "Jews, British, Japanese," etc., the Mormons have "a strong ethnic identity and sense of mutual dependence," "a global network based on mutual trust that allows the tribe to function collectively beyond the confines of national or regional borders."[13] The debate among sociologists as to what term most accurately categorizes Mormonism is not the point here. Clearly, the group transcended merely denominational status fairly early in the nineteenth century and was *represented* as something akin to an ethnic community. The dynamics and uses of that representation are our concern.

Mormonism's peculiar status as a quasi-ethnic group or a global tribe is a sword that cuts both ways. On one hand, it signifies the successful attainment of a group identity that Mormons associated with covenantal status. By common consent, they are accorded a position as a "peculiar people," marked by distinctive traits or behavior. On the other hand, their evolved group identity suggests a threatening difference, a mark of alienation and estrangement from their host society. For its contrived nature, its *quasi*-ethnicity, reveals a lack of full distinctness that is dangerous. Like tares that grow up among the similar-looking wheat, and do not reveal their true nature until their roots are already entangled with others, so do Mormonism's indigenous origins and imperfectly realized identity make its extraction from the body politic an urgent but difficult affair in the nineteenth century.

To attribute quasi-ethnic status to this new religious minority (whether as a sociological pronouncement or through scores of literary representations) is to recognize a process by which threatening proximity has been successfully transformed into manageable difference. This reification of religious difference into ethnic status might easily be interpreted as a reflection of Mormonism's own religious genius, the making of a sect into a people, were it not for certain facts. The history of colonialist discourse and the malleability of ethnic categories (of which Mormonism is an example), the prevailing ideological systems under which Mormonism evolves, and the role of popular fiction in shaping this evolving identity—all suggest something different is at work in Mormonism's acquisition of ethnic status than self-presentation as a "peculiar people." As the viper on the family hearth motif suggests, the more ominous implications of Mormonism's image as a quasi-ethnic group won out in the popular culture of the day. The religion's identity was largely shaped by external rhetorical, political, and literary strategies aimed at solving the core dilemma represented by "the Mormon problem": How does a people respond to an intolerable heresy in a pluralistic society?

Mormons were first and foremost members of a religious community, and their challenge to American values was therefore initially a religious challenge. It is not a coincidence that the peculiarly vexing threat the not-quite Other poses to ideological construction has one of its more urgent manifestations in the realm of the heretic. One of the most important battles being waged in the antebellum years was between religious orthodoxy and a proliferating heterodoxy. Nowhere are these challenges and ironies of defining heresy in a pluralistic society more evident than in the religious response to Mormonism. Just as anti-Catholicism would be subsumed under the nobler banner of nativism, so can we construe the civic anxiety provoked by an alien (yet not foreign) culture rooted in American soil (as Mormonism came to be characterized) as the projection of religious outrage against a full-blown "heresy" that stakes a vexing claim to being the authentic Christianity.

THE POLITICS OF INTOLERANCE

This construction of ethnicity does, it is true, facilitate the Mormon project of self-definition as a covenant people. But this differentiation of the Mormons as Other also gives sanction to any number of measures exercised against them; it serves to render the "heretics" more susceptible to recognition and exorcism as well. For while religious zeal for orthodox purity may be at least as impassioned as any nativist sentiment, the latter is much easier to defend in American political history. Religious intolerance and jingoism may be equally repugnant, but they have never been viewed as equally un-American. This fact was starkly manifest five years after Mormonism's founding, with the appearance of two political treatises. Gustave de Beaumont had spent almost a year touring the United States with Alexis de Tocqueville, studying the workings of American prisons and democracy. Beaumont's assignment was to concentrate on race relations and religion in particular. Though his work never achieved the recognition or influence accorded that of his colleague, Beaumont published some of his findings in an essay on "Religious Movements in the United States." He noted,

> In general [Catholics and Unitarians excepted], perfect harmony is seen to prevail among members of different communions; the mutual goodwill that Americans bear toward each other is not at all altered by the divergence of religious beliefs. The prosperity of a congregation, the eloquence of a preacher, may well inspire in other communities less fortunate, or whose orators are less brilliant, some feelings of jealousy; but these sentiments are ephemeral and leave behind no real bitterness; the rivalry certainly does not go so far as to become hatred.[14]

We could say Beaumont wrote too soon. By the essay's 1835 publication, the mobbings and expulsions of the Mormons had already begun in Missouri. But that raises precisely this point: we must not only ask *why* such animosities developed, but *what rationales* were necessarily invoked, given the investment American society had in religious diversity, and its expressed commitment to religious pluralism. Certainly, early America was never the epitome of religious tolerance. From Anne Hutchinson's seventeenth-century expulsion from the Massachusetts Bay Colony to the anti-Catholic acts of the nineteenth century, religious discrimination was legally implemented and enforced. But certainly by the time of Joseph Smith, American views of religious liberty were better represented by Jefferson's Virginia Statute for Religious Freedom than by, for example, New Jersey's anti-Catholic statutes. As Beaumont himself adds, what "infringements upon religious freedom" remain "are disappearing daily." Massachusetts, for example, had just abolished its religious test in 1833.

That Beaumont's remarks could appear the same year as Samuel Morse's vitriolic anti-Catholic book *Foreign Conspiracy against the Liberties of the United States* and his collection of essays *Imminent Dangers to the Free Institutions of the United States* is at first glance paradoxical. We certainly cannot point to Morse's tirades as atypical, or explain them away as unprecedented salvos in the soon to erupt anti-Catholic crusade. On the contrary, Michael Chevalier, another foreign observer who spent two years in the early 1830s studying "the workings of our social and political machinery," was dismayed by a society that too seldom confined itself to mere rhetorical violence against unpopular minorities:

> Unfortunately the reverence for the laws seems to be wearing out with the Americans.... They have, therefore, been driven in the United States to deny

that there is any principle true in and by itself, and to assert that the will of the people is, always and necessarily, justice; the infallibility of the people in every thing and at all times, has, in fact, become the received doctrine, and thus a door has been opened to the tyranny of a turbulent minority, which always calls itself the people.[15]

Not only was such violence distressing to Chevalier in and of itself; its blasé acceptance he found appalling. "And, I repeat it, the worst and most fatal symptom of the times is, that the perpetration of these outrages, however frequent they become, excites no sensation." Referring to arson, beatings, and lynchings committed against groups from abolitionists to bankers, blacks and Catholics, he concludes: "In a word, the *reign of terrour* is begun in the United States."[16] And this appraisal comes one year before his countryman Beaumont's essay on American religious harmony.

We could simply dismiss Beaumont's assessment of religious toleration in America as naively sanguine, if it were an isolated instance of the apparent contradiction it poses to Morse's essay or to Chevalier's observations. But at least two contemporaries endorsed Beaumont's version of America as a sea of religious harmony disturbed only occasionally by the ripples of religious discord. Just the year before Beaumont's essay appeared, Governor Daniel Dunklin of Missouri had wondered why, in an era full of impostors and fanatics, the Mormons alone were deprived of their "clear and indisputable right[s]."[17] And in a *Scribner's Monthly* editorial a number of years later, J. H. Beadle confirmed the Frenchman's judgment, referring to the Mormon conflict as "anomalous" in the history of American religion: "Americans have but one native religion and that one is the sole apparent exception to the American rule of universal toleration."[18] But anomalies are simply events that haven't yet yielded to explanation, and Beadle offered this incisive view of how the Mormon conflict and universal religious toleration (like Morse's invective and Beaumont's verdict) could be reconciled: "Of this anomaly two explanations are offered: one that the Americans are not really a tolerant people, and that what is called toleration is only such toward our common Protestantism, or more common Christianity; the other that something peculiar to Mormonism takes it out of the sphere of religion and necessarily brings it into conflict with a republican people and their institutions."[19]

The thesis of this book is a modification and an elaboration of Beadle's second hypothesis: "something peculiar to Mormonism takes it out of the sphere of religion." That something *does* bring the church out of the religious sphere is evident not by virtue of any sociological analysis of Mormonism that reveals it to be more an ethnic than a religious group.

To phrase the explanation in those terms and leave it at that avoids a most complex dimension of America's confrontation with Mormonism— the dynamics by which a new religion becomes constructed, under the pressures of pluralism and toleration, into an entity that can justifiably be exorcised from the American body politic. Beadle's formulation may lead to the mistaken impression that categories like "Christian" or "American," and the identities they imply, are objective realities, outside of negotiation or manipulation, rather than the products of political conflict and ideological construction. The how and why of the process by which Mormonism came to be defined as something other than, or in addition to, a religion, tend to be elided in scholarly disputes about what that definition is.

It is precisely the casting of Mormonism in nonreligious terms, then, that explains why anti-Mormonism is not an exception to the rule of toleration; the dissociation of Mormonism from religion, in fact, reinforces the authority of tolerance as a value that constrains and shapes the terms of social conflict. In other words, toleration and nationalism can coexist more comfortably than tolerance and religious bigotry. Accordingly, what "takes [Mormonism] out of the sphere of religion" may be driven more by external than internal factors; the shift may be as much a function of rhetorical strategies as a consequence of some morphological or sociological evolution.

The American investment in this ideal of religious tolerance has been a part of our self-presentation, our shared American mythology, for two hundred years and more. Sanford Cobb's 1902 study, *The Rise of Religious Liberty in America*, for example, argues that the modern ideal of a "pure Religious Liberty...may be confidently reckoned as of distinctly American origin." Cobb goes so far as to claim that "among all the benefits to mankind to which this soil has given rise, this pure religious liberty may be justly rated as the great gift of America to civilization and the world."[20] Reviewing this country's own history of religious strife, Cobb asserts that our soil "was never drenched...with the blood of men fighting and dying for conscience and creed." What "few instances of colonial persecution" occurred "were speedily followed by such a revulsion of the public mind that the after-occurrence of similar cruelties was made forever impossible."[21] These words were written decades after the Haun's Mill massacre and Missouri expulsions of the Mormons, in the wake of recent federal legislation designed to expropriate and disenfranchise the Mormons, at the close of a half century of anti-Catholic agitation, propaganda, and riots, and only a year before the U.S. Congress would refuse to seat the Mormon senator from Utah, Reed Smoot.

My purpose is not to dispute Cobb's (or Beaumont's) assessment of American religious tolerance. On the contrary, I wish to explore the sense in which their observations are true. Morse's books do not prove an exception to the rule of universal religious tolerance any more than anti-Mormonism does. On the contrary, they demonstrate the necessary contortions that religion must be subjected to, the rhetorical strategies that must be deliberately and ingeniously applied, in order to maintain the underlying value system of pluralism and religious toleration intact while the aberrant group is proscribed. That strategy was so successfully employed in the case of anti-Catholicism that it apparently didn't even occur to the writers cited above (Dunklin and Beadle, or Cobb) to mention that campaign as a blatant exception to the "universal" rule. Morse's work is a textbook example of how to take a sect "out of the sphere of religions" *so as to place it* "into conflict with a republican people and their institutions."

Morse's assault on the Catholic church is vicious. He assails the pope, the Jesuits, the "increase of Roman Catholic cathedrals, churches, colleges, convents, nunneries," and warns against "the evil, the great and increasing evil that threatens..." But rhetorically, he shows acute awareness of the need to cast the issue in strictly secular terms. He even apologizes for mentioning "a particular religious sect, the Roman Catholics," by name, and insists that with their *"religious tenets*, properly so called, I have not meddled."[22] Of course he hasn't, for by the time they have been processed by his rhetorical mill they are no longer religious tenets. The pope has become a "foreign despot," the Jesuits are now political "agents," the foreign political "conspiracy" is identified with "that creed," and not American churches but "democratic republicanism" is being threatened. And Morse's coup de grâce? He invokes the only American icon with the weight and moral authority to refute Thomas Jefferson, author of the Virginia Statute for Religious Freedom. His champion? Thomas Jefferson, anti-immigration "apostle of democratic liberty." "*Mr. Jefferson*," he writes triumphantly, "*denounced the encouragement of immigration....* Let me show that Mr. Jefferson's opinions in relation to emigration are proved by experience to be sound" (emphasis in original).[23]

Under the banner of nativism, then, patriotic Americans could equate Catholics with foreignness rather than heterodoxy, the papacy with antirepublicanism rather than theocracy. Thus, the religious dimension to the conflict was neatly sanitized by the rhetoric of patriotism, transposed into political rather than theological differences. This is not to say that the underlying hostilities were or were not really more religious than economic or political. It *is* to say that such hostilities, to be culturally acceptable, were more effective in being cast in terms of political rather than denominational interests.

The strategy successfully used to justify anti-Catholicism under the rubric of nativism suggests a model for the anti-Mormon rhetoric of the same era. But Mormonism was home-grown, not foreign born, and its members were indistinguishable from typical Americans. So relief from the disturbing proximity of this "moral leprosy" and justification for its excision depended upon the creation of distinctions that would change what was disturbingly pervasive into the more manageably marginal. Nevertheless, when it came to this cultural conflict, Americans found it impossible to employ the standard repertoire of nativist and xenophobic responses to this demonized Other. For Mormonism's origins and composition—unlike Catholicism's—were inextricably bound up with American institutions, ideals, and gene pools. Consequently, a particular kind of anxiety was fostered that, we shall see, fictional strategies engaged— sometimes to exploit, and sometimes to combat.

In addition to its problematic status as a group that was distressingly different yet disturbingly similar, other aspects of Mormonism presented its opponents and detractors with an array of colliding imperatives. Nineteenth-century Mormonism was clearly alien to and incompatible with fundamental American values—both religious and cultural. And its emerging status as a quasi-ethnic group coupled with its aggressive proselytizing made Mormonism especially threatening as an example of radical otherness that did not blatantly manifest otherness. But the ideological imperative to construct such heterodoxy into a manageable shape was thwarted by those same factors that made such exorcism necessary. In other words, the impulse to construct Mormons as a distinct ethnic community was matched, in the early Republic, by an impulse to display tolerance of nonconformity as part of the recent independence ideology. So, that very difference that was exaggerated to serve as a foil in American self-fashioning also had to be embraced. Thus, this cultural conflict was marked by a compulsion to exorcise a threatening Other regarded as hostile to American values, while its marginal position and the ideological contradictions it provoked made it impossible to readily identify and banish the sinister otherness.

In sum, sociohistorical accounts of the Mormon image in American culture have scarcely considered the ideological role of fictional representation in American political life. On examining the *uses* to which such representations of Mormonism have been put, it becomes clear that America's ongoing process of self-definition has been facilitated by the appropriation of images of a handy, purpose-built Other. The Mormon villain, it turns out, is integrally related to an evolving American self-definition. Not only must the typical American hero be consistent with the image of Pilgrims, Puritans, and the Quest for Religious Freedom, but so must the enemy represented be conducive to America's self-concept. Party platforms, debates about manifest destiny, Utah's struggle for statehood: all are forums where the American hero evolves in the context of caricatured foils, of which the Mormon is a prominent example.

The history of fictional *representations* of Mormonism in particular must be central to any complete accounting of Mormonism's history and place in American life. Some of the questions we must ask are: How were Mormons represented? What patterns of depiction and distortion emerged? What ends did these sometimes creative shapings serve, and what do they tell us about the anxieties, fears, and hostilities of an American public? What did the public see as being at stake, and what interests were furthered by representing Mormons in certain ways? How did political, religious, and literary motives converge to create a distinctive identity for the Mormon people? Asking these questions may illuminate what was typical and what was distinctive about the invention of one of the most interesting Others in American history. The construction of Mormon identity was not, of course, purely a matter of forms imposed from without. Mormons told their own story as well, and sometimes in ways that had more than casual affinities to the depictions of their enemies.

Mormon founder and martyr, Joseph Smith. His challenge was to
endow the claims of the restored gospel with a privileged status in
the midst of an American scene described by a contemporary
journalist as "the paradise of heterodoxy."
(Archives of the Church of Jesus Christ of Latter-day Saints,
Salt Lake City, Utah)

*"I had actually seen a light, and in the midst of that light
I saw two Personages, and they did in reality speak to me;
and though I was hated and persecuted
for saying that I had seen a vision, yet it was true. . . .
I knew it, I knew that God knew it, and I could not deny it."*
—Joseph Smith,
"Joseph Smith—History," *Pearl of Great Price*
(Salt Lake City: Deseret, 1981)

The discredited prophet "Matthias" (Robert Matthews) sought solidarity with
Joseph Smith in an 1835 meeting in Kirtland, Ohio.
(*Memoirs of Matthias the Prophet*, New York: *New York Sun*, 1835)

"Had we not seen in our own days similar impostures practiced with success,
(that for instance of the celebrated Matthias ...) [Mormonism] would
have excited our special wonder; as it is, nothing excites surprise."
—Henry Brown, *The History of Illinois,*
from Its First Discovery and Settlement to the Present Time
(New York: Winchester, 1844)

Page 41.

William Miller, fellow New Yorker and contemporary of Joseph Smith,
preached the imminent return of Christ to a growing millennialist movement
that eventually spawned the Seventh-Day Adventist Church.
(Isaac Wellcome, *History of the Second Advent Message and Mission,
Doctrine, and People*, Yarmouth, Maine: Wellcome, 1874)

*"One day the world represents Mormonism and Millerism as twin brothers.
The next, they hear that 'Joe Smith' has wiped all the
stain from his pure skirts which a belief in Christ's
near coming would attach to him."*
—*Midnight Cry*, March 13, 1843

Margaret and Kate Fox launched the era of rappers and spirit mediums.
(A. Leah Underhill, *The Missing Link in Modern Spiritualism*,
New York: Thomas R. Knox and Co., 1885)

*"We called at Kirtland, found a few that called themselves Saints,
but very weak, many apostates, who have mostly joined the rappers."*
—Mormon missionary Thomas Colburn, letter,
St. Louis Luminary, May 5, 1855

Shaker communities shared with Mormonism clannish isolation, economic
communalism, radical family organization, and other heterodoxies
that elicited both amusement and opposition among the wider public.
One heterodoxy Mormons didn't share was the Shakers' belief in a
female incarnation of Christ. (Henry Howe, *Historical Collections of Ohio*,
Cincinnati: Derby, Bradley and Co., 1848)

*"Go and preach my gospel which ye have received, even as ye have
received it, unto the Shakers.... And again, verily I say unto you,
that the Son of Man cometh not in the form of a woman."*
—Revelation to Joseph Smith, 1831,
Doctrine and Covenants, section 49

James Gordon Bennett, editor of the *New York Herald* and "founder of a new school of writing." (Don C. Seitz, *The James Gordon Bennetts*, Indianapolis: Bobbs-Merrill, 1928)

"Wonders never case. Hereafter, I am James Gordon Bennett, Freeman of the Holy City of Nauvoo, LL.D. of the University of Nauvoo, and Aid-de-Camp [sic] to the Major-General, and Brigadier General to the Nauvoo Legion, with the fair prospect of being a prophet soon, and a saint in Heaven hereafter."—Bennett on his newly acquired honors, in the *New York Herald*, August 13, 1842

Warren Foote, Mormon convert, diarist, polygamist, and colonizer
(Archives of the Church of Jesus Christ of Latter-day Saints)

"I have kept a journal of my life untill [sic] the present day in which I have recorded the most important events of my life, and the corespondence [sic] I have had ... on the topics of Mormonism."
—Warren Foote, letter, September 8, 1898

CHAPTER 2

"This Upstart Sect": The Mormon Problem in American History

"Is there any group you wouldn't pick on?"

"Mormons. You don't pick on Mormons. They've been picked on enough. I mean look at Marie Osmond. She's a Mormon."

Interview with Andrew Dice Clay

On the afternoon of October 30, 1838, after weeks of skirmishes between Missourians and Mormon militia, a mob attacked the Mormon settlement of Haun's Mill. Eighteen or nineteen Mormons were killed, including two as young as eight or nine and a Revolutionary War hero some eighty years of age. Artemisia Sidnie Myers was a nine-year-old girl when she experienced what came to be known as the Haun's Mill massacre.

> About dark word came to us that the mobbers were coming, and that men, women and children had better hide in the woods as they intended to kill all they could find.... The men were told to hide by themselves. After the men were gone, the women took the children and went about a mile and a half to the woods, and after the children were got to sleep and lights put out, my mother put on a man's coat and stood guard until one or two o'clock when word was brought to us that they had had a battle at the mill and two of my brothers were wounded.... When we came to [my brother's] house, we went in and found him lying on the bed. When mother saw him she exclaimed, "O Lord have mercy

on my boy." He replied, "Don't fret mother, I shall not die." He was very weak from loss of blood. I will here relate the manner of his escape in his own words as he told to us after he got better. Our guns were all in the blacksmith's shop when the mob came upon us unexpectedly. Orders were given to run to the shop. The mob formed a half circle on the north side of the shop extending partly across the east and west ends, so as to cover all retreat from the shop. They commenced firing before we could escape with our arms....I made two or three jumps for the door when a bullet struck me a little below the right shoulder blade and lodged against the skin near the pit of my stomach. I fell to the ground. Mother, if ever a boy prayed I did at this time. I thought it would not do to lie there, so I arose and ran for the mill dam and crossed over it, and ran up the hill; the bullets whistling by me all the time. When I came to the fence and was climbing over it a ball passed through my shirt collar. I walked as far as I could but soon became so weak from loss of blood, I had to get on my hands and knees and crawl the rest of the way home....After mother had dressed George's wounds, we went to the mill, where we arrived just at break of day. I shall never forget the awful scene that met our eyes. When we got to Haun's house the first scene that presented itself in his dooryard was the remains of Father York and McBride and others covered with sheets. As we went down the hill to cross on the mill dam, there stood a boy over a pool of blood. He said to mother, "Mother Myers, this is the blood of my poor father." This, with the groans of the wounded, which we could distinctly hear, affected my mother so that she was unable to make any reply to the boy. We made our way to my brother Jacob's house....From my brother's house we went to the blacksmith's shop where we beheld a most shocking sight. There lay the dead, the dying, and the wounded, weltering in their blood, where they fell. A young man, whose name was Simon Cox, who lived with my father lay there, four bullets having passed through his body above the kidneys. He was still alive. He said to mother, all he wanted was a bowl of sweet milk and a feather bed to lie on. He had just got a pair of new boots a few days before, and he told mother how they dragged him about the shop to get them off. He told us to be faithful, and said to me, "Be a good girl and obey your parents." He died in the afternoon about 24 hours after he was shot. After we went back to my brother's house, my father, David Evans, and Joseph Young, with one or two more came and gathered up the dead and carried them to my brother's place and put them into a well which he had been digging, but had not yet come to water. They brought them on a wide board and slid them off feet forward. Every time they brought one and slid him in I screamed and cried. It was such an awful sight to see them piled in the bottom in all shapes. After the dead were buried, (which was done in a great hurry,) father and the brethren went away and secreted themselves for fear the mobbers would come on them again.[1]

The tragedy described here by the young Myers arose out of the same explosive environment that three days earlier had led Lilburn Boggs, the governor of Missouri, to sign an infamous executive order. Directed to General John B. Clark of the Missouri Militia, it read in part: "The Mormons must be treated as enemies and must be exterminated or driven from the state....Their outrages are beyond all description. If you can increase your force, you are authorized to do so, to any extent you may think necessary....You will proceed immediately to Richmond and there operate against the Mormons."[2]

How was it possible that an armed massacre, sanctioned by the governor of the state, could come to be carried out against its own citizens? Mormons were complicit in aggravating the intensity of conflict, but the weight brought to bear against them was disproportionate by any measure. Although Haun's Mill was in some ways the most dramatic example of religious intolerance directed against the Mormons, it was far from unique in its scope or the cloak of legal authority that made it possible. Within a decade, fifteen thousand Mormons were evicted from Nauvoo, Illinois; a decade later a federal army marched against their mountain refuge in Utah; and legislative sanctions later stripped the church of its possessions and many of its people of their civil rights.

The Mormons often expressed bewilderment at their repeated failure to coexist peacefully with their "gentile" neighbors. Their account of the aspirations and persecutions of Mormonism of course stands in stark contrast to Mormonism's rendering in popular fiction. It is against the backdrop of Mormonism's self-presentation that we may gauge more fully the ways in which popular representations of Mormons both reflected and exacerbated the conflicts and anxieties behind the "Mormon problem" in American history.

NEW YORK ORIGINS

The roots of the Mormon conflict must be traced to the origins of the Mormon church itself. At the time of the Haun's Mill massacre, and eight miles to the east, lived a young man Artemisia Sidnie Myers would marry five years later—Warren Foote. While Artemisia was hiding from the mobbers in the woods with her mother, Foote and his father were spending what he described in his journal as a "cold frosty night" in the woods near his home, in Shoal Creek, having been informed of the massacre by two fleeing survivors. His record is a particularly useful insider's account of Mormonism for a number of reasons. Foote was a meticulous diarist, and as a contemporary of Joseph Smith who would live to the age of eighty-four, he was eyewitness to most of the shaping events and personalities of Mormonism's first generations. While his record was freely shared with friends and correspondents, he never intended it to be published, even resisting encouragement to do so.[3] He first grew interested in the church in 1830, and even though he would soon move into the Mormon community, he did not formally associate himself with the Saints until 1842. His perspective is therefore that of a seeker, sympathizer, and eventually faithful member, attempting to make sense of the Mormon experience to himself and an audience composed largely of friends and relatives. If, as we shall see, the standard genre into which anti-Mormons wrote their stories is the captivity narrative, Foote's account is a conversion narrative. If the captivity narrative represents, as has been argued, the safe perusal of the abyss by one who has successfully entered there and escaped, the conversion account represents a description of that same abyss from the far side.

Warren Foote's account traces Mormon history back to the same origins Joseph Smith would point to as the ferment out of which Mormonism would spring forth—the wave of spiritual fervor and proselytizing zeal ensuing from the Second Great Awakening. This American religious revival is often traced to an 1801 series of camp meetings at Cane Ridge, Kentucky, from which it soon spread in all directions. Methodist circuit riders vied with Disciples of Christ preachers, Presbyterians clashed with Baptists, camp meetings swept the whole countryside, and everyone seemed to be competing for converts in a scene vividly described by the young Joseph Smith:

> There was in the place we lived an unusual excitement on the subject of religion. It commenced with the Methodists but soon became general among all the sects of that region of country. Indeed, the whole district of country seemed affected by it, and great multitudes united themselves to the different religious parties, which created no small stir and division amongst the people, some crying, "Lo, here!" and others, "Lo, there!" . . . Great zeal . . . was manifested by the clergy, who were active in getting up and promoting this extraordinary scene of religious feeling, in order to have everybody converted.[4]

Joseph lived in Palmyra, in upstate New York. A hundred miles to the south was the small town of Dryden, where Warren Foote had been born in 1817. The seekerism so common in his generation was captured in his journal as well: "I could not believe in the gospel as taught by any of the sects. I often went to the Methodist revival meetings to see them jump and hear them shout and sing, and when they all got to praying, shouting and singing at once it was fun to me to hear them, I could not see any thing in such proceedings, like the gospel as taught by the ancient apostles of Christ."[5]

In 1820, fourteen-year-old Joseph Smith recorded that he went to the woods near his home in prayerful search of answers to his religious questions. When he returned, he claimed to have experienced the most sublime epiphany since Stephen the martyr. In Smith's First Vision, as it came to be called, God the Father and Jesus Christ appeared to him and commanded him to remain aloof from all sects, as they were teaching "for doctrines the commandments of men."[6]

The next major development occurred in 1823, when Joseph was visited by an angel who identified himself as Moroni, a resurrected ancient American prophet who told him that God had a mighty work for him to do, and that "[his] name should be had for good and evil among all nations."[7] Moroni further promised to deliver to Joseph a sacred record, which he himself had buried over fourteen hundred years previously. These "golden plates," which lay buried in a hillside in Manchester, New York, were entrusted to the young prophet in 1827. They purported to contain the history of an offshoot of the house of Israel that migrated to the Western Hemisphere six hundred years before Christ. Here the immigrants developed distinct cultures; one group followed the Mosaic law, anticipated the Messiah, and was visited by Christ after his ascension in the Old World. Generations of internecine battles finally resulted in the extermination of Moroni's people, the Nephites (around A.D. 400), while the surviving Lamanites were purportedly assimilated into Native American populations.

Working intermittently at the translation of this record, Joseph called the inspired process complete in 1830, and in the spring of that year E. B. Grandin of Palmyra published five thousand copies of the Book of Mormon. With a new canon to resolve the diversity and deficiencies of orthodox theologies and to testify to the divine nature of his calling as a modern prophet and seer, Smith next undertook the formal organization of a church. On April 6, 1830, the Church of Christ, as it was originally called, was legally organized. In Smith's view, the stone cut without hands prophesied by Daniel was about to roll forth and fill the earth, and the restitution of all things foretold by Peter had begun.[8]

From its inception, the Mormon church (or Church of Jesus Christ of Latter-day Saints, as it was called from 1838 to the present) conceived of itself as the fulfillment of biblical prophecy and the precursor of a millennial era. A revelation received on the day of the church's organization designated Smith as "a seer, a translator, a prophet, an apostle of Jesus Christ," and called upon the church to receive "all his words and commandments...as if from" the mouth of God himself.[9] This was not to be just another sect, or the reformation of a Christianity gone astray. Joseph Smith insisted the church he was restoring was the authoritative embodiment of the kingdom of God on earth.

Accordingly, Mormonism was a zealously proselytizing church. Foote recalled that in 1830 his father borrowed a Book of Mormon ("which went by the name of Golden Bible"), and three years later, now living in Greenwood, New York, Foote borrowed one from his uncle and read it again.[10] In the fall of that year, two missionaries came to Greenwood teaching the restored gospel. In November, Foote's father, David, was baptized into the new faith.

In 1834 and again in 1835, Foote recorded additional visits of traveling Mormon missionaries to his New York town, among them Mormon luminary Orson Pratt and George A. Smith, cousin of the prophet. Foote adds, "My Father having been ordained an Elder had been preaching some during the winter, and some were believing"[11]—enough, apparently, that a branch was organized, with his father as president.

THE "GATHERING" IN OHIO AND MISSOURI

Even before the church's founding in 1830, the restoration of the gospel was seen by Smith as making possible a gathering of the righteous, "as a hen gathereth her chickens."[12] The anomaly of a church as a gathering struck Charles Dickens, who observed of the Mormons: "It sounds strange to hear of a church having a 'location.' But a 'location' was the term they applied to their place of settlement...in Jackson County, Missouri."[13] Nevertheless, that the gathering was meant to be literal, and not metaphorical, was soon made clear. In December of 1830 the Saints were commanded to "assemble together at the Ohio," and in March, from Kirtland, Ohio, Smith revealed that "the remnant [of Israel] shall be gathered unto this place....Wherefore, I, the Lord, have said, gather ye out from the eastern lands, assemble ye yourselves together."[14]

With conditions in New York increasingly inhospitable, and now with the sanction of Smith's revelation, the main body of Mormonism's first converts moved to Kirtland early in 1831. At the same time, Ohio was proving an especially fertile field for Mormon missionaries. Parley P. Pratt was one of a group of four elders who had been sent to the western frontier to proselytize the Native Americans. They had little success with that group, but their travels took them through the town of Kirtland. Pratt later recollected, with some exaggeration perhaps, that "the interest and excitement became general in Kirtland, and in all the region round-about. The people thronged to us night and day, insomuch that we had no time for rest and retirement...and multitudes came together soliciting our attendance, while thousands flocked about us daily."[15] Pratt and his companions performed well over a hundred baptisms over the next few weeks, with the number of converts reaching one thousand soon thereaf-ter.[16] Among the number was former Campbellite preacher Sidney Rigdon, along with a substantial portion of his congregation. His leadership and oratorical skills would soon be put to good use in the fledgling Mormon church.

Within months, however, the gathering in Ohio was seen as provi-sional, or preparatory for the real gathering about to take place elsewhere. In June of the same year, the command came designating Missouri as "the land which I will consecrate unto my people"; a revelation the following month was even more emphatic: "Hearken, O ye elders of my church, saith the Lord your God, who have assembled yourselves together, according to my commandments, in this land, which is the land of Missouri, which is the land which I have appointed and consecrated for the gathering of the saints."[17]

Most of the remaining New York Mormons moved to Missouri by the summer of 1832. Some lagged behind, and not until the spring of 1836, Foote records, did "most of the Saints in Greenwood remove..., some to Kirtland, and some to Missouri. My father and sister Almira went to Kirtland."[18] The next year, after a visit from his father, Foote decided to make the trip to Kirtland himself, "being anxious to see that country, and especially the prophet Joseph Smith."[19] Smith's reputation was already such as to attract a steady stream of the curious, the seekers, and the skep-tics. By the time Foote's steamer arrived at Fairport, in May of 1837, he recorded that "the rest of our company being somewhat anxious to see the Prophet Joseph, and the Temple, [they] concluded to accompany Father, and myself to Kirtland."[20]

After meeting Smith, Foote sought employment in the town, but complained that "times were very dull, and there was but little build-ing going on. The Kirtland Bank was going down which made it still worse."[21] Rampant land speculation had been sweeping the nation and soon infected the Ohioans. In the ensuing panic of 1837, bank failures in New York City alone surpassed $100,000, and the Kirtland wildcat bank quickly went under in the general collapse. The failure of this institution, in which Smith had been involved, caused many of the Saints, especially those in leadership positions, to revolt against the prophet. Disaffection and outside opposition alike soon caused Smith to change his headquarters to Missouri, early the next year.

Unemployed and homesick, Foote returned home to New York. That fall, the family decided to move permanently to Ohio, although the situation there was precarious. In December, Brigham Young was chased from town by an angry mob furious at his public support of Joseph Smith, and three weeks later the prophet and his counselor fled as well. In May of 1838, after a residence of a few short months, Foote and his family (absent now his unbelieving brother and mother) left for Missouri with a group of sixty others.

Meanwhile, the young church had been experiencing problems of its own in Missouri. Assembling there the year after the church's organization in New York, the Mormons had at first settled in Jackson County. They lasted two years, before anti-Mormon activity drove them to several neighboring counties, but principally Clay County. By June of 1836 they had overstayed their welcome in that county as well, and a mass meeting of citizens was called to act upon the problem. They unanimously passed a resolution calling for the Saints' removal. A new county, Caldwell, was created to accommodate them, and from his headquarters in Kirtland, the prophet urged his followers to peacefully remove to the prairie regions to the northeast. By September 1836 this resettlement was under way.

It was to this location, Far West, Missouri, that Foote and his party arrived at the end of August 1838. Under the leadership of Joseph Smith's close friend Stephen Markham, they covered 835 miles in three months of traveling.[22] In early October most of the remaining Kirtland Saints, some five hundred in number, arrived.

Once in Far West, Foote immediately found himself in a hornet's nest of agitation. Just weeks prior to Foote's arrival, violence had broken out at Gallatin when a group of Missourians attempted to prevent Mormons from casting their ballots in a local election. On September 6, wrote Foote, the Mormon militia gathered in Far West "to take measures to defend themselves against the mob, who were still actively engaged in spreading false reports, to incite the Missourians to arise and drive the 'Mormons' from the state. The report was, that they had set this day to begin their driving."[23]

On September 8, Mormon militia were sent to defend Adam-ondi-Ahman to the north, and another contingent intercepted a shipment of weapons and ammunition going to the mob gathering in Daviess County, and returned with the arms and three prisoners. Hundreds of state militia were called up under General David R. Atchison in order to restore order, but to little avail. The bloodiest stage of the Missouri War was just beginning. Both sides burned and pillaged in the weeks that followed.[24]

The attitude of the Saints toward their persecutors had taken a tragic turn with leading elder Sidney Rigdon's inflammatory Fourth of July speech. In it, he defiantly declared that

> from this hour we will bear it no more; our rights shall no more be trampled on with impunity; *the man, or set of men who attempt it, do it at the expense of their lives. And that mob that comes on us to disturb us, it shall be between us and them a war of extermination; for we will follow them until the last drop of their blood is spilled; or else they will have to exterminate us, for we will carry the seat of war to their own houses and their own families, and one party or the other shall be utterly destroyed* [emphasis in original].[25]

By now accustomed to opposition, many Saints were clearly not anticipating removal again anytime soon, in spite of deteriorating conditions. On October 7, Foote recorded, "we bargained for 80 acres of...land." And in the next sentence, "We heard today, that the mob commenced firing on the 'Mormons' at De Wit [sic], in Carroll county."[26] The governor sent a force with General H. G. Parks to the scene, who reported that he found hundreds of men with artillery poised to attack the town. His men were more sympathetic to the besiegers than to the besieged, so he soon withdrew. Joseph Smith, who had recently arrived to encourage his followers, described the result: "We had now no hopes whatever of successfully resisting the mob, who kept constantly increasing; our provisions were entirely exhausted, and we being wearied out.... Some of the brethren...perished from starvation; and for once in my life, I had the pain of beholding some of my fellow creatures fall victims to the spirit of persecution."[27] On October 11, the Mormons were forced to cede the town to the mob forces. Seventy wagons of the exiles and their possessions soon filed into Caldwell County.

Violence again erupted a few weeks later, when a group of Caldwell militia led by the Reverend Samuel Bogart raided a residence south of Far West and made off with three prisoners. The Mormons sent an equal force to rescue them. Foote wrote on the twenty-fifth, "This morning there was a battle fought between a company of 60 mormons commanded by David W. Patten, and about the same number of Mobbers on Crooked river. The mobbers were driven across the river, and several of them killed. The 'Mormons' had one killed...and seven wounded two of which were fatal."[28]

By this time, peaceful resolution of the conflict was impossible. But when hysterical and distorted reports of the engagement came to the attention of Governor Lilburn Boggs, he responded with the "extermination order" cited earlier, ensuring a violent finale. Even before learning of Boggs's order, the mob was en route to the hamlet. Foote was among the first to learn of the consequences: "Oct. 30...two men came up from Haun's Mill, going to Far West. They reported, that a mob came on them that afternoon at Haun's mill, and had killed nearly all the 'Mormons' gathered at that place.... They had also ascertained, very late in the evening, that 4000 some say 6000 Malitia [sic] had camped that night, one half mile south of Far West with orders from the Governor of the state to exterminate the Mormons."[29]

Even allowing for exaggeration, the Mormons could not hope to match such firepower. Foote and his father spent the next few nights sleeping in a hollow sycamore, hiding from the mobbers. On November 1, they learned that "they had made a treaty at Far West, and the Mormons had surrendered and agreed to leave the State in the Spring."[30] What actually happened was that Smith and several leading elders accepted an invitation to parley, but were immediately apprehended, subjected to a court-martial, and sentenced to be shot. Alexander W. Doniphan, the militia general receiving the order, refused to carry it out, and the prisoners were remanded to jail in Richmond. Mob depredations and plundering increased, with Mormons claiming thirty dead and a hundred missing in the days following.[31] After delays and changes of venue, Smith and his fellow prisoners made their escape in April of the next year, while in transit to Columbia.

NAUVOO THE BEAUTIFUL

Before the end of winter, the first Saints were already wending their way eastward across the Missouri River and into Illinois, where sympathies at that time ran toward the Mormon cause. On the first day of April, Foote began the two-week journey in company with his father and sister. About this time he received a letter from his nonmember brother George, in which George offered a northerner's view of the Mormon wars: "I believe...the Mormons have been shamefully abused, but at the same time, I also believe that the Mormons have provoked the inhabitants of Missouri, with their doctrines, in declareing [sic], that they are the only true people on earth: assigning the others as doctrines of men, and devils."[32]

Within days of the Footes' arrival in Quincy, Illinois, Smith and his companions arrived as well, and the decision was soon made to situate in Commerce, a swampy settlement of six buildings on a panoramic bend of the Mississippi. Although the advice of General John B. Clark of the Missouri Militia had been to mix with general society, the Mormons in their Illinois period only consolidated their position as a distinct, independent people. They changed the name of Commerce to Nauvoo, petitioned the Illinois legislature for a city charter, and were awarded one that granted them unprecedented powers of self-government.[33] Operating as a virtual city-state with an extraordinary degree of judicial and military autonomy, the Saints now had official legitimation of their status as a distinctive, privileged community. Over the next five years, thousands of new converts—many from England—joined the Missouri refugees in their new place of gathering. A U.S. artillery officer passed through and reported to the *New York Herald* in 1842 that "there are probably in and about this city, and adjacent territories, not far from 30,000 of these warlike fanatics."[34] The city would eventually boast its own militia and university, as well as numerous foundries, steam mills, businesses, and a temple. Foote settled down to a peaceful life ten miles south of Nauvoo, working at various times as a stage driver, a schoolteacher, a chair maker, and a sawmill worker.

He finally joined the Mormon church in 1842, and married Artemisia Sidnie Myers the following year. Only two entries in the next few years indicated the worsening relationship of the Mormons with their neighbors. In March of 1844, Foote read a pamphlet of Joseph Smith's titled *Views of the Powers and Policy of the Government of the United States*. It was a campaign brochure, for Joseph Smith was a candidate for the coming presidential elections. Failing to secure national redress for his followers' persecutions, and with no hope of more sympathetic treatment from the major candidates, Smith decided to run himself. It is doubtful that he harbored any illusions about his chances, but the venture was a bold publicity move. Unfortunately, it played into the hands of critics who claimed his powers as prophet, mayor, and commander of the Nauvoo Legion, Nauvoo's militia of thousands, were going to his head.[35]

On June 16, Foote learned that "the citizens of Nauvoo have destroyed the printing press of the 'Nauvoo Expositor,' and there is a great excitement in Hancock Co." Disaffected Mormons had started the press as an opposition newspaper. It was declared a city nuisance by the Nauvoo council, and its destruction ordered.[36]

This was not the first time that frontier justice refused to recognize the right to a free press as inviolate. The printing press of abolitionist Elijah P. Lovejoy had been damaged and dumped in a river by a Missouri mob (who followed him into Illinois) in 1836. The destruction ruffled few feathers, other than those of the injured owner. Other attacks followed, and a year later, Lovejoy was murdered by another mob, who then proceeded to destroy his fourth press. No one was convicted for either crime, and those who undertook to defend the press were themselves brought to trial.[37] The Mormons had, in fact, had their own press destroyed by a Missouri mob in 1833. With the publication of a compilation of Smith's revelations imminent, their print shop was reduced to rubble, the press ruined, and the type and galley sheets scattered. All told, perhaps sixteen violent attacks on presses or editors occurred in Illinois between 1832 and 1867, and another handful in other states.[38]

MARTYRDOM AND EXODUS

Precedents notwithstanding, in the case of the destruction of the *Expositor*, repercussions were explosive. Newspaper editors throughout the state called for war, mobs began to assemble, and warrants were sworn out for Smith's arrest in nearby Carthage. The governor, Thomas Ford, rejected Smith's defense of the Mormons' actions and charged him with violating the Constitution. He insisted that Smith come to Carthage for trial, since conviction in Nauvoo was obviously impossible. Fearing for the safety of Nauvoo's inhabitants, and deterred from fleeing by his friends, Smith delivered himself to the authorities after expressing premonitions of his impending death.[39]

The next day, Foote was cutting wheat in the field when he heard the news:

> My wife came out and told us that word had just come that Joseph Smith and his brother Hiram [Hyrum] was shot in Carthage Jail yesterday afternoon. I said at once, "that it cannot be so." Yet it so affected us that we dropped the cradle and rake and went home. We found that the word had come so straight that we could no longer doubt the truth of it. We all felt as though the powers of darkness had overcome and that the Lord had forsaken His people. Our Prophet and Patriarch were gone! Who now is to lead the Saints! In fact we mourned "as one mourneth for his only son."[40]

In August of 1844, only a few months after the death of the prophet, Foote noted in his journal a meeting that refers to the most famous cause of anti-Mormon agitation:

> We went to see Bro Duncan McArthur, with whom we were well acquainted. Having learned that he was one of the number who had been appointed to

teach the principle of Celestial Marriage to the saints, according to the revelation given to Joseph Smith on that subject we disired [*sic*] to get some correct
information on that principle. The doctrine having never been taught publicaly
[*sic*] there were all sorts of reports concerning it. He very willingly taught and
explained to us that doctrine in such a simple manner, as to remove all prejudice we had against the doctrine of plural marriage.[41]

Smith first taught the principle of plural marriage to a small circle of asso-
ciates a few years before his death. He probably married his first plural
wife, Fanny Alger, in the mid-1830s, and then several more beginning in
April 1841.[42] The facts and public perceptions were easily clouded, given
the contemporary prevalence of related practices[43] (the spiritual wifery
of the Perfectionists, the free love inclinations of some spiritualists), the
resentment of ex-Mormons excommunicated on charges of immorality,[44]
and the public appetite for the sensational and prurient. Accusations and
public denials had been rampant by 1842 and contributed to the climate
of tension and suspicion that culminated in the mob violence in Illinois
and the murder of Joseph and Hyrum Smith two years later.

After the Carthage martyrdoms, the friction continued unabated. In
September of the next year, Foote noted that the mobbers had burned "70
or 80 houses" in recent days, and at an October church conference, "it was
voted unanimously that the Church enmasse [*sic*] move from the United
States, where we have had nothing but persecution from the beginning,
and go to a country far to the west where we can serve God without being
molested by mobs."[45] What Foote neglected to mention (he may not have
known) was that three weeks earlier, Smith's successor Brigham Young
had offered to hostile forces a spring exodus in exchange for a stop to the
burnings and violence.[46]

Hearing that the federal government meant to disarm them first, and
facing continuing harassment, the Mormons began a wintry departure
instead. On February 12, 1846, a correspondent for the *Warsaw (Ill.)
Signal* reported that "one thousand or twelve hundred had already crossed
the river, amongst whom were the TWELVE, the High Council and all the
principal men of the Church and about one hundred females. They had
been crossing night and day for several days and were still crossing when
[I] left."[47] Foote followed in May, and the few remnants were forced out
the following September.[48] The exiles wintered at Council Bluffs, Iowa,
and Winter Quarters, Nebraska. In the spring of 1847, Brigham Young
led the first party of pioneers into the Salt Lake Valley, arriving in July.
Many would remain at Winter Quarters for months or even years. Foote
would himself lead a wagon train of one hundred families, but not until

the spring of 1850. That September, after 101 days of traveling, and losses amounting to more than twenty dead (one by stampede, one by a wagon accident, the rest by sickness), Foote's train arrived in Salt Lake.

UTAH AND POLYGAMY

The Saints had intended to find refuge and independence by leaving the United States. In a rather perverse irony, the Saints, while on their westward migration, were asked to raise a battalion to participate in the Mexican War. Foote recorded the recruiting visit of "Colonel Allen of the U.S. Army...to raise 500 men to go to California to fight against Mexico," and added with some bitterness that "no one felt like fighting for a Government that would not protect us in our rights." Nevertheless, the Saints, whether from begrudging patriotism, dire necessity, or political self-interest, voted unanimously to raise the volunteers.[49] As a consequence, the Mormons participated in a war that resulted in the American flag flying over their new refuge in Salt Lake. A few weeks before Foote's party entered the valley, Utah was organized as a U.S. territory. Utah petitioned for statehood in 1849 as "Deseret," but the request was overwhelmingly rejected. A compromise territorial government was established in 1850, with Brigham Young as governor.

In the latter part of 1851, Foote mentions in passing that his sister Clarissa was herself a plural wife to one George Gates. Although Foote does not mention it, the church would publicly acknowledge the practice the next year. In 1856, sandwiched between an account of his family's health and a description of the harvest, Foote made the following entry: "I went to Provo after Eliza Maria Ivie Daughter of James N. Ivie and Eliza M. Fawcett Ivie. I returned the 20th. The roads were very muddy."[50] "Sealed" to him by Brigham Young, Maria became Foote's second wife. The arrangement, as was so often the case, was almost immediately fraught with tensions and difficulties. (She finally left him in 1877.)

With the public announcement of polygamy, those opposed to Utah statehood and Mormonism generally had new and unimpeachable support for their claim that Utah was outside the pale of American institutions. At the same time, tensions between Mormon officials and federal appointees intensified. The non-Mormon administrators found themselves superfluous, ignored, or impeded in their work. This was the case with federally appointed judges Lemuel Brandebury and Perry Brocchus, who lasted only months into their 1851 appointment to the territory. One of Brocchus's final gestures while in the territory revealed the catastrophic consequences of imposing tactless eastern political appointees on a devout Mormon populace. Combining extreme arrogance and shocking political naiveté, Brocchus went so far as to usurp the podium at a semiannual church conference to lecture the stunned audience on the immorality of polygamy and their duty to display more properly patriotic attitudes toward then president Zachary Taylor. Brigham Young immediately delivered a stinging rebuke, and Brocchus very shortly thereafter departed from an appointment intolerable to himself and Mormons alike. Along with many of his judicial colleagues, Brocchus returned to Washington, where they relayed horror stories of Mormon polygamy and disloyalty, adding fuel to the fire of controversy about the growing "Mormon problem."[51]

The situation became critical with the appointment in 1855 of three new federal judges, two of them virulent anti-Mormons. The most hostile of these, William Wormer Drummond, was a libertine with an exhibitionist flair. Bringing in tow a Washington prostitute, who shared his bench as well as his bed (he had abandoned his family in Illinois), Drummond flouted Mormon mores while endeavoring to establish federal judicial authority. After two years of contention, these judges too returned to Washington, furious and intent on revenge. They circulated rumors of Brigham Young's tyranny and of massacres by "avenging angels," whipping up public opinion to a fever pitch.[52] Drummond was especially effective in enlisting journalistic allies in the anti-Mormon campaign, calling for a "crusade...against this foul horde which would soon put an end to their sway" and pledging to return as their governor.[53]

In the meantime, a new governor had already been dispatched to replace Brigham Young, and a new stage of the Mormon conflict began. Young had already addressed such a possibility: "Though I may not be Governor here my power will not be diminished. No man they can send here will have much influence with this community, unless he be the man of their choice."[54]

On July 24, 1857, the Saints were celebrating their annual Pioneer Day, commemorating the arrival of the first Mormons in the valley, when "two men came in from the States with the express and brought word that an army was on the way to Utah for the purpose of fighting the Mormons.... It came upon them like a clap of thunder in a clear sky. Governor Young had not received any intimation of any thing of the kind before."[55] President Buchanan had sent an army of twenty-five hundred under Colonel Albert Sidney Johnston to bring the rebellious Mormons to terms. The Republican Party had taken an official stand against Mormon polygamy in its platform of 1856, and this may have been a partisan attempt by the Democrat Buchanan to show equal zeal.[56] At least one adviser of the president encouraged him to undertake the campaign because he anticipated that the public's enthusiastic support of the effort would divert attention from the more vexing and contentious slavery issue: "Should you," Robert Tyler unabashedly wrote, "with your accustomed grip, seize this question with a strong fearless and resolute hand, the country I am sure will rally to you with an earnest enthusiasm and the pipings of Abolitionism will hardly be heard amidst the thunders of the storm we shall raise."[57]

More recently, it has been argued that the expedition may have been a ploy by southern conspirators. With the federal army numbering only five thousand at this time, the Utah force constituted a substantial portion of the total, and was strategically near California, poised under southern commanders to bring that state into the Confederacy, should Civil War erupt.[58]

Under Brigham Young, defenses were erected, but neither battle nor capitulation was an acceptable option. Engaging in an early version of guerrilla tactics, Mormon rangers so successfully burned vast stretches of prairie grass before the soldiers' line of march that three thousand head of livestock perished. Another eleven hundred animals were captured or run off. Surprise raids destroyed over three hundred thousand pounds of foodstuffs.[59] The Mormons succeeded in bringing the troops to the verge of starvation, but managed to avoid bloodshed. The troops settled into winter quarters as the crisis simmered on. The next spring, substantial federal reinforcements arrived. Finally, Foote records, "President Young preached yesterday at the Tabernacle that he thought it best to move southward and if the United States were determined to send their army into the Valley without some treaty, or agreement, we would burn our houses, cut down our orchards and make the country as desolate as it was when we came here. He then called for a vote of the congregation. They all voted aye."[60]

Thousands of refugees were soon moving southward, but further conflict was narrowly avoided in part by the timely intervention of skilled negotiator and Mormon friend Colonel Thomas Kane. The army soon retired to a discreet distance, but not before the atmosphere of hysteria and provocation led to the tragic massacre of an immigrant wagon train by a combined force of Mormon militia and Indians.[61]

In the last phase of the Mormon conflict, polygamy continued to be a festering sore addressed by legislative rather than military or mob action. In 1874, the Poland Bill reduced the power of the Mormon-controlled courts by establishing federal control over courts and juries. The next year, George Reynolds became the first Mormon convicted under federal anti-polygamy statutes. In 1882, Senator George Edmunds of Vermont

sponsored a bill that disenfranchised polygamists and made plural marriage a crime, as well as established an electoral commission to supervise
Utah's voting. In 1887, the Edmunds-Tucker Act went far beyond the
Edmunds law; it disincorporated the church, abolished female suffrage,
and required a more stringent voter registration oath. Three years later,
in the church's General Conference of 1890, President Wilford Woodruff
issued a manifesto proclaiming an end to the practice of plural marriage
within the borders of the United States. Foote correctly predicted in his
journal that while such a move might mean the beginning of a tolerable
coexistence with the "gentiles," the way ahead would be rocky. "I suppose,"
he wrote, "they will conjure up something else in order to keep up their
warfare."[62]

CHAPTER 3

"Manners, Habits, Customs, and Even Dialect": Sources of the Mormon Conflict

Would you murder me? What is my offense?
I believe in God and revelation?

Samuel McBride, victim of the Haun's Mill massacre

On October 2, 1881, the Reverend De Witt Talmage gave a sermon in the Brooklyn Tabernacle on the subject of President Garfield's recent assassination. Attempting to console those shaken by the ineffectuality of their prayers for his recovery, he solaced them with the thought that "if the death of Garfield shall arouse the nation to more hatred of that institution of Mormonism, . . . he will not have died in vain." For though Talmage couldn't be sure of the assassin's affiliation, the villain clearly "had the ugliness of a Mormon, the licentiousness of a Mormon, the cruelty of a Mormon, the murderous spirit of a Mormon."[1]

Talmage's remarks came more than three decades after the Saints' expulsions from Missouri and Illinois and during the final years of Mormonism's polygamous period. When that practice was banned by church manifesto in 1890, the last waves of national indignation began to exhaust themselves. One final act of public resistance to the church's legitimation came in 1903, after Reed Smoot was elected to the United States Senate from Utah. Because of his position as a high official in the Mormon church, Smoot was denied his seat. Hearings raged on for four years. When the issue finally resolved in 1907, the Mormon problem was at last beginning to wane.

Still, old rancor and stereotypes continued to emerge from time to time. Over a hundred years after the pulpit bombast of Talmage, a prominent scholar and social critic bemoaned the state of America's spiritual wasteland: "We are living in a moment teeming with raucously overvalued emptiness and trash," he wrote. His book was not merely an account of "the death of American sensibility and taste," but probed the causes as well. In his concluding comments, he conjectures as to the origin of ills as diverse as "BAD Advertising" and "BAD Airlines" to "BAD Public Sculpture" and "BAD Television." He finds the culprit in a rather unlikely place. "When did the dumbing of America begin?...Some rude skeptics might want to locate the origins of 'creeping nincompoopism'...in the 1830s, when Joseph Smith took from dictation a number of miserably written narratives and injunctions conveyed to him by the angel Moroni and then persuaded a number of hicks to begin a new religion."[2]

What is it about Mormonism that accounts for such an enduring and tenacious fixation on this marginalized and relatively minor denomination as one of the most significant threats to presidents, Christianity, and good airlines that America has ever known? The history of religious and ethnic prejudice in American culture is vast indeed, and perhaps this is but one more monotonous example of the more pernicious aspects of the Jacksonian inheritance. But there are grounds for believing otherwise.

The history of anti-Mormonism has much to distinguish it, both in the intensity and variety of its manifestations, and in the origins of the hostility. In no other case in American history has a governor signed an order for the expulsion or extermination of a segment of his state's own citizenry (Governor Lilburn Boggs of Missouri in 1838),[3] a state militia forced the evacuation of a city of thousands (Nauvoo, Illinois, in 1847), the United States sent an occupying army against its own citizens ("Buchanan's blunder," 1857–58) or dissolved a church as a legal corporation and disenfranchised thousands of its members (Edmund Tucker Act, 1887).

From its founding in 1830 to the turn of the century, Mormonism was the subject of persecutions, "mobbings," state extermination orders, editorials, religious pamphleteering, congressional committee hearings, federal legislation, and several national political platforms. Many accounts of "the Mormon problem" in American history have been written, and the sources and shape of the Mormon conflict explored. Several of these interpretive histories seek to answer the question the Mormon experience recurrently invites: Why an influence and reaction out of all proportion to the sect's relatively small numbers?

Some have seen Mormonism as merely one of several new and unortho-dox American religious and quasi-religious groups that sprang to life in the 1800s. Spiritualism, Christian Science, Mesmerism, utopianism, to name a few, also gained large followings to their unconventional value systems and teachings. Some of them engendered hostility and opprobrium. None elicited pogroms, disincorporation, and disfranchisement.

As to whether Mormon accounts of their conflict with the American people and government were exaggerated, it is doubtful. Certainly *empha-sizing* their persecutions had the effect of writing them more effectively into the history of the beatitudinally blessed. Group cohesion and loyalty undoubtedly were strengthened by a collective sense of shared suffering. But the Mormon experience is well enough documented to make clear a pattern of religious persecution and violence without parallel in American history.

Historians have suggested a wide array of factors contributing to hos-tility toward Mormonism.[4] Religious intolerance, clerical jealousies, a predisposition to resolve conflict by violence on a tempestuous frontier, defensiveness about traditional economic and social practices, all contrib-uted. So, too, did Mormon missionary work that was extensive and ener-getic, a vocabulary of exclusion that cast Mormons as "covenant people" and outsiders as "gentiles," and the fact that areas settled by Mormons, from Nauvoo, Illinois, to Salt Lake, were too near theocracies for popu-lar taste. In the case of one horrific atrocity perpetrated by Mormons, the aforementioned wagon train massacre, at Mountain Meadows, Utah, church leaders did more to conceal Mormon involvement than aid fed-eral prosecution of the responsible parties. Mormonism has a history that spans almost two centuries of American social and political history, and the Mormon church has passed through a number of stages in its own theological and institutional development. It is clear that the conflict has too many variables to admit of reductive explanation. Nevertheless, the continuing challenges the church has faced in its efforts to be accorded legitimacy and respectability among sister religions and the public at large suggest the possibility of a common thread that pervades the history of representations of Mormonism from the journalistic outrage in Palmyra, New York, to twentieth-century popular anti-Mormon films like *The God Makers*, to twenty-first-century resistance to a Mormon presidential candidate.

Warren Foote's vision of Mormon history was informed by his fervent conviction that the church he had joined was "the only true and living church upon the face of the whole earth" and must inevitably arouse the wrath of the powers of darkness. Accordingly, he saw the sources of the conflict in fairly simple terms: "This war was waged against the Latter Day Saints, because they believed in prophets and professed to have revelation from God. This was the statement of General Clark in his address to the Saints at Far West, after the surrender."[5]

Critics, on the other hand, had a vested interest in framing their objections to Mormonism in nonreligious terms. The legitimacy of their position depended on its being founded on more than religious prejudice. What this means is that both sides had enormous stakes in contesting the other's explanation of the sources of the conflict. But paradoxically, both contributed to the Mormons' emerging status as a distinctive ethnic community. The conversion narrative of which Foote's account is a type emphasizes the disparity between the Babylon left behind and the New Jerusalem the convert has found. For a people who stake a serious claim to being a covenant people, some basis for their identity as a "peculiar people" is essential. For Mormons, who lacked racial or other conspicuous markers of difference, the peculiarity outsiders imposed on them worked to affirm the very status of chosenness they sought. The Mormon practice of referring to all outsiders as "gentiles" is seen in this light not as historically naive posturing, but as a way of reinforcing a difference that is entirely constructed.

For the nineteenth-century opponents of Mormonism, a favorite mode of representing Mormonism, working in counterpoint with the conversion narrative, was the captivity narrative. It, too, is constructed around radical opposition between incompatible social and religious worlds. The horrors of enslavement and the raptures of escape depend for their effect upon the enormity of the chasm that the victim successfully navigates in her homeward journey. So from the Mormon perspective, this radical difference is the believer's sign of blessedness. But from the opposite perspective, such difference is threatening and dangerous; opposing it becomes a display of patriotism, not intolerance.

VISIONS AND "CONTEMPTIBLE GIBBERISH"

Joseph Smith himself recorded that within days of his first vision, he was imprudent enough to share the account with a local minister, who dismissed the episode as being of the devil.[6] Soon, he writes, the entire religious community was stirred to anger against him. It has been common to dismiss as overly self-important Joseph's estimate of the uproar he created as a young boy claiming to have seen a vision, and perhaps, until the church assumed official status, actual persecution to members other than the Smith family was minimal. But the press began fulminating against Smith even before the Book of Mormon was published in 1830; "Blasphemy!" trumpeted the *Rochester Daily Advertiser*, inaugurating a trend that would continue unabated for decades. Months after the April organization of the church, a mob destroyed a baptismal dam and threatened Smith and some of his converts in the Colesville, New York, area, where the prophet was preaching and baptizing. Within days, a constable appeared on the scene and arrested Smith for "being a disorderly person by preaching the *Book of Mormon*, and setting the country in an uproar."[7] Church headquarters soon removed to Ohio, where New York members relocated and new converts from the surrounding areas began to gather. In the spring of 1832, disaffected Mormons and religious leaders organized an attack on Smith and his associate Sidney Rigdon, who were savagely beaten, tarred, and feathered.

Meanwhile, as the place of gathering shifted to Jackson County, Missouri, the first full-scale persecutions soon erupted. A number of new factors were added to the sources of religious conflict. With the growing size and cohesion of the Latter-day Saint population, political and cultural frictions developed. From this point on in the Mormon story, historians have increasingly focused on nonreligious explanations for the conflict. Nevertheless, before the organized depredations and expulsions that came to be called the Missouri War began, the hundreds of mobbers involved at the outset committed their complaints to paper.

The document, drawn up at a mass meeting in Jackson County, Missouri, in July 1833, makes it clear that religious difference was never far from the minds of the old settlers, however substantial their other objections were. They cite a number of motives as justification for the imminent expulsion of the Mormons from the area. First, the Mormons had the impudence to refer to Missouri as their rightful inheritance (Smith had in 1831 referred to Missouri as "the land of [the Mormons'] inheritance, which is now the land of your enemies").[8] The document on the one hand contemptuously dismisses such doctrine as empty bombast ("whether this is to be accomplished by the hand of the destroying angel, the judgments of God, or the arm of power, they are not fully agreed among themselves"). On the other hand, the document at the same time refers to the influx of Mormon "swarms" and raises a specter that brings the religious issue right to the foreground. Imagine, the authors implore, "the fate of our lives and property, in the hands of jurors and witnesses, who do not blush to declare, and would not upon occasion hesitate to swear, that they have wrought miracles ... and supernatural cures, have converse with God and His angels, and possess and exercise the gifts of divination and of unknown tongues."[9]

Second, the residents accused the Latter-day Saints of "an indirect invitation to the free brethren of color in Illinois, to come up ... to the land of Zion."[10] This was one of the explanations given by the visiting Englishman Edward Abdy. Mormon settlements were attacked, he reported having heard, because they had "invited the free people of color to join them."[11] Such a practice would not only have been inflammatory in a slave state like Missouri; it also would have been, as Mormon apostle Parley P. Pratt pointed out in a rebuttal to the claims of the mob, illegal.[12] In fact, LDS editor W. W. Phelps had published a statement of Mormon policy regarding free blacks, indicating that the Saints sustained Missouri law, which disallowed immigration of free blacks unless they could produce proof of citizenship.[13] If the Missourians had taken their own charge more seriously, they would have highlighted such dangerous subversive activity in a pro-slavery state. Instead, the accusation is sandwiched between an attack on the Mormons' religious practices and a stubborn reiteration of that attack at the document's conclusion. Because there are no laws against religious claims, no matter how incredible, even frontier justice cannot pretend to justify itself in the name of bigotry. Yet the Missourians cannot ignore the religious irritants, even to legitimate their collective act of violence. Rather than mount a serious attack on Mormon racial views in a way that *would* legitimate—or at least mitigate—their violent solutions, the mobbers repeatedly invoke and caricature the real source of friction, Mormon religious heterodoxy.

Studies like that by Kenneth Winn have attempted to downplay or dismiss altogether the religious component to the Missouri persecutions. Winn goes so far as to claim that "despite heated Mormon protests to the contrary, the Missourians displayed a relative indifference to the actual content of Mormon theology."[14] As evidence, he cites the same mob document, which claims to leave "to God alone" the matter of this "grossest superstition." But Winn fails to mention that this generous remark follows hard upon the gratuitous return to that very subject of Mormon beliefs, which are supposedly a matter of indifference: "Of their pretended revelations from heaven—their personal intercourse with God and His angels—the maladies they pretend to heal by the laying on of hands— and the contemptible gibberish with which they habitually profane the Sabbath, and which they dignify with the appellation of unknown tongues, we have nothing to say."[15] Obviously, the Missourians have already said a great deal. Given the investment the Missourians—and American critics of Mormonism in general—had in their status as freedom-loving exemplars and defenders of American individualism, it would be surprising if they did *not* attempt to present their case in terms of nonreligious issues.

To take these references to nonreligious sources of the conflict as reliable evidence of a purely secular conflict is to acquiesce a little too readily to the Missourians' exculpating rationale. To blithely discount religious motivations because we are asked to is to ignore the mechanisms by which ideology and acts of self-fashioning work to conceal inherent tensions and inconsistencies that arise when espoused values and political imperatives collide.

The Saints themselves expressed no uncertainty about the source of their oppression. "We believe that these persecutions have come in consequence of our religious faith, and not for any immorality on our part," asserted a number of leading Mormons in Caldwell County in a petition to a committee of the Missouri Legislature on December 10, 1838.[16] Smith wrote to Isaac Galland, a land broker in southeastern Iowa, that Missouri judges and the Saints' lawyers corroborated this view:

> The Judges have gravely told us from time to time that...if we deny our religion, we can be liberated. Our lawyers have gravely told us, that we are only held now by the influence of long faced Baptists; how far this is true, we are not able to say; but we are certain that our most vehement accusers, are the highest toned professors of religion. On being interogated [sic] what these men have done? their uniform answer is, we do not know, but they are false teachers, and ought to die. And of late boldly and frankly acknowledge, that the religion of all these is all that they have against them.[17]

Obviously, just as the persecutors' moral authority depended upon their suppression of the religious dimensions of the conflict, so did the Mormons' depend upon its centrality. Of course, nonreligious factors contributed to the problem, and in significant ways. The mob, however, was neither willing nor able to downplay the outrage of Mormon claims to their religious sensibility. It is abundantly clear, from their initial reference to the Mormons as "this singular sect," to their concluding salvo about "contemptible gibberish," that religious difference of a particular kind aggravated, if it did not generate, the conflict.

Other factors, too, suggest that anti-abolitionist rhetoric was more of a red herring—or at best an explosive issue easily and cynically exploited—than genuinely central to anti-Mormon sentiment in Missouri. For example, Clark Johnson, in his work on the Missouri Redress Petitions (773 affidavits that served as the Mormons' paper trail to document both the history of their persecutions and their good-faith effort to work within the system for redress of their wrongs), concludes that the testimonies are unanimous in specifying religious belief, not political views or cultural tensions, as the explicit catalyst for mob attacks. The testimonies Johnson has assembled constitute the most impressive body of firsthand accounts concerning the violence perpetrated against Mormons during the Missouri conflict. Time and again, they demonstrate that "religious differences were the prime cause of LDS troubles," as they record that the mobbers made Mormon beliefs the focus of and justification for their actions.[18]

Smith often referred to the role of the clergy as prime instigators of anti-Mormon violence. He frequently recorded in his journal history the names of preachers active in actions against the Mormons. An affidavit signed by three representatives of the church in 1842 records that when Smith was court-martialed by the Missouri Militia at Far West and sentenced to death, "seventeen preachers of the gospel were on this court martial; and, horrible to relate, were in favor of this merciless sentence."[19]

Even Winn does not deny the involvement of the clergy in the Missouri religious tensions, but he asserts that "the growth of anti-Mormonism" might not have "depended upon this encouragement."[20] That is hardly a reason to diminish the significance of religious factors in the conflict. Contemporary characterizations of frontier preachers lend some credibility to Smith's claims. A gazetteer of Illinois, published in 1834, grants that the "qualifications of the clergymen are various. A number of them are men of talents, learning, influence, and unblemished piety. Others have but few advantages in acquiring either literary or theological information, and yet are good speakers and useful men. Some are very illiterate, and make utter confusion of the word of God. Such persons are usually proud, conceited, fanatical, and influenced by a spirit far removed from the meek, docile, benevolent, and charitable spirit of the gospel."[21] A year later, Tocqueville's companion Gustave de Beaumont was equally unimpressed. "Nothing," he remarked, "is more unusual than to see a Protestant minister with white hair. The major goal that the American in the ministry pursues is his own welfare and that of his wife and children. When he has materially improved his condition, his end is achieved; he retires."[22]

Edward Abdy noted that in Missouri, a Mormon bishop claimed in a local newspaper that "there are already 20,000 converts to the doctrines he professes." Abdy goes on to remark on the dynamics of such rumors: "Absurd as this 'account' is, or perhaps because it is absurd, it has imposed upon many."[23] Clearly, the Mormons, with their aggressive and phenomenally successful proselytizing, presented a serious threat to contemporary preachers. That economic considerations compounded the threat to doctrinal purity is more than likely.

NATIVISM AND ANTI-CATHOLICISM

Popular treatment of ethnic minorities in general, and of Catholics in particular, who came to be increasingly associated with Irish immigrants, suggests other nonreligious dimensions to anti-Mormonism. Mormons and Catholics were both charged with what Gary Bunker and Davis Bitton refer to as a "ritually recited litany" of offenses: "(1) deliberately subverting American values; (2) posing a threat to the constitutional separation of church and state; (3) submitting to autocratic control from Rome and Salt Lake City—the latter labeled 'A Yankee Vatican' in the pages of the English humor periodical *Punch*; (4) sponsoring secret ceremonies of dubious repute; and (5) encouraging the licentious or economic exploitation of women."[24]

Because of these alleged affinities between Catholicism and Mormonism, the nativist hostility against the Catholics in the mid-nineteenth century was soon targeting the Mormons as well. At least two scholars have written of anti-Catholicism and anti-Mormonism (along with anti-Masonry) as "separate waves of a common current"—nativism.[25] One classic study of American religious bigotry even situates the Mormon problem in a chapter titled "Nativism."[26] Undoubtedly, some anti-Mormon authors framed their attacks in nativist terms, as we will see. Mormons were at times tarred with the same brush as the "papists," as in the case of Robert Richards's *The Californian Crusoe* (1854). In fact, Richards portrays the Mormon leaders as conceiving, together with Jesuit conspirators, "the bold design of introducing the whole Mormon community into the Romish fold."[27] Mormon doctrines are seen as thinly veiled Catholic heresies; baptism for the dead is thus "a preparation for a belief in purgatory and masses for the departed," and Mormon miracles are viewed as reminiscent of the portents and visitations that characterize much of Catholic history. In 1842, the Reverend John Clark had similarly lamented the "Mormon Jesuitism,"[28] by which he apparently meant Mormon conspiratorial and deceptive practices generally.

Occasionally, then, nativism was a common ground in the anti-Catholic and anti-Mormon campaigns, and a perception that the same values were at stake in the two causes led some writers to participate in both. Such was the case with Orvilla S. Belisle. In 1855 she published *The Prophets; or, Mormonism Unveiled*. Her *The make Arch Bishop; or, Romanism in the United States* had been dedicated "to the American people who have the perpetuity and prosperity of our institutions at heart: To those who are opposed to the suppression of the Bible in public schools and legislative halls, of free thought, free speech, and a free press."[29] Her anti-Mormonism, like her anti-Catholicism, was part of her campaign to make America safe for democracy.

As late as 1909, a lingering nativism would still motivate—or at least be invoked by—some anti-Mormon writers, like Gertrude Keene Major. In that year, she collected a virulent series of anti-Mormon essays in *The Revelation in the Mountain*. She uses her dedication to insist upon a political rather than religious motivation: "To the American Party, which is striving to bring the majesty of the Country's law to despotic Utah."[30] Charles Pidgin's *House of Shame* (1912) is a little more creative in making its point. The (American) hero's name is Madison. His (American) brothers' names are Washington, Adams, Jefferson, and Monroe. His (American) son's name is Franklin. Typical Mormon characters are Jason and Samson.

Nineteenth- and early twentieth-century writers were prone to sprinkle their work liberally with allusions to other non-American ethnic groups, further driving home the point that Mormons were but one more alien culture, undeserving of political or social toleration in a time of economic and social tensions. Pidgin provides a good example of this guilt-by-association strategy. He situates his story in Salt Lake but manages to refer, in none-too-favorable terms, to "Mahometans," American Indians, Turks, and Chinese (referred to by a character as "rat-eaters").[31] Gary Bunker and Davis Bitton have traced this same practice of associating Mormons with undesirable ethnic groups in periodical illustrations. "The specific groups most frequently linked to Mormons in prints," they write, were the "Irish, Catholics, blacks, Chinese [and] Native Americans."[32]

Certainly the references to ethnicity suggest a nativist complexion to these and similar works. Pressures besides opposition to immigration directed attention to questions of group identity and character. Mormonism flourished during the high point of American expansion and in the shadow of that crucible of American self-definition, the Civil War. The Republican Party held its first national convention; manifest destiny was still unfolding; territories—Utah would soon be one of them—were petitioning for admission to the Union. Against this historical backdrop, the question of American identity was moved from the realm of abstract Tocquevillian conjecture to explicit political debate. And it is in this context that the first and formative generation of anti-Mormon literature was spawned.[33]

Anti-Mormonism, however, was also distinct from nativism. In 1856, a year when both Mormonism and nativism provided grist for the political mills, three parties enunciated their official platforms. The Republican Party expressly vowed "to prohibit in the Territories those twin relics of barbarism—Polygamy and Slavery."[34] Certainly the party was committed to an unambiguous stand on the controversial issue of slavery, and perhaps it was merely convenient to link that issue to a religious custom readily metaphorized as white slavery. Such rhetoric had the advantage of furthering the Republican position as enlightened crusaders against oppression. Still, the linking of nativism and anti-Mormonism would have been just as timely, given the xenophobic frenzy of the period. It would doubtless have been less divisive an allusion than that to slavery. That neither the Republicans nor any other party made such a connection, even when circumstances invited one, suggests that nativism was not entirely credible as a basis for anti-Mormon agitation.

Nativism *was* made a part of the platform of one political party in 1856—the American Party (Know-Nothings). The party stipulated that *"Americans must rule America*; and to this end, *native*-born citizens should be selected for all...offices of government employment, in preference to naturalized citizens" (emphases in original). The platform goes on to hint darkly of those who would enter into "alliance or obligation of any description to any foreign prince, potentate, or power."[35] No allusions, however, were made to Mormonism. So two of the three parties of the period were willing to tackle the problems of nativism and Mormonism head-on, but neither platform connected them.

It is of course possible that anti-Catholicism and anti-Mormonism were nonetheless related, that the prejudices against both drew from a common well. What is beyond doubt is that both currents were presented to the public in ethnic terms—regardless of the degree to which ethnicity and the immigration chimera it evoked were the genuine sources of alarm.

THEOCRACY AND POLYGAMY

Finally, at the court of inquest subsequent to Joseph Smith's arrest in Far West, the testimony against the Saints raised an issue to which recent scholars have given increasing weight. Wrote Pratt: "Our church organization was converted, by the testimony of the apostates, into a temporal kingdom, which was to fill the whole earth, and subdue all other kingdoms."[36] The inflammatory July Fourth speech by church leader Sidney Rigdon, unremitting talk of Missouri as a place of gathering and land of inheritance for the Saints, their potent political solidarity—all these factors produced a recurring charge that Klaus Hansen claimed was *the* central cause of Mormon persecutions: a theocratic social system with aspirations to political empire.[37] Discounting the more intuitive explanation that polygamy was a major culprit, Hansen cites the testimony of anti-Mormon Frederick Dubois as representative of a subterfuge that employed the plural marriage issue as a weapon in the moral crusade against Mormonism:

> Those of us who understood the situation were not nearly as much opposed to polygamy as we were to the political domination of the Church. We realized, however, that we could not make those who did not come actually in contact with it, understand what this political domination meant. We made use of polygamy in consequence as our great weapon of offense and to gain recruits to our standard. There was a universal detestation of polygamy, and inasmuch as the Mormons openly defended it we were given a very effective weapon with which to attack.[38]

Pointing to the Saints' millennialism, and a theocratic vision backed up by a Mormon "Council of Fifty" poised to function as an effectual government, Hansen's argument gains credence from Brigham Young's defiance of the federal government when LDS leaders were de facto leaders of a federally administered territory. Whether or not such Mormon power dynamics were more symbol than substance, and reflected "millennial anticipations" rather than "temporal realities," as some have argued, the virtual theocracy was real enough to alarm American observers.[39]

As for Dubois's statement that the anti-polygamy crusade was really a ploy by clever critics whose real concern was Mormon political power, it is hardly an effective argument against polygamy's centrality in anti-Mormon sentiment. For his explanation acknowledged the moral repugnance the practice engendered in the many (the "recruits"), but added to the volatile equation a political concern on the part of the elite ("we who understood the situation.") The plausibility of his conspiratorial scenario aside, the strategy he alludes to reinforces rather than diminishes the role of polygamy in the history of Mormon persecution.

However, even into the polygamous period and during Utah's quest for statehood, opposition continued to emphasize the religion-making aspects of Mormonism. Writers as diverse as contemporary LDS scholar Hugh Nibley and *Scribner's* anti-Mormon editor J. H. Beadle, writing during the height of the anti-polygamy period, have agreed that other factors were responsible for far more persecution than polygamy ever was. Nibley, in his exhaustive survey of anti-Mormonism, discounts polygamy and politics as root causes of the conflict, since these were "rapidly changing circumstances." He finds only one constant: "the religious teaching of the Mormons, and the persecution is always explicitly leveled at the teaching."[40] Writing in 1877, Beadle editorialized about the causes of Mormon persecution. He discounts polygamy as an explanation, noting that the record clearly shows "the Mormons had more trouble with the world before they adopted polygamy than since.... Polygamy will do for a scape-goat, but the trouble is far more radical than that."[41] Finally, historian of bigotry Gustavus Myers agrees that "in the earlier stages, the feeling against the Mormons was not dominantly because of polygamy."[42]

After their expulsion from Jackson County in July 1833, the Saints moved north into Clay County. The arrangement was supposed to be temporary. When it became obvious that the Mormons would not be returning to Jackson County in the foreseeable future, the residents of Clay held their own mass meeting. Though opposition did not turn violent, the residents threatened that civil war was imminent if the Mormons did not move on. In a token nod to constitutionalism, they acknowledged they did not have "the least right under the constitution and the laws of the country to expel them by force." Nevertheless, intimidating the Mormons with the specter of "ruin, woe, and desolation" if they did not relocate was, in light of their recent experiences, quite enough.[43] The Saints moved into the uninhabited areas northward.

CLASH OF CULTURES

As justification for this second expulsion, the residents of Clay County, like their Jackson County neighbors, drafted a document in which they named the factors that rendered coexistence impossible. This document, too, began with a critique of the Mormon religion: "Their religious tenets were so different from the present churches of the age, that this always had and always would excite deep prejudice against them in any populous country where they might locate." In addition, the settlers cited the Mormons' "manners, habits, customs, and even dialect" peculiar to "eastern men." Third on the list was the familiar charge of opposition to slavery, and last was their "constant communication with the Indian tribes on the frontier" and Mormon belief that Indians were "a part of God's chosen people."[44]

It was true that most of the church's early converts came from the states of New York, Pennsylvania, and Ohio, the first areas of church headquarters and proselytizing efforts, as well as from a number of other eastern states to which missionaries had traveled as early as 1830. At least in the case of the Missouri War, much friction was undoubtedly a consequence of very different cultures coming into conflict.

One of the most prevalent of the many stereotypes of Mormon converts held that they were drawn from the dregs of American and European society. Objective accounts of such observers as Charles Dickens were quite to the contrary. The novelist visited an emigrant ship about to sail for America "in order to see what Eight hundred Latter-day Saints were like, and I found them (to the rout and overthrow of all my expectations) . . . a very fine set of people." In fact, he found them, "in their degree, the pick and flower of England." "It would be difficult," he went on, "to find Eight hundred people together anywhere else, and find so much beauty and so much strength and capacity for work among them."[45] Perhaps a celebrity like Dickens was merely defying popular impressions. Still, enough disinterested accounts exist to suggest that Mormons' level of intellectual aspirations—if not actual attainments—were so far above the average frontiersman as to aggravate social tensions. The same army officer who was alarmed at the prospect of "30,000 of these warlike fanatics" recently arrived from Missouri in Nauvoo, was also moved to admiration. Three years after the settling of Nauvoo, he wrote: "Ecclesiastical history presents no parallel to this people, inasmuch as they are establishing their religion on a learned footing. All the sciences are taught, and to be taught in their colleges, with Latin, Greek, Hebrew, French, Italian, Spanish, &c. &c. The mathematical sciences, pure and mixed, are now in successful operation, under an extremely able Professor of the name of Pratt, and a graduate of Trinity College, Dublin, is President of their University."[46]

The idea of a vagrant religious minority already dispossessed three or four times in ten years setting up a university in the midst of recently drained swampland along the Mississippi frontier in order to study Hebrew and Italian is so incongruous as to strain belief.

Missouri in 1831, the year of the Saints' arrival, was still very much a frontier state, with all that that implied. The English traveler J. S. Buckingham remarked in 1842 that "no one can approach the frontier settlements . . . without being struck with the lawless spirit . . . everywhere manifested by the inhabitants."[47] Carlyle Buley, in his study of the Old Northwest during the period 1815–1840, concedes that the impression of these inhabitants as "coarse, ignorant, lawless, and violent" was true at all times for some and at some time for most. The collision of old cultures with new was the result, he continues, of a "failure of law made for the older societies to function under the peculiar conditions of the frontier."[48]

Joseph Smith himself arrived in Missouri in the summer of 1831. Long before the first hostilities were manifest, his observations caused him great foreboding:

> Our reflections were many, coming as we had from a highly cultivated state of
> society in the east, and standing now upon the confines or western limits of the

United States, and looking into the vast wilderness of those who sat in darkness; how natural it was to observe the degradation, leanness of intellect, ferocity, and jealously of a people that were nearly a century behind the times, and to feel for those who roamed about without the benefit of civilization, refinement, or religion.[49]

These perceptions were not limited to European visitors and Yankee prophets. William Walker, at one time the provisional governor of the Nebraska Territory, visited Independence, nerve center of the Mormon gathering in Missouri, a few years after the Saints' expulsion. He found the citizens "the most *selfish, exacting, grinding, mercenary people* I ever saw in any country, barbarian or Christian. Hospitality is an utter stranger and foreigner to them" (emphasis in original).[50]

An inescapable feature of life on the frontier was a social leveling born of necessity, the total irrelevance of class and rank once the entertainments and amenities of eastern culture were left behind. "The leveling spirit of Western democracy," writes Ray Allen Billington, "sought not only to elevate the lowly but also to dethrone the elite. Any attempt at 'putting on airs,' was certain to be met with rude reminders of the equality of all men." In fact, he continues, "new settlers were warned by guidebooks to mingle freely and familiarly with neighbors, and above all to pretend no superiority, if they wished to be accepted."[51] Edward Pessen similarly challenges the notion that the characteristic type of the early nineteenth century was "an inner directed American, marching to his own music, living his life according to his own and his family's notions of how it should be lived. Observers during the Jacksonian era saw a very different American, indeed. The American was a conformist, in the opinion of foreigner and native, to the sympathetic as well as the jaundiced."[52]

Not only did the Saints not mingle or conform—they emphasized by word and deed their radical distinctness from their neighbors. Their principle of "gathering," their self-identification with the House of Israel, and their relegation of all others to the status of "gentiles" did not help. According to Joel Kotkin, "what distinguished the Mormons and offended their 'gentile' neighbors was a kind of clannishness, what one mid-nineteenth-century writer described as their Jew-like 'separation from their great brotherhood of mankind.'"[53]

Richard Burton, the writer Kotkin refers to, may have been the most successful European ever to blend into the Arab cultures he studied, and he was the first outsider to explore such forbidden cities as Harar in Somaliland, as well as Mecca and Medina. But even he sensed that "there is in Mormondom, as in all other exclusive faiths, … an inner life into which I cannot flatter myself or deceive the reader with the idea of my having penetrated."[54] The exclusiveness of Mormon society was a predominant feature of the public's perception of the sect, and provoked reactions both humorous and tragic.

After the debacle at Far West, at least one central participant in the Missouri persecutions saw "the gathering" as a major factor in the conflict. Upon the occasion of the betrayal of Smith and his colleagues into the hands of the militia at Far West, General Clark went so far as to prophesy that tragedy would again befall the Saints if they did not give up the practice: "I would advise you to scatter abroad, and never again organize yourselves with Bishops, Presidents, etc., lest you excite the jealousies of the people, and subject yourselves to the same calamities that have now come upon you."[55] Some Mormon leaders were persuaded that Clark was right. Sidney Rigdon, Edward Partridge, and others advised scattering, while Brigham Young felt the principle of gathering was still vital for purposes of mutual support. When the opportunity to purchase large tracts of land in the region of Commerce, Illinois, arose, Smith resolved the dispute by writing from his basement dungeon in Liberty jail. He wrote to Isaac Galland, a land broker, asking him to "hold it in reserve for us."[56] Commerce (soon to be renamed "Nauvoo") would quickly outstrip Far West as the new place of gathering.

Clark's advice was echoed in a humorous fashion in Warren Foote's encounter with a simple but well-intentioned woman he met on his exodus from Nauvoo to Winter Quarters in Nebraska eight years later. The exchange reveals both the estrangement and apprehension that accompanied popular impressions of Mormon solidarity: "She asked, 'How many do you suppose there are of the Mormons.' I answered, I cannot tell, some thousands I suppose. She said with surprise, 'Do you not know them all?' O no madam, but a few of them I replied. 'You *don't*,' said she 'I thought they all knowed one another.' I said that they were like other folks about that." She went on to add, tellingly, "If the Mormons would scatter around amongst the white folks, they could live in peace."[57]

In a number of ways Mormons were clearly not "like other folks," and aspects of their clannishness were disturbing for several reasons. By adhering so zealously to the principle of the gathering, the Mormons were, of course, complicit with their detractors in emphasizing the apartness of Mormon culture that would later flower into the quasi-ethnicity remarked upon by O'Dea and Kotkin. And in addition to the offensiveness of a vocabulary of "chosenness" in the midst of an emphatically egalitarian culture, there were Mormon economic practices that emphasized self-sufficiency and independence from the larger economic order and their embrace of theocratic principles in the midst of frontier individualism; in all respects they reaffirmed their status as a people set apart. In retrospect, it is virtually inconceivable that a clannish, religious people with deeply held convictions about their elect status could hope to successfully establish themselves in the midst of such surroundings.

RACE RELATIONS

This clash of cultures had its specifically political tensions as well. The Mormons' reputation for abolitionist sympathies was an issue that wouldn't easily die in the skittish context of antebellum Missouri. Few states in American history would be so divided by the slavery issue. The fractious debate over its admission as a slave or free state had produced the Missouri Compromise of 1820, with its admission as a slave state the next year. Although that temporarily resolved the problem in Missouri, conflict and eventually violence would swirl around the borders, as opposing factions contended for the surrounding territories. Within Missouri, internal dissension would increase as the balance of pro-slavery sentiment shifted with the influx of immigrants from the Northeast and from Europe. By the Civil War, the tide had turned enough to consign Missouri to the Union side. Into the midst of this turmoil came the Mormons at the close of 1831.

As mentioned above, the complaint of Mormon opposition to slavery had first been leveled by the Missourians of Jackson County in July 1833. Supposedly an article in the *Evening and Morning Star*, the church newspaper, had invited freed slaves to settle there. In actual fact, the article in question had reprinted the law prohibiting such settlement, warned church members of the penalties associated with transport of free Negroes or mulattoes, and encouraged Saints to "shun every appearance of evil." At the same time, however, the editor, W. W. Phelps, was also impolitic enough to refer to "the wonderful events of this age," in which "much is doing towards abolishing slavery."[58]

Sensitive to the political winds, Joseph Smith responded to the mob's allegations about Mormon abolitionism the next year (1835) with a "Declaration of Belief regarding Governments and Laws," in which he insisted that "we do not believe it right to interfere with bond-servants, neither preach the gospel to, nor baptize them contrary to the will and wish of their masters, nor to meddle with or influence them in the least to cause them to be dissatisfied with their situations in this life." Such meddling, he added, no doubt with some irony, was "dangerous to the peace of every government allowing human beings to be held in servitude."[59]

Nevertheless, that Phelps's careless words accurately reflected Mormonism's inherent opposition to slavery, Smith could not deny. As

Abdy himself noted, Smith's own Book of Mormon made it clear it was against God's law "that there should be any slaves."[60] Undoubtedly the slavery issue was grist for the anti-Mormon mill. Still, as we shall see, the anti-Mormon tradition in popular literature, like the Republican platform of 1856, tied slavery to Mormonism by citing Mormon practice of, not their opposition to, a system of alleged servitude (polygamy).

The charges of communicating with Indians and giving them a special place in God's plan were not easily laid to rest either. From 1821 until Texas was granted statehood in 1845, Missouri was the westernmost state in the Union, and attitudes and behavior of the old settlers toward the various Indian tribes inhabiting the area were brutal. One writer, James Coates, refers to "hunting parties" that "ranged across the nearby Indian Territory border where they shot the Indians like they were game animals."[61] As early as 1830, Joseph Smith had sent a party of four on a mission to the "Lamanites," the name given in the Book of Mormon to the Native American descendants of colonizers from Israel who arrived here in the time of the prophet Jeremiah. Considering the Indian nations to be rightful heirs of the Abrahamic covenant and the promises made to Joseph of old, Mormons saw it as an imperative duty to reclaim these lost sheep of Israel. Accordingly, Oliver Cowdery and his companions journeyed fifteen hundred miles to preach to the Wyandots in Ohio and then crossed the Missouri frontier to proselytize the Shawnee and Delaware tribes before being expelled from the Indian country by government agents.

The elevation of the "savage" to the status of Israelite was offensive enough to the old settlers. Not that Mormons were the first to assert this connection; Ethan Smith had published his *View of the Hebrews* in 1825. In it he argued that the lost ten tribes of Israel "are *the aborigines of our own continent!*"[62] Its second edition even bore the subtitle "The Tribes of Israel in America." Even earlier, James Adair had published his *History of the American Indians* (1775), in which he argued that the continent's native inhabitants were "lineally descended from the Israelites."[63] Other versions of the theory appeared in print going back to the sixteenth century. But Mormon fraternizing with the tribes and their attempts to win them to the Mormon fold were clearly beyond the pale of tolerance. The combination of Missouri's vulnerability to Indian unrest with an apparently imminent Mormon/Indian alliance was easily recognized by even a foreign observer as a key ingredient in the Missouri conflicts. The English traveler Abdy, writing in the midst of these Missouri troubles, commented:

> As the promulgators of this extraordinary legend maintain the natural equality of mankind, without excepting the native Indians or the African race, there

is little reason to be surprised at the cruel persecution by which they have suffered, and still less at the continued accession of converts among those who
sympathize with the wrongs of others or seek an asylum of their own. The
preachers and believers of the[se] ... doctrines were not likely to remain, unmo-
lested, in the state of Missouri.[64]

The Missourians' worst fears were confirmed in the years ahead as the
Mormons continued with their rhetoric of dispossession.

In 1846, as the Saints deserted Nauvoo, Illinois, en route to present-day
Omaha, rumors of Mormon machinations to unite with the Indians were
still rampant. When Warren Foote encountered the Nebraska woman
mentioned earlier, she was clearly disturbed by such reports:

> The inhabitants are very much scared. They are afraid that the "Mormons" will
> soon be upon them and slay men, women, and children. I called into a house
> to see if I could sell any thing. The man was not at home. As I turned to go
> out the woman said "You are a Mormon I suppose it is a fair question." Yes
> Madam I replied. She said "There are a great many Indians up there where you
> are camped." I replied that I had not seen any. Said she, You have not seen any!
> Why we hear that you are building forts and your women are marrying in with
> the Indians, and that you are combining togather [sic] and are coming down
> here to kill us all off." ... She then said, "There are a great many women here that
> are almost scared to death, they are just ready to run." Well, Said I, if they are
> not killed until the "Mormons" kill them they will live a long time.[65]

Two years later, alarmists persisted in their claims. In 1848 Catherine
Lewis published her *Narrative of Some of the Proceedings of the Mormons.*
Her subtitle read, in part, "With Particulars concerning the Training of
the Indians." Among her allegations was the claim that at "about the time
the Smiths were shot, ... there were two or three tribes of Indians all ready
to go through, avenge, and destroy the people of Carthage [Illinois]; they
only waited for the word of command from the Church."[66]

PREEMPTION AND MILITIAS

Besides the cultural and religious clashes between Mormons and
Missourians, two historical circumstances contributed to the conflagra-
tion known as the Missouri War. One was the context for Pratt's reference
to the "common boast that, as soon as we had completed our extensive
improvements ... they would drive us from the State, and once more enrich

themselves with the spoils."[67] Preemption rights, based on laws first passed
in 1830, allowed impoverished settlers to acquire unsettled land, with no
payment required until a survey was completed and the land went on sale
at a specified date. If they improved and inhabited the land they settled
on, it gave them preferred status to buy it. By 1838, most of the land in
Caldwell had been fully surveyed and was not eligible for preemption pur-
chases. But the land in Daviess County had not been, hence thousands of
impoverished Mormons settled across the county and immediately began
improvements. Months later, as surveys in those areas neared comple-
tion and the date of public sale (November 12) neared, the very preemption rights that had attracted the Saints became, in the words of one legal
scholar, "an impetus for non-Mormon land speculators to force Mormons
out of Missouri." As he explains, "The imminent vesting of those property
rights further explains the frantic efforts to dislodge Mormons from their
lands in Missouri altogether in late 1838."[68] Even observers who found the
Mormons a "weak and credulous people" recognized those motives in the
expulsions:

> The Anti-Mormons were determined the Mormons should yield and abandon
> the country. Moreover the land sales were approaching, and it was expedient
> that they should be driven out before they could establish their rights of pre-
> emption. In this way their valuable improvements—the fruit of diligence and
> enterprise—would pass into the hands of men who would have the pleasure of
> enjoying without the toil of earning.[69]

The ploy was successful. Those who played key roles in the Mormon expulsions immediately swept in and bought up nearly eighteen thousand
improved acres in Daviess County alone.[70]

Another important element was the role and behavior of state militias. The federal Second Militia Act of 1792 had mandated the conscrip-
tion of able-bodied white male citizens ages eighteen to forty-five into
state-sponsored militias, under the command of each state's governor.
By the 1830s, most citizens resisted or ignored mandatory militia service, and volunteer militias generally displaced the common militia.[71]
Volunteers who organized themselves into units of sufficient size, equip-
ping themselves and electing their own officers, could apply for a state
charter under names they chose. Militia service was particularly popular in Missouri, partly as a consequence of Native American unrest; three
times in the 1830s the governor called out the militia to deal with Indian
disturbances. In addition, it reflected a frontier ethic that tended toward
rough-hewn independence and even violence. Militia units had been

notoriously ill-trained and unreliable dating back to Revolutionary times, and Missouri's Black Hawk War of 1832 revealed the same weaknesses. As a result, men were required to muster with the militia four times a year, though the occasions generally took the form of diversion and public spectacle, more than serious military training.[72]

On the Missouri frontier in antebellum America, the line between mobs and these militia units was sometimes fluid or nebulous. The operative principle seemed to be that anything public opinion considered a threat to American values was fair game; depending on the moment and setting, that could mean Irish shantytowns, Catholic convents, abolitionist newspapers, or Mormons. In New York, at the height of the Missouri conflict, a Democratic congressman led a mob that destroyed an abolitionist newspaper office. Two years earlier in 1834, armed Democratic Party loyalists chased Whigs from a polling place, foreshadowing the Gallatin polling violence that launched the last stage of the Missouri War.[73] In fact, the 1830s have been called the high point of extralegal violence in America, with dozens of public riots, some of which involved volunteer militias.[74] In the Jacksonian era generally, political and economic leaders, "gentlemen of property and standing," led both mobs and the local militia—and sometimes both, rendering distinctions almost meaningless.[75] In Missouri, Mormons repeatedly identified prominent leaders at the head of mobs and militias alike. The blurring raised a crucial legal question: did the call to action formally originate in state authority? This was the implicit question recognized by the judge in a case where a mob led by Grandison Newell in Mentor, Ohio, disrupted Mormon apostle Parley Pratt's preaching. He wrote in his opinion that Newell "issued orders to march, and halt, and keep time, but gave no orders to fire. The jury, however, came to the conclusion, that, holding them under military command, he was responsible for their acts."[76] Since on the Missouri frontier the modus operandi of mobs and militia turned out to be the same, uncertainty as to the legal status of an armed group could confuse both sides. Missouri militia often behaved against the Mormons like mobs, and Mormon militia reprisals gave little appearance of being within the law.

In the battle of Crooked River, the blurred boundaries between mob and militia had especially tragic repercussions. The Missouri men attacked by a Mormon unit led by David Patten officially operated as a unit of state militia, even if their actions were more vigilante than soldierly. On the other side, Patten was a captain in a different unit of the state militia, and his men acted under authorization of Elias Higbee, Caldwell County judge. Mormons thought themselves legally constituted as a militia unit to defend themselves against lawless aggressors. State officials saw the

Mormons as lawless fanatics operating against authorized militia units. Weeks later, when John B. Clark, major general in command of the Missouri Militia, prepared to court-martial Mormon leaders in Richmond, he seemed astonished to learn they had themselves been acting as part of a militia unit. In a discussion with Pratt, he referred to Mormon George M. Hinkle as "your commanding officer." Pratt replied in dismay,

"Colonel Hinkle, our commanding officer! What had he to do with our civil rights? He was only a colonel of a regiment of the Caldwell County Militia."

"Why! was he not the commanding officer of the fortress of Far West, the head-quarters of the *Mormon forces*?"

"We had no *'fortress'* or *'Mormon forces,'* but were part of the State militia."

At this the general seemed surprised, and the conversation ended.[77]

Nevertheless, in the eyes of Missouri officials, Mormons had attacked state militia at Crooked River, thereby crossing a line that put them squarely outside the law and made them enemies of the state. That perception, added to exaggerated reports of the Crooked River casualties, led to the famous extermination order of Governor Lilburn Boggs dated October 27. The denouement to the Missouri tragedy followed quickly.

ECONOMICS AND POLITICS

Another source of friction resulted from the Mormons' communitarian economic experiments. In Missouri and Ohio (from 1831 to 1834) "the Law of Consecration," as the underlying principle was called, mandated that Mormons deed over to the church all personal assets, in return for which a portion was deeded back, appropriate to the needs of that family or individual. Thereafter, yearly surplus would continue to be placed at the disposition of the presiding bishop.[78] In spite of tentative efforts at implementation in Ohio and then Missouri, a combination of human foibles, a steady influx of often destitute converts, and, by April 1833, persecutions and forced relocation defeated the practice.

Certainly the communitarian aspirations of the Mormons were sufficient to arouse the suspicion and displeasure of frontier individualists, but it is unlikely that the economic fruits of the short-lived practice were sufficient to provoke envy or resentment, in spite of assertions by historians to the contrary. The historian of religious bigotry Gustavus Myers, for example, felt that "animus was directed at Mormons partly because their ideas and ways differed so greatly from the customary, and in part because of their phenomenally industrious co-operative system which, while essentially individualistic, was planned harmoniously for the common benefit."[79] The Missourians, on the contrary, claimed the indigence of church members was a legitimate factor in their being expelled from Jackson County.

Apart from economic solidarity, Mormonism represented a very potent threat as a political bloc as well. As J. H. Beadle editorialized about the persecutions, "The same results would soon overtake the Methodist or any other church, if it should concentrate its forces in one state, every man voting…at the command of the bishop."[80] Illinois governor Thomas Ford would later repeat this opinion that the greatest public outrage against the Mormons was caused by this bloc voting, which gave them effectual veto power over any aspirant to public office.[81] As politicians were to learn, that was no exaggeration. Mormons did, in fact, vote en bloc, and had the numbers to swing any close Missouri election. In Mormon-dominated Caldwell County, Missouri, for example, in the 1838 race for congressional representative, the Democratic candidate received 337 votes, the Whig, 2.[82]

The volatility of the slave issue, political challenges to American republicanism, and the institution of polygamy contributed to anti-Mormon sentiment, but much remains to be explained in the history of Mormonism's relations with the rest of the world. Slavery, theocracy, and polygamy do not of themselves constitute continuous threads in the Mormon story. The observation of Charles Dickens is a reminder that the constant irritant in relations with Mormonism was always beliefs, not practices. "What the Mormons do," he wrote in 1851, a year before the polygamy proclamation, "seems to be excellent; what they say, is mostly nonsense."[83] Before Mormonism existed as a coherent community, it presented itself as a religion, and the earliest opposition to the church was to its beliefs, not its practices.

As we have seen, opposition to the Mormon church would take many forms, culminating in legislative sanctions and military actions, and would be precipitated by many causes, most notably the church's theocratic ideals and unconventional marriage practices. But long before polygamy was ever an issue, or Johnston's army headed for Utah, the media campaign was in full swing, and its impetus was initially religious.

On June 18, 1830, only weeks after Smith had organized the church, a very concerned Rev. Diedrich Willers, pastor of a German Reformed Church on the outskirts of Fayette, wrote a letter to two ministerial colleagues. The letter gives us a glimpse of what anxieties and criticisms the church provoked from its very inception. Two characteristics of the new faith stand out as theologically most objectionable to Willers. First, Joseph Smith "claims to associate with spirits and angels." One of the first converts and "witnesses" of the Book of Mormon plates, David Whitmer, was known to Willers personally, and Whitmer also "claimed to have seen an angel of the Lord."[84]

Second was the publication and promulgation of the Book of Mormon itself. Joseph Smith, Willers lamented, "wants to elevate his book to the status of a canonical work,...and thereby expects it to be acknowledged that the Word of God is not complete."[85] Soon, Smith's claim to prophetic authority was added to the list of offenses against respectable Christian notions.

With the new church only months old, Joseph Smith was arrested for "setting the city in an uproar by preaching the Book of Mormon." As we saw in the origins of the Missouri War, these same particular features of Mormonism ("miracles," contact "with God and his Angels," "the gift of Divination and unknown tongues") were invoked as justifying the mobbers' wrath and the loss of the Mormons' civil rights. As late as 1898, the multidenominational League for Social Service published its manifesto of anti-Mormonism, *Ten Reasons Why Christians Cannot Fellowship the Mormon Church*. Their major objections? Belief in modern prophets, continuing revelation, an authority vested in the priesthood, and a repugnant doctrine of deity.[86] To an observer like Dickens, what situated Mormons outside the mainstream was equally clear: "Mormons seem to differ from other sects chiefly in believing the continued inspiration of their prophets."[87]

Religious intolerance is the most recurrent and explosive feature of anti-Mormon sentiment and clearly the most complicated. How are we to understand the acceptable range of religious innovation when orthodoxy and religious conformity are not a part of a country's heritage or ideology? The nineteenth century witnessed a flood of new religious movements, from the Grahamites and Millerites to spiritualists and Christian Scientists. And consequent upon this religious heterodoxy came a vast outpouring of popular fiction that targeted various religious and ethnic groups associated with them, from the Shakers to the Irish. Still, the ferocity of the Mormon persecutions, and of anti-Mormon representations in literature, was not matched in the case of other aberrational nineteenth-century groups. This was true even though the Shakers' concept of God was more radical, their celibacy and the free love practices of the "Perfectionists" equally hostile to traditional family values, and the prophetic claims and canon-busting of Christian Science and Adventism as pronounced as the Mormons'.

Why were the rules of religious tolerance held in abeyance for the anti-Mormons, while elsewhere in the nineteenth century equally unorthodox religious movements were proliferating, movements that were in many ways as indifferent to contemporary notions about orthodoxy and patriotism as Mormonism was? How are prevailing distinctions between essential tenets and accidental features of religious orthodoxy derived? An examination of the range of religious pluralism that characterized Joseph Smith's America in 1820 is necessary to ascertain what was *not* especially noteworthy or objectionable about Mormon heterodoxy. Only then can we proceed to examine more closely the nature of those differences that exempted Mormonism from the toleration accorded scores of contemporary sects with equal claims upon orthodox indignation. Finally, we consider how transgression comes to be represented when unacceptable difference manifests itself in the midst of a community or society that has already founded its identity on ideals of pluralism and tolerance.

CHAPTER 4

"An Age of Humbugs": The Contemporary Scene

America is the paradise of heterodoxy.

J. H. Beadle, *Life in Utah*, 1870

The rise and fall of gold is believed to be a surer index in politics than any other expression of opinion. But that judgment is only true in reference to events of routine. If a new and unknown contingency occur,—disturbances from Mormonism, or Antimasonry, or Spiritism, or a Know Nothing Party, or a new Civil War like ours in 1861, the bankers are then on the like footing with other people, and as likely to go wrong.

Ralph Waldo Emerson, journal entry, 1867

Many Mormons see their history as a long record of oppression and exclusion. To the non-Mormon, the LDS past is more often marked by mystery, peculiarity, or what a scholar like Laurence Moore considers a pattern of exaggerated and cynical self-promotion as a deviant and persecuted people. "The Mormon strategy for survival," he writes, was "to risk destruction by straining to advertise Mormon deviance." For Moore, in other words, the construction of a Mormon image is central to any understanding of Mormon history. But the image is one artfully contrived by the Mormons themselves, "an imaginative space created by rhetoric."[1]

Two truisms of revolutionary philosophy are that martyrs are harder to kill than leaders, and persecution more often serves to strengthen resolve than to stifle it. When Joseph Smith protested to the *Quincy Whig* in Illinois that he was unjustly linked to the assassination attempt on ex-governor

Lilburn Boggs of Missouri, the friendly *New York Herald* counseled acquiescence: "We advise Joe Smith to be quiet—his enemies and slanderers
will make him a better prophet than he could hope to be made by any
other process. Opposition was the making of Moses—of Mahomet—of
Napoleon—of every great master spirit that has appeared in this dirty
world below."[2] From asserting that out of the crucible comes resiliency, it
is but an easy step to claiming that persecution may be exaggerated for the
sake of sympathy or even deliberately invited as a strategy to galvanize a
beleaguered minority. Indeed, the politics of marginalization and collective guilt as they operate today make it clear that status as an oppressed
group may have its political advantages. In the case of Mormons, however,
to interpret their reputation for deviance as a desire to serve as lightning
rods of opprobrium is to miss the crucial point: deviance of a theological
sort is central to their very raison d'être.

When the young boy Joseph Smith retired to a grove of trees in upstate
New York to pray for guidance about religion, he was perhaps no different
from thousands of other seekers who were responding to religious stir-
rings inflamed by the Second Great Awakening, which gave to that area
the telling name "the Burned-Over District." But when Smith emerged
from the woods, it was with the conviction that no church then on earth
preached the gospel of Jesus Christ in its purity.[3] The church he would
soon found never claimed to be anything less than the reinauguration of
the original Christian church. The fact of a universal apostasy was the
condition that proved the need of a restoration; Mormonism was thus
erected on the premise of radical difference.

Mormon self-presentation in the church's first generation thus required
something of a balancing act. Articulation of theological uniqueness was
necessary to legitimize the church's entry onto a crowded religious stage.
The absolutist position of the church was one way to define the place of
Mormonism relative to contemporary religions. Unlike the reformers who
had preceded him, Joseph Smith insisted that his role was to usher in a
new dispensation, a full restoration of Christianity in its original form. He
proclaimed a general apostasy from primitive Christianity, the apostolic
succession long broken, and authority to act in God's name completely
removed from the earth. A reinstitution, not merely a reformation, of
Christianity was called for. New scriptures, doctrines, and practices rapidly
followed, effecting further differentiation from contemporary Christian
faiths. At the same time, Mormonism's claim to be a return to original
Christianity necessitated conformity with Christian ideas, rooted in the
Bible and in tradition, of church and doctrine. An appeal to the familiar
was integral to this claim, as well as being necessary for both survival and

growth. The first formal proclamation of Mormon tenets therefore began with an apparent endorsement of the Trinitarian creeds, but one that skirts the controversial details: "We believe in God, the Eternal Father, and in his Son, Jesus Christ, and in the Holy Ghost."[4] However, those persons are separate and distinct in Mormon thought.

Further complicating this project of self-presentation was the number of reformers competing with Joseph Smith in 1820s America. So great was the stampede to renovate Christianity that we could say Mormonism did not risk destruction by advertising deviance—it risked oblivion if it did not. Even with its baggage of supernaturalism—or perhaps because of it—Mormonism was just one more religious innovation in a sea of sectarian ferment. In an age when religious deviance was almost the norm, exaggerating its own distinctness from Christianity only situated the church more securely within the host of proliferating heterodoxies. This fact suggests that ascertaining the exact nature of Mormonism's deviance and the hostility it engendered requires first seeing what it shared with competing heterodoxies of the nineteenth century. Only then can we move on to examine the peculiarity of the Mormon church that moved it out of the realm of difference to rupture, from heterodoxy to heresy.

THE "PARADISE OF HETERODOXY"

Before Mormonism's message to the world could be condemned, it had to be heard. This was no mean feat, given the prevailing cynicism with which new religions were coming to be greeted. One Illinois historian writing in the early 1840s was probably representative of countless contemporaries who adamantly refused to take note of one more new faith:

> The frequent communications of "the prophet" with an angel, the gold plates, the discovery, and afterward the translation of the Book of Mormon in the manner above related; had we not seen in our own days similar impostures practiced with success, (that, for instance, of the celebrated Matthias, in New-York, a few years since, and several others more recently,) [Mormonism] would have excited our special wonder; as it is, nothing excites surprise.[5]

Similarly, an English observer remarked that Mormonism was but another "curious illustration of the facility with which religious frauds can be perpetrated in this country."[6]

The early nineteenth century may well be associated with an industrial revolution in full swing and what one author calls the "Birth of the

Modern."[7] But the Illinois historian called it "an age of humbugs," and at least one writer saw the period beginning with 1820 as "the Age of the Irrational."[8] Paul Fussell, as we have seen, dates the "dumbing of America" to that same moment. If religion and rationality are incompatible, the name of the dawning age was appropriate. For certainly the proliferation of new, heterodox religious movements was unprecedented in American history. The period saw a mushrooming percentage of Americans who claimed religious affiliation, with the repercussions felt to this day. Of the established religions, Baptists, Methodists, Quakers, and Presbyterians saw their numbers grow from a combined total of 320,000 at the turn of the century, to 1,764,000 by 1840.[9] Even given the 300 percent increase in population for this period, such growth is phenomenal.

The burgeoning of such newcomers as the Campbellites and scores of flash-in-the-pan churches was even more striking. All told, the percentage of Americans actively affiliated with a church grew from 7 percent in 1800 (the lowest proportion in American history) to 13 percent in 1830 and 23 percent in 1860.[10] By the time Mormonism was formally organized in the spring of 1830, it was too late to be a conspicuous arrival on the scene.

Five years before the Book of Mormon was published, local newspapers had announced a new religious group, the Osgoodites, with the headline "Fanaticism." The arrival of the Osgoodites was followed a few months later by that of the Davidites. "Singular Sect," trumpeted the *Livingston Register*. Soon a "New Delusion in Baltimore" was noted by two other papers. This unnamed sect was criticized for its practice of healing with consecrated oil and water. Numerous other groups emerged, were noted briefly in skeptical newspaper accounts, and then disappeared from the scene.[11]

Lieutenant Colonel A. M. Maxwell was a British officer who toured the United States in 1840. One of his first observations was that "there seems to be no lack of churches nor of persuasions, and church-going seems to be the rage."[12] But after some time in the States, he had had his fill. He found the Episcopalians and Presbyterians, even the Universalists, respectable enough. But a Shaker service left him "sick and indignant," and he passed near a meeting of "about 4000 mountebank Methodists, commonly called Campers," which he found a "sauntering sect." In exasperation, he finally complained that he was "really sick of hearing of the Mathiasites and Mormonites, Jumpers, Shakers, Lynchers, Saturday Saints," and others.[13] No doubt it was hard to keep track. The 1844 American edition of *History of All Christian Sects* lists as some of the denominations then current, in addition to more orthodox varieties, Dunkers, Sabbatarians, Hicksites, Shakers, Sandemanians, Swedenborgians, Campbellites, Bereans,

Come-Outers, Millenarians, Millerites, Wilkinsonians, and Mormonites.[14] An 1849 almanac adds River Brethren and Schwenkfelders to the list.[15]

If Maxwell had been more attentive to developments in his native country, he might not have been so contemptuous of American sectarian proliferation. The poet laureate of England, Robert Southey, published a series of letters purporting to be from a Spanish traveler in Great Britain, in which he mocked the explosion of heterodoxy:

> The heretical sects in this country are so numerous, that an explanatory dictionary of their names has been published. They form a curious list! Arminians, Socinians, Baxterians, Presbyterians, New Americans, Sabellians, Lutherans, Moravians, Swedenborgians, Athanasians, Episcopalians, Arians, Sabbatarians, Trinitarians, Unitarians, Millenarians, Necessarians, Sublapsarians, Supralapsarians, Antinomians, Hutchinsonians, Sandemonians, Muggletonians, Baptists, Anabaptists, Paedobaptists, Methodists, Papists, Universalists, Calvinists, Materialists, Destructionists, Brownists, Independents, Protestants, Hugonots [sic], Nonjurors, Seceders, Hernhutters, Dunkers, Jumpers, Shakers, and Quakers, &c. &c. &c. A precious nomenclature! only to be paralleled by the catalogue of the Philistines in Sanson Nazareno, or the muster-roll of Anna de Santiago's Devils, under Aquias, Brum and Acatu, lieutenant-generals to Lucifer himself.[16]

Many of these new sects migrated across the Atlantic, but America had no shortage of home-grown denominations. Some were too short-lived to make it into the almanacs, like the Bowery Hill followers of the remarkable Robert Matthews, known as "Matthias," a New York neighbor of Joseph Smith who in 1830 proclaimed himself a messiah, but fell from grace a few years later and ended his career incarcerated for feeding arsenic-laced blackberries to some of his flock. His career was sensationalized in the penny press of the day and was the subject of an exposé published in 1835, by which time the discredited prophet was meeting in Kirtland with Joseph Smith, presumably in hopes of finding solidarity with another of God's anointed victimized by bad press.[17]

Indeed, so many were the outbreaks of religious nonconformity in Joseph Smith's neighborhood alone that David Reese published in 1838 a volume called *Humbugs of New York: Being a Remonstrance against Popular Delusion; Whether in Science, Philosophy, or Religion*. Mormonism merited barely a mention, given the "kindred enormities of Matthias" and the "multitudes who believe in 'Animal Magnetism,' subscribe to 'Phrenology,' are the willing victims of every form of 'Quackery,' and have adopted the creed and practice of 'ultraism.'"[18]

Also in this decade, Macon County, Illinois, witnessed an even briefer ministry than that of Matthias in the founder of the "New Light" doctrine. The anonymous farmer turned revelator of this "plan entirely new" was soon discredited as a charlatan, providing to at least one writer's mind the moral that Mormonism was but one more instance in a growing tradition of unsavory religious fanaticism.[19]

In 1844, John Greenleaf Whittier spent the fall in Lowell, Massachusetts. He wrote a series of essays inspired by "the common incidents of daily life" he observed there as *The Stranger in Lowell* (1845). His encounters include a pair of Mormon missionaries in mourning for the recently martyred Joseph Smith, and a stagecoach driver easily filling his coach (at seventy-five cents each) for a quick run to a Millerite campground; he attends a home meeting of Swedenborgians and relates stories of Mesmeric detectives searching for a lost child. In this period of religious questing, remarks Whittier, "there are many who have not yet marked the boundaries, or set up the pillars and stretched out the curtains of their sectarian tabernacles; who, in halls and 'upper chambers,' and in the solitude of their own homes, keep alive the spirit of devotion, and, wrapping closely around them the mantles of their order, maintain the integrity of its peculiarities."[20]

Unlike the earlier Great Awakening of Jonathan Edwards's colonial America, more was in the air this time than a simple return to religious devotion, or even the competition for converts. The lapse of time and the atrophy of religious purity were seen as requiring a new dispensation, new revelation, new doctrinal emphases, and new forms of worship. Thus the early 1800s saw not just increased devotion, but religious innovation.

Primitivism, the effort to return to a purer form of Christianity, was a particularly strong current in the Awakening. Founding fathers like Franklin and Jefferson had reflected the increasing dissatisfaction with institutional accretions to original Christianity. The former lamented the "various corrupting changes" wrought by the centuries, and Jefferson desired to go back to Christianity's roots and retrieve "the diamonds from the dunghills."[21] Blaming the "mythologists of the middle and modern ages" for corrupting the original church, he was nonetheless "happy in the prospect of a restoration of primitive Christianity."[22] Waiting in the wings were a number of figures willing to fill that apostolic calling. And not all the new movements were as ephemeral as the now forgotten Osgoodites and Wilkinsonians.

Not far from Joseph Smith's home in Palmyra, New York, and only months after Smith's first vision, William Miller announced in 1831 that the world would end in 1843. Like a second John the Baptist, Miller galvanized an anxious public ready to behold the greatest event in the universe since the Nativity. The prophecy's failure did little to dampen the ardor of a movement that would soon claim to have fifty to a hundred thousand Adventist followers. The sense that the world was on the verge of apocalypse fueled a fervor and devotion that survived numerous other failed predictions, finally settling into the institutionalization of such expectations as the Seventh-Day Adventist Church.

In 1838, Charles Poyen, a French lecturer on animal magnetism and Mesmerism, visited several New England towns and successfully imported what had until then been a European sensation. Franz Anton Mesmer (1734–1815) and his disciples had tried unsuccessfully to create the basis for a new science, organized around the assertion that a superfine fluid pervaded the universe like a primeval ether, which could be controlled and exploited for a variety of purposes. This fluid was seen as a mechanism for the transmission of everything from electricity and magnetism to spirit communications from the dead. The proper regulation of this fluid's flow through the body was deemed the key to physical and emotional health.[23]

Gradually, the interest aroused by the "science" focused on the hypnotic trance that Mesmer had pioneered (and which was soon popularized in such literature as Coleridge's *Rime of the Ancient Mariner*). Though originally used for diagnostic and therapeutic purposes, increasingly the trance state was exploited for the communication with a world of spirits that it seemed to make possible. Propitiously, Mesmerism found its way to America just in time for the celebrated Hydesville spirit rappings, which would begin in 1848. The young Fox sisters captured public attention with their ability to attract and communicate with departed spirits by a series of mysterious tapping sounds. Not surprisingly, hundreds of other people were quick to discover that they were capable of serving as mediums of communication for the world of spirits as well. The transition from an emphasis on Mesmer's fluidic theory to a fascination with supernatural communion was immediate. With the advent of spiritualism, many Mesmerists considered that they were already on to the force behind the mysterious rappings and table-turnings and allied themselves with the rapidly growing spiritualist movement.

Public interest was so widespread and the demonstrations of paranormal phenomena so sensational that the spiritualists were soon by far the largest of the new religious groups. Enlightenment thought had made atheism popular with the intellectual class, and the dawning age of modern science and technology made it increasingly difficult to package and sell religion to a smugly "modern" mentality. (Charles Dickens was incredulous that anyone could believe in miracles "in the age of railways."[24])

Spiritualism seemed uniquely suited by its proponents to blend the religious impulse with the quest for scientific certainty. The tangible, demonstrable fruits of this faith were as much a matter for public exhibition as the wonders of a burgeoning technology. Indeed, not only the popularity of the movement, but its pretensions to a kind of modern respectability, are ironically suggested in Emerson's disarming list of the new professions that careening change had brought to the decade of the fifties; he listed "the sorcerer, rapper, mesmeriser, [and] medium" along with "the railroad man" and "the daguerrotypist."[25]

The Society for the Diffusion of Spiritual Knowledge was founded in 1854, but few of the adherents claimed formal affiliation with any organization. Still, one historian of American religions claims that "scarcely another cultural phenomenon affected as many people or stimulated as much interest as did spiritualism in the ten years before the Civil War and, for that matter, through the subsequent decades of the nineteenth century."[26]

A contemporary, Theodore Parker, speculated that "in 1856, it seems more likely that spiritualism would become the religion of America than in 156 that Christianity would be the religion of the Roman Empire, or in 756 that Mohammedanism would be that of the Arabian population."[27] Howard Kerr thinks an estimate of one million adherents by the 1850s not unreasonable.[28]

The Shakers never approached the impressive number of adherents spiritualism claimed, though they had settled in this country on the eve of the Revolution. But these same decades before the Civil War saw their most rapid growth and the establishment of many of their communistic, celibate communities. Their first society had been established at New Lebanon, New York, in 1787. Ten more followed, scattered throughout the Northeast. When the frenzied revivalism began in Kentucky in 1801, the Shakers became zealous missionaries like so many other religionists, and soon had over a thousand new converts of their own. Shaker communities spread in the next years to Kentucky, Ohio, and Indiana. Although the Shakers were never as numerous as Millerites or Mormons—their peak membership probably never exceeded six thousand[29]—their unorthodox and highly efficient communities attracted considerable attention.

In another few decades, Christian Science would emerge to reinvigorate Mark Twain's satirical pen. Although, like Artemus Ward, Twain would get lots of mileage out of his Mormon jokes, only Christian Science aroused in him enough indignation eventually to elicit a book-length attack (*Christian Science*, 1907). Christian Science was the most successful of the religious movements that foregrounded health as a spiritual concern, a tendency also found in both early Mesmerism and the later Grahamites. (Sylvester Graham was a Presbyterian evangelist who believed spiritual and physical health were interdependent. In 1830 he developed a vegetarian diet that was embraced for a time by institutions as diverse as Brook Farm and Oberlin College.[30]) Christian Science claimed modern revelation and additional scripture, and had a woman prophet to boot. As E. G. White built upon the foundations of Millerism to create Seventh-Day Adventism, so did Mary Baker Eddy adapt many principles of Mesmerism (or animal magnetism) in articulating the most emphatically antimaterialist sect in Christian history. But by then, heterodoxy had become the rule rather than the exception in American religious life. America's orthodox indignation was mostly spent.

MORMONISM AND HETERODOXY

Relative to these contemporaries of the eighteenth and nineteenth centuries, Mormonism's deviance from orthodoxy was greater than some and less than others. Emanuel Swedenborg, for example, claimed that the Lord had manifested himself to him "in a personal appearance in the year 1743," and that for decades following, he was privileged to "converse with spirits and angels."[31] Unlike Joseph Smith, he never made his revelations an instrument of aggressive proselytizing, and that may have been the telling difference in their receptions. In fact, it was not until 1760, when he was seventy-two, that rumors of his visions began to spread. And when a friend asked him how many converts he had obtained, "he said, after reflection that he thought he had about fifty in this world and about the same number in the other."[32]

Nevertheless, in his capacity as seer he did effectively expand the Christian canon by adding to the Bible some seventeen visionary books. He went even further: he *removed* from the canon the Acts, the Epistles, and many Old Testament books as well. In spite of such radical revisionism, an 1844 handbook credits the denomination with six to eight thousand American members and describes reaction as varying from ridicule and contempt on the one hand, to Kant's respect for the founder's "miraculous proofs" on the other.[33]

While few claimed personal visitations from deity, visions and revelations were also claimed by Miller and the Shakers. In 1863, Ellen Gould White claimed to have received the first in a series of more than two thousand such visions.[34] The spiritualists also claimed to receive revelations and spirit communications.[35]

A version of Mormonism's claim to be a restoration of primitive Christianity was made also by most of the revivalists of the Second Great Awakening, and the Campbellites (later Disciples of Christ) in particular. In fact, Alexander Campbell accused Mormonism of being a Satanic imitation of his own version of primitive Christianity.[36]

In 1879 Mary Baker Eddy of Christian Science would, like Joseph Smith, profess to be a prophet and revealer of new scripture. Shakers did Mormonism one better by claiming not merely a prophet, but a second incarnation of God himself, in the person of "Mother" Ann Lee. Thus the millennialism of Miller's Adventists and so many of their contemporaries took a new twist in the Second Coming, which the Shakers saw as an accomplished event. But a celibacy that extended to the entire laity could be just as destructive of traditional family structures and values as the free love practices of some of the spiritualists and utopians. At least one anti-Mormon writer considered the "moral perversion ... [of] the anti-marriage Shakers, [and] the celibate Harmonists" as great as that of "the wife-communists of Oneida, or the polygamous Mormons."[37] "It seemed that everywhere the Shakers went," writes one critic, "homes were being torn asunder by the message of celibacy they preached."[38] So discovered Mother Lee herself, whose husband deserted her when she persisted in her refusal to cohabitate.

Shakers also shared with the Jumpers the distinction of the most unusual form of worship service of any nineteenth-century movement. Increasingly formalized over time, their dancing (or "laboring," to use their term) included several types, from "Square Order Shuffle" to "Skipping Manner."[39] The tempo accelerated and the volume of accompanying singing increased as the meeting progressed, until the dance became what Horace Greeley described as a "wild discordant frenzy."[40] The Englishman Abdy noted both the ceremony's offensiveness to public ideas of religious decorum and the trend toward greater propriety: "The sight of rational beings cutting capers to the glory of God must be rather humiliating than amusing. These peculiarities are becoming less preposterous; and, as the distortions of the body are exchanged for movements more natural and graceful, the attention of the inquisitive to these ceremonies will be lessened."[41]

Mormonism's experiments in communalistic societies came years after the Shakers' first such settlement in New Lebanon in 1787. The Sandemanians, followers of the Scotsman Robert Sandeman who had published his ideas back in 1757, established communities in Boston, Nova Scotia, and throughout New England, and practiced a "community of goods, so far as that every one is to consider all that he has in his possession and power liable to the calls of the poor and the church; and the unlawfulness of laying up treasures upon the earth, by setting them apart for any distant, future, or uncertain use."[42] In addition, there were of course the experiments such as Oneida and Brook Farm, along with the experiments of the lesser-known Ephratists, Wilkinsonians, and Rappites. The poets Samuel Coleridge and Robert Southey never managed to pull off their dream of an American "Pantisocracy," but their designs (and Coleridge's poem on the subject) nonetheless bore witness to the prevalence in theory and practice of experimental utopianism. Indeed, Emerson wrote to Carlyle in 1840 that "We are all a little wild here with numberless projects for social reform. Not a reading man but has a draft of a New Community in his waistcoat pocket."[43] When Joseph Smith outlined the principles of the Law of Consecration in February of 1831, he stipulated that each member "consecrate" his property to the church, and receive back "sufficient for himself and family," with "the residue" to be used "for the poor and needy."[44] When the principle was implemented, the Mormons followed the Shaker practice of formally deeding over freely "themselves and services, with all their temporal interest for the mutual support and benefit of each other."[45]

Doctrinally, the Mormons were neither orthodox Trinitarians nor Unitarians. Their belief in an anthropomorphic God and Christ was at least a literalist reading of the Old Testament; the Shakers' view of God as dual, father and mother together, had not even that appeal to precedent.[46] In their Articles of Faith, the Latter-day Saints certainly did not present themselves as religious deviants. They claimed, among other things, belief in faith, repentance, baptism, and the Holy Ghost. They accepted the atonement of Christ and the Bible ("as far as it is translated correctly"), and personal accountability for sin (though denying original sin). As primitivists, they proclaimed "the same organization that existed in the Primitive Church," and as millennialists they anticipated that "Christ will reign personally upon the earth." As charismatics, they believed in spiritual gifts. Of the tenets described in this published synopsis of their creed, only their acceptance of the Book of Mormon as "the word of God," and their belief in divine revelation present and yet to come put them at odds with most contemporaries (polygamy would come later).[47]

As zealous proselytizers, Mormons were no more than typical of their day. As mentioned above, even the Shakers were aggressive missionaries, though only sporadically. One Issachar Bates, Shaker missionary, claimed to have traveled thirty-eight thousand miles in the course of his proselytizing and to have won eleven hundred converts.[48] In 1831, the Mormons even sent missionaries to the Shakers in Ohio.[49] Though there is no record of a reciprocal effort, early Mormon leader Martin Harris, after a falling out with his fellow Saints, did join the Shakers for a time.[50]

HETERODOXY AND INTOLERANCE

In spite of the apparently comparable degrees of religious nonconformity, the public response to Mormonism was clearly remarkable. Certainly, many of these other religious groups experienced persecution in varying degrees. Shaker missionaries complained of being "imprisoned, beaten, mocked, calumniated" and "pursued by cruel and desperate mobs." Ann Lee was herself imprisoned briefly in England before emigrating to America, and was jailed for some months in New York, as were some of her followers during the Revolution, on charges of abetting the British.[51] Their own chroniclers characterize most of their opposition not as mobbers or vandals but "mockers and scoffers," and in alleging persecution ("the usual engine of religious intolerance"), they refer to "every evil report and every wicked device, that falsehood and malice could dictate."[52] In 1781, on at least two occasions, in Harvard and Petersham, Massachusetts, mob violence did break out against the society. Leaders and new converts alike were "scourged with whips, beaten with clubs, stoned, kicked and dragged about by their legs and arms, and sometimes by the hair of their heads, and driven from place to place, in the most cruel and abusive manner."[53] A Believers' meeting was stormed, and Mother Lee abducted and assaulted by a mob of ruffians whose avowed purpose was "to find out whether she was a woman or not."[54] While the Shakers attributed such hostility to "the spirit of Antichrist," it is clear that much of the opposition was a response to their zealous proselytizing and celibate ways. Indeed, at least one elder was whipped for allegedly "going about and breaking up churches, and families."[55]

Writing in 1835, Edward Abdy recorded a major mob action against a Shaker community in Union Village, Ohio, that was forestalled at the last minute by the meekness of the intended victims:

About thirty years ago, an establishment they had formed in Union Village, in the State of Ohio, was attacked by a lawless mob of 500 armed men; led on by officers, and followed by nearly 2000 people, who had assembled to witness this brutal outrage on a peaceable community of religionists. The pretense of all this violence was, as is usual on similar occasions, to protect religion from dangerous fanatics. Such, however, was the patient mildness with which the Shakers conducted themselves towards these turbulent intruders (the real fanatics) that their malice was disarmed, and they retired with far different feelings from those with which they had arrived.[56]

As for the reasons for popular hostility, Abdy felt the charge of threatening the traditional family structure was a red herring: "The Shakers allow no distinction whatever between man and man, but what is founded on moral worth, and admit persons of all colors to the same privileges. Hence, probably, arose those bitter and cruel persecutions to which they were at first exposed, rather than from the charge of alienating children from their parents and disturbing the natural order of society."[57]

What violence did occur against the Shakers apparently was not widespread or sufficiently publicized to receive much notice. An 1844 British publication on American religions noted of the Shakers, "They remain a small and quite obscure community, that must in time utterly disappear instead of growing into something like importance, which would be the probable result if they were persecuted."[58] At any rate, it would appear that what hostility there was soon gave way to amusement over their quaint, celibate communities, and admiration for their simple, peaceful ways. But such acceptance came *after* their proselytizing phase seems to have ended.

Like the Shakers, the Millerites encountered brief but violent mob opposition. In Nashua, New Hampshire, beginning in 1841, and culminating in 1844, critics disrupted meetings and perpetrated violence against adherents. Ruth Doan makes a strong case for Millerism as a "negative referent" by which orthodoxy defines itself. The "general pattern" she perceives is one of peak resistance corresponding to Millerism's "highest level in numbers and influence."[59] Those numbers are hard to pin down, with estimates of their size ranging from ten thousand to one million.[60] But the simplest explanation for the outbreak of real hostilities is the fact that the first major, confirmable failures of Miller's public prophecies had occurred in 1839, by which date he had predicted the Turkish government would fall. He moved the date for the "closing off of grace" and the fall of the Turkish empire to 1840, but was again proven wrong.[61] Critics therefore had plenty of ammunition before the fiasco of his much publicized and popular prediction: that the Second Coming would occur in 1843. The early 1840s may have been the time of Millerism's greatest prominence and influence, but clearly, it was also the period of its greatest susceptibility to charges of fraud or a grand delusion.

Spiritualism made itself vulnerable to disproof in a similarly self-destructive way and with even more fatal consequences. A driving force behind spiritualism was its effort to make itself intellectually respectable.

Like the Mesmerism with which it merged, spiritualism in its beginnings staked a claim to scientific verifiability. But just as Mesmer's petition to be taken seriously by the French Academy ended disastrously in the eighteenth century, so did spiritualism fail to win the support of the American scientific community it tried to enlist in its support two generations later.

Not that the scientists didn't give it what they thought was a fair try. A small group of them did accept an invitation to certify the results of a séance conducted by the celebrated John Buchanan, but the results were inconclusive and only fueled skepticism. Indeed, what is most amazing about spiritualism's appeal is how long it persisted in spite of repeated exposures of frauds and charlatans. As early as 1850, lecturers began to perform debunking exhibitions. The next year, first reports that the Fox sisters had admitted fraud began to emerge (though Maggie would not confess until 1888, whereupon she made even more money as an ex-con doing exhibitions than she had as a spiritualist).[62] In 1857, Frederick Willis was expelled from the Harvard School of Divinity when, in the process of conducting a séance, he was caught cheating by a professor of engineering, Henry Eustis.[63] Scandals and even imprisonments for fraud soon swamped the movement.

The essential spiritualist doctrine was simplicity itself (the New England Spiritualist Association stated in 1854: "Spirits do communicate with man—that is the creed"[64]), and the fortunes of the movement hung on the merits of that one premise alone. For the first time, a posture of empirical skepticism was welcomed into the arena of religious debate, and predictably enough, most of the opposition to spiritualism that ensued took the form of cavalier dismissal by skeptics.

That is not to say that spiritualism was without its religious critics. Orthodox ministers like Charles Beecher rose to condemn spiritualism's assault on such cherished Christian teachings as sin, hell, and the total depravity of man.[65] (Ironically, Beecher himself would soon be subjected to a heresy trial during the Civil War for accepting spiritualism along with evolution and preexistence of souls.[66]) The religious community was hardly united in its opposition, however. Some denounced the spirit communion as fraudulent, some as true but Satanic, and others, like the Unitarian Minot Savage and the Episcopalian R. Heber Newton, went so far as to support the movement.[67]

Newspapers by and large opposed the movement. The *New York Times* attacked spiritualism for its "subversion of all respect and devotion to the only true faith," and Washington's *National Intelligencer* suggested outlawing séances altogether, complaining that the spiritualist fervor was "spreading itself like a pestilence through our borders."[68]

Combined with the lack of a united front against spiritualism was the difficulty in fixing a target for criticism. The spiritualists did not represent a community of believers, like the Mormons or Shakers, or even a formal affiliation in most cases. Séances were attended by the devout, the cynical, the curious, and the con artists—but how to identify the "spiritualist" as such?

As a result, opposition to spiritualism was mostly rhetorical, and the only political threat evaporated in 1854, when Congress tabled a petition with thirteen hundred signatures calling for a national inquiry.[69] The spiritualists claimed their movement had its martyrs, but they were few, and no blood was spilled. John C. Edmonds, a justice of the New York Supreme Court, felt pressured to resign his seat in 1853 when his enemies charged him with consulting with spirits about his decisions. According to the *New York Times*, his affiliation to spiritualism "must render the operation of his intellect utterly unreliable and destroy all confidence in the continued justice and correctness of his judicial actions." And some years later, superintendent of New York City schools Henry Kiddle was fired after publishing a volume of spirit messages.[70]

In another isolated instance, John Murray Spear, an eccentric inventor in Randolph, New York, claimed to have created a perpetual motion machine designed by spirits. He was set upon by a mob of angry neighbors, who broke into his storage shed and "tore out the heart of the mechanism, trampled [it] beneath their feet, and scattered it to the four winds."[71]

Other than such occasional outbreaks of intolerance, opposition to spiritualism was too fragmented to be effective. This opposition was divided among those who readily acknowledged such communication, but feared its Satanic dimensions (like preacher Beecher); those who derided the hoaxsters and opportunists the movement attracted (like the satirists Twain and Ward); and those who feared defections from or contamination of their own Christian sects (some claimed that half the members of the National Spirit Association were former Catholics).[72]

Ultimately, the standards spiritualism had set for itself proved its undoing. By the 1870s, spiritualism had lost most of its credibility, and hence its threatening aspect, with the revelation of a string of hoaxes involving the Eddy brothers, J. V. Mansfield, Henry Slade, and others. Finally, the patron mother, Margaret Fox, confessed in 1888 that her cracking toe joints had supplied the "rapping" of Hydesville fame.

In this period, only Catholicism elicited reactions as intense and violent as those directed against the Mormons. Anti-Catholicism was woven into the legal structure of the colonies long before Joseph Smith's day, rooted in English anti-popery of the sixteenth century and rekindled by the Glorious Revolution of 1688. The eighteenth-century French wars and fears of French and papal collusion produced a spate of new legislation stripping Catholics of many civil rights in several colonies. Even after the Declaration of Independence, many state constitutions (New Jersey, North Carolina, Georgia) barred Catholics from state office, and others, like South Carolina, established Protestantism as the state religion.[73] Only after the federal Constitution was adopted in 1787 did a spirit of tolerance infect the states.

In the years following the Napoleonic wars, the United States experienced its first massive waves of immigration, largely from Ireland and northern Europe. Although the Industrial Revolution had fostered a need for additional labor, the immigrants were not assimilated into the workforce quickly or efficiently enough to avert economic strains. By 1837, there were 105,000 paupers. More than half of them were immigrants.[74] Nativism became the prevailing sentiment of the day, and it had a ready target. As the number of Catholics in America surged, so did the number of parochial schools and new churches. Missionary efforts intensified, and anxieties were inflamed. The Protestant revival, under the leadership of Barton Stone, Charles Finney, and others, converged with an increasingly xenophobic zeal to prosecute a great crusade against Catholicism. What began as a media campaign by the religious and then the secular press soon erupted into violence. Irish Catholic homes were attacked in Boston during three days of rioting in 1829. In 1833, a mob of five hundred attacked the Irish section of Charlestown, Massachusetts, prompting a call-up of troops.[75]

On the other side, at public debates on the Catholic/Protestant issue, Catholics occasionally instigated violence (Baltimore, 1834, and New York, 1835). As a rule, however, they were the victims. In August 1834, the Ursuline convent in Charlestown and an Irish shantytown were burned to the ground by a large mob of townsmen. These attacks on Irishmen, as well as others, such as the Boston Broad Street riot of 1837 involving an Irish funeral procession and a local fire company, were more typical of the emerging pattern. Religious intolerance and ethnic attacks became two faces of the same bigotry, at times overlapping and at other times unrelated. Throughout the thirties and forties, local elections time and again became the scene of ethnic violence, as in the Philadelphia riots of 1844. The conflict escalated, first to the state level, as local no-popery parties were transformed into statewide movements organized around the nativist cause, and then to the national level. By 1856 a national Republican convention had a strong nativist platform, as did, a short time later, a national Know-Nothing Party.

Into the midst of this raucous religious and political upheaval came the Mormons. The unwillingness of Jacksonian America in 1830 to countenance the emergence of yet another religious group can hardly be surprising. However, the foregoing suggests two things. First, within the context of nineteenth-century heterodoxy as a whole, the degree of violence with which Mormonism was challenged is clearly anomalous. Although the distinctive threat that Mormonism posed to orthodoxy has yet to be made clear, something about Mormonism lifted it out of the realm of simple religious nonconformity and into the realm of heresy, thereby provoking what J. H. Beadle, editor of *Scribner's*, referred to as the sole exception to America's rule of universal toleration. We will turn to the problem of heresy next, in chapter 5.

Second, that anti-Catholic violence constitutes the nearest parallel with anti-Mormonism may say more about the conditions necessary for the social legitimization of religious persecution than any inherently shared characteristics between the two groups. For what the two religions undoubtedly do share is identification by the majority culture as ethnic or quasi-ethnic groups, a condition that will be explored further in chapter 7.

CHAPTER 5

"This Great Modern Abomination": Orthodoxy and Heresy in American Religion

Therefore let everyone who can, smite, slay, and stab,
secretly or openly, remembering that nothing can be more
poisonous, hurtful, or devilish than a rebel.

      Martin Luther, *Against the Robbing and Murdering Hordes*, 1525

O merciful God, who hast made all men, and hatest nothing that thou hast made: have mercy upon all Jews, Turks, Infidels, and HERETICS.

      Frontispiece to Rev. Henry Caswell's *City of the Mormons*, 1842

There is scarcely the faintest notion anywhere that unbelief might be changed directly into what the church calls false belief. No, where there is heresy, orthodoxy must have preceded. For example, Origen puts it like this: "All heretics at first are believers; then later they swerve from the rule of faith."

      Walter Bauer, *Orthodoxy and Heresy in Earliest Christianity*, 1971

The heretic has always been a much graver threat to spiritual solidarity than the infidel. Contamination, seduction, corruption, insinuation are hallmarks of the first; mere difference the mark of the second. The fires of the Inquisition scorched the lapsed Christian or deviant believer, not the professing Jew or the Muslim. In the context of sociocultural difference, we have seen that threatening categories often invite a representational response that would emphasize or invent otherness as a means of establishing a tolerable distance. In the religious realm, heresy reflects a similar need to exaggerate disparity so that boundaries can be imposed and enforced. To speak in these terms is to recognize the constructed, artificial, and highly malleable nature of categories like heresy and orthodoxy. Of course, ideology often conceals its own foundations. For example, if the believer accepts whatever is original as by definition authentic, then any deviation is schism or apostasy from the primal, sanctioned order, and authority may legitimately identify and censure such deviance wherever it occurs. This is the implication of the seeming truism Bauer cites, that where there is heresy, orthodoxy must have preceded. Heretics are those who swerve from the *rule* of faith.

In reality, orthodoxy is constituted only after there are choices to be made, with competing, and mutually exclusive, options. Heresy is the choice that lost out. Ecclesiastical history, like any other, is written by the victors. In the case of American religious history, the situation grows more complicated, however. In colonial times heresy and orthodoxy were simple matters. Ecclesiastical authority, at times indistinguishable from the arm of the state, was essentially theocratic. Thus in 1658, the Massachusetts Bay Colony made membership in the Society of Friends punishable by banishment or death. Two went to the gallows in 1659, and one each in 1660 and 1661.[1] With the constitutional rupture of the church-state alliance, orthodoxy and heresy continued as viable categories, but options for punishing the latter were somewhat restricted. Heresy, that difference sufficient to prompt execution or excommunication rather than benign censure or correction, marks the limits of religious freedom that any one particular community will tolerate. Outside the borders of that religious community, the designation is meaningless—or so it would seem.

In the absence of a state religion, and in spite of an American predilection for religious diversity, heresy has persisted as a category that transcends narrow denominational boundaries. By general nineteenth-century consensus, Mormonism was self-evidently beyond the pale of mere difference, a fit candidate for the label of heresy. As Ruth Doan has pointed out, excommunication from orthodox churches of that period was not practiced for "fine distinctions. The cases that came to trial tended to point to rather obvious disagreements—acceptance of universal salvation, for example, or 'imbrasing the *Morman heresy* [sic].'"[2]

Such trials were common among the Baptists and Congregationalists. Thus we have the experience of the recently converted Mormon Isaac Haight, who records that "in the fall of 1839 the Baptist Church sent their priest to labor and reclaim me from the error of my ways.... [He] requested me to meet with the church and answer for myself before the deacons. I gladly accepted the invitation and on the day appointed I met with the church to be tried for heresy."[3] And in the same period, the Mormon William Seichrist was "excluded from the fellowship of this [Baptist] church [of Allegheny, Pennsylvania,] for embracing and maintaining a heresy,—to wit, doctrines peculiar to a late sect called Mormons or Latter-day Saints, that miracles can be wrought through the instrumentality of faith; that special revelations from God are now given to men; and that godly men are now endowed with the gift of prophecy."[4] Such efforts to enforce doctrinal conformity within a community of believers are, to some extent, common to most religious groups. The case of Mormonism, however, presents us with a problem of ampler magnitude. In the rhetoric of the nineteenth century, what is at stake is not merely parish purity, but the national soul. The characterization of Robert Beers was typical: Mormonism "is acknowledged to be the Great Modern Abomination, the most pernicious heresy of this century."[5]

HERESY AND PLURALISM

Given the American tradition of innovation and independence, and of hostility toward authoritarianism and conformity, attacks on heresy in general, and Mormonism's "heresies" in particular, seem odd. In a society characterized by such religious pluralism, how do we distinguish diversity from heresy? When does a sect become a "cult" (a related term of opprobrium used even today of Mormonism)?[6] And what weight or legitimacy does a label like heresy have in a democratic culture? If Mormonism is heresy, what is the American religious orthodoxy from which it deviates? The weight of such unarticulated orthodoxy is considerable. For individualism, even religious individualism, may be an American inheritance, but when religious innovation crosses the threshold of the heretical, the rights of the individual have often been overridden by the greater claims of orthodoxy, as witnessed so abundantly in the religious history of the Mormons.

Clearly, to say that excommunication was not practiced for "fine distinctions" will not get us very far. Not only does such a statement beg the question of how heresy is constructed; it suggests that heresy can be correlated simply with departure from fundamental Christian dogma. In other words, it suggests that we can identify the core of *essential* Christian belief, make that the standard of orthodoxy, and consider variations from *accidental* features of Christianity as constituting tolerable denominational differences. Unfortunately, the historical status of Mormonism does not accord with such a mechanical model of analysis. Rodney Stark and Charles Glock, for example, in their study *American Piety* (after acknowledging the virtual impossibility of finding any "universally acceptable standards" of orthodoxy[7]), selected four "belief items" from which they constructed an "Orthodoxy Index." They were "existence of a personal God, the divinity of Jesus Christ, the authenticity of biblical miracles, and the existence of the Devil." For good measure, they included as "other central Christian tenets: life beyond death, the virgin birth, and Christ's walking on water."[8] In all seven cases, Mormon belief is in unambiguous accord with these core beliefs. Almost entirely lacking from nineteenth-century accusations of Mormon heresy are charges that they deny those beliefs, the Bible, or the Christian sacraments. It would seem, if Stark's and Glock's criteria are valid, that Mormon "heresy" was not a simple matter of their rejecting orthodoxy.

That Mormons claimed to *add* scripture, or reintroduce discarded elements of the Christian tradition, they acknowledged readily enough. But given the dynamics of Protestant church history, the inescapability of tradition, convention, and doctrinal formation all serving to add layer upon layer of accretions to religious institutions, deviation or innovation per se are obviously useless categories for identifying the construction of heresy. And as David Steinmetz, professor of history of Christianity at Duke, reminds us, "Christians have argued, often passionately, over every conceivable point of Christian doctrine from the filioque to the immaculate conception. There is scarcely an issue of worship, theology, ethics, and politics over which some Christians have not disagreed among themselves."[9]

In any case, as religious scholar Stephen Robinson has demonstrated, Mormons are labeled heretics "for opinions and practices that are freely tolerated in other mainstream denominations."[10] To take one example, a favorite target of reproach among Mormon doctrines is the belief that human beings can become gods. In Mormon prophet Lorenzo Snow's words, "As God now is, man may be."[11] Robinson points out that this is a virtual paraphrase of Clement of Alexandria's teaching that "the Word of God became a man so that you might learn from a man how to become a god." Irenaeus, Justin Martyr, Athanasius, and Augustine, as well as popular Christian apologist C. S. Lewis, proclaimed the same principle, and it continues as a mainstay of Eastern Orthodox Church teachings.[12] And the Mormon doctrine of premortal existence was held by Christian theologians as diverse as Origen, Clement of Alexandria, and Augustine in the ancient world to William Benecke, Julius Müller, and Edward Beecher in the nineteenth century.[13]

So at least some Mormon heresies can make a claim to having once been (or to still being) Christian orthodoxies, and are, as Truman Madsen and David Paulsen have demonstrated from the other side of history, in many cases making their way back into the Christian mainstream. In his survey of Mormon doctrines from the nature of God to continuing revelation, Madsen argues that a number of Mormon "heresies" anticipate positions recently articulated by dozens of theologians and philosophers, from Dietrich Bonhoeffer and Charles Hartshorne to Avery Dulles and Dean Turner. Paulsen adds the conception of a social trinity, divine embodiment, and other doctrines to the corpus of doctrines experiencing something of a renaissance.[14]

At the same time, many Christian tenets that Mormonism rejects were patently alien to early Christianity as well—even doctrine as fundamental as the Trinity, as sources as disparate as the *New Catholic Encyclopedia* and *Harper's Bible Dictionary* acknowledge. According to the *Encyclopedia*, "the formulation of 'one God in three Persons' was not solidly established, certainly not fully assimilated into Christian life and its profession of faith, prior to the end of the 4th century.... Among Apostolic Fathers, there had been nothing even remotely approaching such a mentality or perspective." From *Harper's*, we have the assertion that "the formal doctrine of the trinity as it was defined by the great church councils of the fourth and fifth centuries is not to be found in the New Testament."[15]

A more facile solution to the problem of defining heresy is suggested by any number of sociologists of religion who equate heresy with what is new. Frederick Sontag notes that "obviously, existing religions must consider [any] new religion as heresy."[16] Rodney Stark agrees that by definition, "since all new religions begin in obscurity," they are in their "formative days...tiny, deviant, and insignificant."[17] Finally, Martin Marty, prominent historian of religion, also observes that all major religions were considered heresy in their earliest stages.[18]

The difficulty with such an explanation is twofold. First, it does not address the problem this work began by posing—why a violent response to the "Mormon heresy" out of proportion to all other antireligious expressions that were directed at contemporary heterodoxies? Second, it does nothing to explain why after a century and a half, the Mormon church is still labeled a "heresy" (or "cult" or "non-Christian") by its detractors. In fact, according to Gordon Melton, director of the Institute for the Study of American Religion, some four hundred "anti-cult" groups are currently aimed at Mormonism specifically.[19] Many contemporary examples could be cited, but the following is typical of the form such intolerance takes today:

> [In Vail, Colorado,] local churches were forced by high land prices to build an ecumenical chapel overlooking the slopes. Members of the Catholic, Lutheran, Baptist, Episcopalian, Presbyterian, Christian Science, and Jewish congregations all worship there après-ski. The centerpiece is a small cross fashioned out of two ski-tips. When Jews hold services, the cross is easily moved aside, but when the Vail ward of the Church of Jesus Christ of Latter-day Saints applied to use the chapel for its services, the request was denied by a 7–3 vote in 1985 of the Vail Religious Foundation, which oversees the chapel. "This is an interfaith chapel, not an intercult chapel," ... [a] minister told the *Rocky Mountain News.*[20]

One (non-Mormon) researcher noted "how easy it is for one person's faith to be another's heresy. Indeed, that was the basis of my early work on religion and anti-Semitism.... Thus I continue to be astonished at the extent to which colleagues who would *never* utter anti-Semitic, anti-Catholic, or even anti-Moslem remarks, unself-consciously and self-righteously condemn Mormons."[21] Not only is the Mormon church no longer a recent religious innovation; it stands, in the words of this same researcher, "on the threshold of becoming the first major faith to appear on earth since the Prophet Mohammed rode out of the desert."[22]

So rather than equate heresy with doctrinal deviance or threatening novelty, it may be more useful to examine the cumulative *effect* the Mormon innovations had on challenging the very bases of Christianity as it had come to exist by Joseph Smith's day. Discovering how this heresy was constructed, we may thereby come to understand the orthodoxy that it challenged. It is fairly easy to pinpoint the aspects of Mormonism that early detractors found most pernicious. As we noted earlier, the Reverend Dietrich Willers had found offensive the belief in supernatural visitations and continuing revelation, and the Baptist church that excommunicated William Seichrist voiced similar objections, mentioning charismatic gifts in particular. Forty years later, Mormon leader Orson Pratt defiantly concurred about the nature of Mormon heresy: Ministers, he wrote, "from the first century down to the present time...have denied new revelation.... To believe that God would again speak and call men by new revelation...was in their idea a heresy, and they were not to believe in anything except it was bound in their ancient books."[23]

The fairly obvious implication, of course, is that from Pratt's perspective, the entire Christian tradition amounts to one vast heresy. Indeed, three years earlier, Mormon apostle George Q. Cannon had claimed the "pure Gospel [was] lost because of the propagation, for centuries, by so-called

Christian ministers, of the soul destroying and damnable heresy that God cannot or will not speak to man again from the heavens; that God will not reveal his will, send his angels, or exercise his power in the affairs of earth as much as he did in ancient days."[24] In this light, Mormonism's controversial status as a Christian sect may depend on whether "Christian" is taken to refer to a historical tradition or a mode of Jesus-centered discipleship, however idiosyncratic its articulation. The recurrent charge of orthodoxy, even today, is that Mormons are not Christian. Mormons, or members of "the Church of Jesus Christ of Latter-day Saints," as they remind orthodox critics, officially and personally find the accusation repugnant, erroneous, and hurtful. But for Mormons to insist on their Christianity, given that label's evolution as a historically conditioned category of belief and practice, is to minimize Mormonism's innovations, and to subvert its own insistence that restoration rather than reformation was necessary. For Pratt's and Cannon's claim that Christendom has persisted for almost two thousand years in a state of apostasy is tantamount to declaring that Christianity so-called is a heretical charade. Harold Bloom is correct in saying Mormonism's hallmark is its deliberate obliviousness to two millennia of Christian tradition.[25] So Mormonism could be considered, in the context of ecclesiastical history, emphatically not Christian.

Mormonism, however, has chosen the other rhetorical route, asserting its claim to the Christian label, but basing that claim on its unique vision of primitive Christianity. This course is equally daring in its own way. For to insist that Mormons are Christian, but in a sense peculiar to them, is to appropriate the term to their private meaning, and to impudently assert that heresy is orthodoxy, and orthodoxy heresy. Such a move is not difficult for a religion that has from its beginnings referred to the Jews as gentiles. But such claims do suggest that heresy in American religious discourse is not merely a function of additions, accretions, fine points of doctrine, or institutional practices. Rather, Mormonism sees itself as redefining in a radical way the essence of Christianity, and both Mormonism and its critics deny the possibility of accommodation because of the way Mormonism reconceptualizes religion itself.

INEFFABILITY AND THE SACRED

Only taken in the collective do the assaults on Mormonism's heresies reveal their common theme: opposition to the Mormon disintegration of that distance that separates the sacred and the profane, that defines religious experience as unfathomable mystery, that constitutes religious feeling in the presence of the ineffable, that renders such terms as holiness, worshipfulness, and reverence as constituting the very essence of religion. Such distance comes close to being the sine qua non of all Western religious faith and practice.

Rudolf Otto is emphatic on this point. In *The Idea of the Holy*, he insists that this category of experience, this *mysterium tremendum*, is not merely an attribute of divinity, but "the deepest and most fundamental element in all... religious devotion." It is something "beyond conception or understanding, extraordinary and unfamiliar," "before which we therefore recoil in a wonder that strikes us chill and numb." In sum, the mysterious is "that which lies altogether outside what can be thought, and is, alike in form, quality, and essence, the utterly and 'wholly other.'"[26]

Such mystery has not traditionally been characterized as merely incidental to God's nature or to our fallen condition. In Emil Brunner's words, "God's revelation of Himself always occurs in such a way as to manifest more deeply his inaccessibility to our thought and imagination. All that we can know is the world. God is not the world.... He is Mystery."[27] As Elizabeth Johnson writes:

> The history of theology is replete with this truth: recall Augustine's insight that if we have understood, then what we have understood is not God; Anselm's argument that God is that than which nothing greater can be conceived; Hildegard's vision of God's glory as Living Light that blinded her sight; Aquinas's working rule that we can know that God is and what God is not but not what God is; Luther's stress on the hiddenness of God's glory in the shame of the cross; Simone Weil's conviction that there is nothing that resembles what she can conceive of when she says the word God; Sallie McFague's insistence on imaginative leaps into metaphor since no language about God is adequate and all of it is improper.[28]

A sense of the sacred is inseparable from a sense of radical discontinuity, be it temporal, rational, experiential, or a combination of the three. The mystification that is usually a concomitant of such discontinuity is at the very heart of the Christian tradition especially. Whether it takes the form of Christianity's *"credo quia absurdum est"* (inaccurately attributed to Tertullian) or the more subtle form of fundamentalism's ahistorical canonicalism, distance is the guarantor of the sacred's status as sacred. The difference between a contemporary and a historical prophet, a contemporary and a historical canon, and a contemporary and a historical Messiah has always been the difference between excoriation and adoration. So it was that in the early history of Mormonism, at least, it was the context rather than the content, timing rather than tenets, that led inescapably to charges of heresy. For if anything is clear, it is that the targets of scathing denunciation were beliefs absolutely central to Christianity—at least to New Testament Christianity. Scriptural formation, the prophetic calling, heavenly visitations, miracles, and spiritual gifts—these were explicitly and repeatedly made the focus of the anti-Mormon crusade.

This is not to say Mormonism had a monopoly on such unorthodox tendencies or that they alone constituted the faith's heretical status. It is to say that when these same tendencies have been manifest in other religions, they have contributed to those religions' marginalization by American Protestantism as well. Examples would range from Emanuel Swedenborg to the Reverend Sun Myung Moon, two of many who have believed that God has revealed himself through special, personal revelations from time to time.[29] In the 1800s, as now, heterodoxies besides Mormonism shared billing as premier examples in "the Kingdom of the Cults"[30] But when Mormonism's reenactment of Christian origins, its collapse of sacred distance, was combined with a potent, growing, and highly visible presence, the combination proved catastrophic.

From the Reverend Willer's first objections, to those of the League for Social Service and beyond, religious protests were directed against early Christian claims and practices occurring "in the age of railways," to use Charles Dickens's words. Mormonism's radicalism can thus be seen as its refusal to endow Christianity's origins with mythic transcendence. The *effect* of this unflinching primitivism, its resurrection of original structures and practices, is nothing short of the demystification of Christianity itself. For Mormonism replicates the process of canon formation, prophetic utterance, communion with supernatural entities—all this *without* the veil of intervening history, mythic origins, or murky tradition. The church is reintegrated into the ongoing flow of human history, origins are concrete and proximate, the process of doctrinal formation is laid bare.

Thomas O'Dea remarks of the Mormons that "they in fact re-enacted in the sociologically conducive conditions of nineteenth-century America the experience of the biblical Hebrews, whom they sought to emulate."[31] But while they were sociologically reenacting Exodus (and much of the gospels and Acts besides), few recognized the irony—or the danger—of effectively attacking Mormonism on that basis. John Russell was a rare exception in being attuned to the potential for theological self-detonation in the way those beliefs and practices were vilified. As he complained, anti-Mormon rhetoric was a sword too easily turned against its wielder as well: "The secret enemies of the Christian religion, whom a regard for their own reputation restrained from uttering their sentiments openly against the divine revelation, were loud against the Mormons. In assailing their claims to working miracles and other professions, they leveled many a blow, safely, that bore equally hard upon the miracles of Scriptures."[32]

For most observers, however, the whole Mormon "restoration" seemed blasphemous parody rather than mere anachronism. Even the prophet's name seemed calculated to resist any comforting aura of antiquity or exoticism—not Abraham or Hezekiah, but Joe Smith, of all things, compounding the insult to religious sensibility. More than one literary character reacts dismissively: "'Smith!' said Miss Priscilla, with a snort. 'That's a fine name for a prophet, isn't it?'"[33] And as another author's piqued character remarked, Smith didn't even *look* like Isaiah.[34] Having met the Mormon prophet, a writer of an Illinois history bristles with similar indignation, the indignation that any attempt to demystify religion elicits: "He is, upon the whole, an ordinary man; and considering his pretensions, a very ordinary man."[35] Another visitor to Nauvoo responded similarly to the disillusion: the prophet was clearly a man of "the nineteenth century, when prophets must get a living and provide for their relations."[36]

The omnipresent charge of blasphemy in anti-Mormon rhetoric is but another way of acknowledging this feat—the dissolution of that very distance that constitutes the essence of the sacred. Demystification, the devaluing of radical distance as a positive attribute of divinity and its workings, is precisely what critics charged and what Mormons acknowledged.

In one of his religious allegories, C. S. Lewis has suggested the enormous psychological investment we have in maintaining the fundamental distinction separating the human and the divine, and hints at the crisis their conflation would occasion:

> The distinction between natural and supernatural, in fact, broke down; and when it had done so, one realised how great a comfort it had been—how it had eased the burden of intolerable strangeness which this universe imposes on us by dividing it into two halves and encouraging the mind never to think of both in the same context. What price we may have paid for this comfort in the way of false security and accepted confusion of thought is another matter.[37]

In the ancient church, a similar heresy had been known—cosmism, or what Hugh Nibley calls the association of religion with the physical universe in any way, or seeing God as a part, rather than the ultimate source, of reality: "The idea was that anything spiritual or anything divine had nothing to do with the physical world whatever, because God is pure spirit, and matter is vile." In this view, ex nihilo creation is a necessary premise to avoid this taint of cosmism, the idea that God actually participates in this physical realm as an artisan or shaper of materiality.[38] Nibley goes so far as to suggest that Smith's essential work was the revival of this heresy. Accordingly, the hostility directed at him was a response to "the crude literalism of his religion—not only talking with angels like regular people, but giving God the aspect attributed to him by the primitive prophets of Israel."[39]

In his classic study of Mormonism as a theological system, Sterling McMurrin finds this cosmist view aligns Mormonism more nearly with Greek naturalism than with typical Christian thought. In fact, he argues, "this is a radical departure from the position of traditional theism, whether Christian, Jewish, or Islamic." His elaboration of this "somewhat distinctive quality of Mormon theology" is worth quoting at some length:

> The naturalistic disposition of Mormonism is found in the denial of the traditional conception of the supernatural. It is typical of Mormon writers to insist that even God is natural rather than supernatural, in that there is not a divine order of reality that contrasts essentially with the mundane physical universe of ordinary experience known to us through sensory data, which is the object of scientific investigation and is described by natural law. The naturalistic facet of Mormon thought is indicated by the Mormon denial of miracles in the traditional sense of an intrusion of the supernatural that suspends the natural processes. The typical Mormon conception of a miracle is that the miraculous event, though entirely natural, is simply not understood because of deficiencies in human knowledge. From the perspective of God there are no miracles.
>
> The denial of the supernatural is not simply a terminological issue in Mormonism, for reality is described qualitatively as a single continuum.[40]

Joseph Smith's teachings and writings certainly amounted to a re-materializing of Christianity. But his work went beyond this to a re-historicizing of Christianity as well. By serving as the conduit for a putative restoration of Christianity, he reenacted its origins. The authenticity of his call is really beside the point. Not to believers, certainly. But to a Christian world generally, the genie cannot be put back into the bottle. Detractors could fume and shout and label him impostor and charlatan, but the unavoidable features of religion-making themselves were there for everyone to see, and *they* become the source of ridicule and fury. Time and again, the brute scope of his claims has served to obscure the contents; the forms, the modes of revealing and constructing his system, far overshadow any question of inherent value pertaining to the particulars constituting that system.

To put Joseph Smith's "canon-making originality" on a par with the Jewish scribe J's "creation" of Yahweh, Mark's "invention" of Jesus, and

Mohammed's revelation of Allah, as Harold Bloom does, may seem extrav-
agant.[41] But Bloom's lack of any personal religious engagement with Joseph
Smith's message at least makes it possible for him to admire as grand daring that which is itself so blasphemous from any orthodox perspective.

Thus Orson Pratt's sardonic observation: "For men a few centuries ago
to hunt up a few scattered manuscripts and compile them into a Bible was
considered a very laudable undertaking, but for any man to find a sacred
book since that time is considered the highest blasphemy."[42] And in Oliver
Cowdery's words, "To talk of heavenly communications, angels' visits,
and the inspiration of the Holy Spirit, *now*, since the apostles have fallen
asleep, . . . is a novel thing among the wise, and a piece of blasphemy."[43]

Indeed, the very first recorded reaction to the Book of Mormon (before
its publication, even) was a headline in the *Rochester Daily Advertiser*:
"Blasphemy—Book of Mormon, Alias the Golden Bible."[44] And one who
dared to teach such things, as Elder Theodore Curtis did in England, was
guilty of the only appropriate charge one could make: he spent five days in
prison in Gloucester on a charge of "blasphemy."[45]

A series of editorials in the Baptist *Religious Herald* is especially revealing of the dilemma such orthodox mortification represents. The April
9 issue for 1840 has an editorial under the heading of "The Mormons":
"A correspondent requests information as to the peculiar tenets of this
modern sect. We have never seen a copy of the book of Mormon, nor any
abstract of their creed upon which we could fully rely, as a fair exposition of their opinions." This frank admission does not, however, pre-
clude a summary verdict: "The book of Mormon is a bungling and stupid
production. . . . It contains some trite, moral maxims, but the phraseology . . . frequently violates every principle and rule of grammar. We have
no hesitation in saying the whole system is erroneous.[46] As O'Dea wryly
but accurately noted, "The Book of Mormon has not been universally considered by its critics as one of those books that must be read in order to
have an opinion of it."[47]

Clearly, it is not *necessary* to see the contents of the new revelation. In
fact, those contents would invariably prove disappointing as evidence in
any heresy trial. As one religious scholar remarks, "The Book of Mormon,
first published in 1830, may not have added enough doctrinal novelty to
the Christian tradition to have made Mormonism more than a Protestant
sect."[48] That doesn't matter; the new revelation is itself taken as proof of
the fraud. This unblushing indifference to the book's *content*, the sanguine
a priori condemnation of the text, suggests that the Book of Mormon
functions for the orthodox as an empty sign, intimating a divine origin, but devoid of any substance that might be internally persuasive one

way or the other. Points of doctrinal disagreement are obviously quite beside the point. But Christian editorialists who would vehemently condemn Mormons, Seekers, and other canon-breakers, are in something of a quandary. To repudiate divine revelation as a principle is to undermine the basis of Christianity itself. So the ostensible grounds for the rejection become the most tangible but inconsequential of red herrings: bad "grammar" and awkward "phraseology."

When a subsequent reader of the *Herald* editorial complains that the writer has unduly compared Mormonism to the Campbellites, the paper responds with its list of definitive and distinctive proofs of Mormonism's heresy, and again intimates a peculiar antipathy to Christian origins. It cites "belief in the book of Mormon [that is, canon development], and in the power of working miracles, and the establishment of a separate community of saints on earth"[49] (which system the editors had already compared to "the primitive disciples and modern Shakers"[50]). Many other contemporary accounts could be cited, such as the 1835 guidebook for Ohio immigrants, warning Englishmen of this "wildest fanaticism" called Mormonism, which espouses belief in miracles, new revelation, gifts of healing and of prophecy.[51]

Heresy may be a little passé as a term of opprobrium today—but a new one has emerged to take its place—"cult." Not surprisingly, defining the parameters of Christian "cults" becomes as elusive a task as defining heresy; ultimately it becomes more self-referential than descriptive of the Other.[52] Current popular attempts to define the category have a way of being self-incriminating. As a result of the 1993 David Koresh incident near Waco, Texas, religious experts rushed to provide litmus test kits to the public for identifying "dangerous cults." One typical example is unblushing in its irony. After claiming that "cults...are heretical" in unspecified doctrinal ways, the author goes on to the more easily identifiable hallmarks, listing the "behavioral traits" of destructive cults:

—Preaching the coming of the Apocalypse...
—Attacking churches and synagogues for false teachings and not practicing what they preach.
—Relentlessly proselytizing new members.
—Making demands of followers of absolute commitment of time and money.
—Having an absolute leader whose word is law and who often claims to be a prophet...
—Requiring participation in a continuous system of mind-bending lectures, prayers, chants, speaking in tongues or meditation.

—Exploiting members...

—Having a system of secrecy in which members do not know the real aims of the group.[53]

It can hardly go unobserved that the New Testament portrays a Christ who preached an imminent apocalypse (Matthew 24:15), reproved the scribes and Pharisees as hypocrites (Matthew 23:13), commanded his followers to preach the gospel to all the world (Mark 16:15), commanded the rich young man to give away all that he had (Mark 10:21), proclaimed himself the Messiah (Luke 4:21), exhorted his disciples to fast and to pray always (Mark 9:29; Luke 18:1), and so forth. And yet here Christian heresy is defined in those very terms.

Heretics teach doctrine that is heretical, and heretics are just like early Christians, except they aren't. And since they aren't, they are certainly exploitative and deceptive. And by the way, we know they aren't real Christians because they are exploitative and secretive. With "cult" as with "heresy," the semiotic value of the term has been entirely neutralized, but the term's political value is incalculable.

It is most curious that emulation of early Christian forms by a "cult" is itself taken as prima facie evidence of heresy, rather than as initially suggestive of authority. Certainly one could argue that the singularity of the church's historical appearance consigns all other manifestations to ecclesiastical limbo—there can be only one inauguration of Christianity, as there was only one Incarnation. But as the history, not to say diversity, of Christianity amply demonstrates, moving *beyond* those original forms is itself legitimized. Indeed, such development is sanctioned by virtue of a paradigm that sees Christianity as the unfolding of the original deposit of faith. What John Henry Cardinal Newman calls the "want of accord between the early and late aspects of Christianity" is precisely the problem that he attempts to theorize in his famous *Essay on the Development of Christian Doctrine.*[54]

The intrinsic merits of Mormonism's claims seldom surface as a debatable issue, however. Not because there is no case, but because these claims are themselves taken as a sign of heresy. As the Mormons learned to their surprise, the content of the Book of Mormon was irrelevant. The record seldom elicited serious discussion, because its claim to divine authorship was its own condemnation.

Strangely enough, then, it would appear that it is not deviation from an origin, but disclosure of those origins—the re-presentation of sacred beginnings—that may effectively constitute the transgression of orthodoxy, at least in the increasingly secularized world in which Mormonism appeared and grew. This state of affairs may be explained if we consider prevailing modes of religious faith to be a condition made possible by the various forms of obscurantism that tradition leaves in its wake. Indeed, religions seem to carry as part of their own self-conceiving the means of obscuring seminal moments of their history, thereby creating an opening for the divine, the transcendent, the eternal, to intervene and create the rupture with historical reality that is the root of the sense of the sacred. Like Christ's empty tomb or Moses's mysterious burial, mystification, as the precondition for religious faith, must provide a metaphor pregnant with all the possibilities of true mystery. The weight of centuries, the poetry of creeds, and the rhythm of ritual create of themselves a sense of timelessness and sanctity that further dematerializes such founding ruptures. The immediacy and nakedness of Mormonism's foundations—like those of any contemporary religious movement—make possible a condition that critics call gullibility. But what separates orthodox faith from heretical credulousness are the layers—historical, conceptual, or psychological—that intervene between institutional origins and the call to discipleship. That the *objects* of belief are essentially the same in both cases is not a comfortable thought.

In this context, Christian orthodoxy emerges as a category defined not so much by articles of faith, as by the conditions that make faith possible. The heterodoxy of Mormonism and other "cults" challenged the construction of religious belief more than the value of its particulars. Of course certain core beliefs are essential to any conception of Christian orthodoxy: the Bible as inspired scripture, God as creator, and Christ as divine redeemer of mankind. But neither Mormonism nor other heterodox movements challenged these fundamental tenets. More to the point, as we have seen, Mormonism at least was not attacked for its departures, but for its retrogressions. What Mormonism and similar heresies did challenge—implicitly—was the fantasy that religious belief can circumvent its own historical conceiving: that God spoke to man but not in a moment that was ever the present, or to a man who was anyone's contemporary; that the canon records God's word, but God never spoke a pre-canonical utterance.

This insistence on maintaining the illusion of religion as timeless self-givenness is implicit in Christian allusions to "the canon" as if it were the same for Catholics and Protestants, and of course this while forgetting Saint Gregory's rejection of Revelation, Luther's repudiation of James, and the arguments of some contemporary scholars that the Gospel of Thomas should be added.[55] When a group of seventy liberal religious scholars called the "Jesus Seminar" at the Westar Institute in Sonoma, California, completed work on a radical revision of the gospels, they came under fire not just for their conclusions but also, perhaps even more so, for their reminder to us that all canons are necessarily the product of historical process. As Norman Hjelm, director of faith and order for the National Council of Churches, put it: Christian resistance to revisionism like that of the "Jesus Seminar" results from the tendency of most denominations to see the canon as "a given in history."[56] Popular Christian thought seldom encompasses the notion that the Apostles were Christian (that is, disciples of Christ) before there were councils, creeds, or even a New Testament.

This Christian frame of mind is not merely incidental, but is essentially and inescapably related to Paul Tillich's claim that "the intention to speak unsymbolically of religion is irreligious."[57] Symbolic language is certainly lacking in Mormonism's self-presentation. Indeed, Joseph Smith's whole language was startling—and unapologetic—in its hostility to the tradition of religious discourse. Given the language of Smith's spiritual autobiography, one must doubt the comment of the otherwise accurate writer on Mormon history William Mulder. Referring to Smith, he sympathized that "his was the perennial despair of visionaries striving how to say the unsayable." Mulder goes on to describe Smith and his peers (Jonathan Edwards, Emerson) as "nearly blinded by God's waylaying light, [turning] to analogy and metaphor, finding in nature 'images and shadows of divine things.'"[58] Here Mulder has missed the essential core of the Mormon heresy. For it was precisely the ease and brazenness with which Smith appropriated heavenly matters to his simple, direct discourse that got him—and the church he founded—into hot water to begin with.

When the visionary William Blake described celestial realms, he was keenly aware of the poverty of secular language and material eyes to describe it. "'What,' it will be questioned, 'When the Sun rises do you not see a round Disk of fire somewhat like a Guinea?' O no no, I see an Innumerable company of the Heavenly host crying 'Holy Holy Holy is the Lord God Almighty.'"[59] Not so Joseph Smith. True enough, of his encounter with the angel Moroni, he would write that the personage's countenance was "truly like lightning." But such a description is no more than common metaphor, given the description that precedes it: "His hands were naked and his arms also, a little above the wrist, so, also were his feet naked, as were his legs, a little above the ankles. His head and neck were also bare. I could discover that he had no other clothing on but this robe, as it was open, so that I could see into his bosom."[60] Neither Smith's gaze nor his language scrupled to invade celestial space with artless spontaneity. Contrast his description with Otto's pronouncement: "A spirit or soul that has been conceived and comprehended no longer prompts to 'shuddering' . . . [and] thereby ceases to be of interest for the psychology of religion."[61]

Smith's unrelenting anthropomorphizing; the chronological and geographical specificity of his encounters with the divine; his commitment of heavenly revelation to the process of transcription, publication, and marketing; his enactment of prophetic restoration through the medium of legal incorporation—these and related aspects of his work rendered religious allegorizing of his message impossible.

The stone cut out of the mountain without hands and seen by Daniel might have been figurative, but its fulfillment was not: it occurred "one thousand eight hundred and thirty years since the coming of our Lord and Savior Jesus Christ in the flesh" (to the day) when the kingdom of God was "regularly organized and established agreeable to the laws of our country" (and the state of New York).[62] When God commanded Hosea to take a harlot as a wife, the act presumably symbolized something about spiritual apostasy and devotion (Hosea 1:2). But when God commanded Joseph Smith to have Sidney Gilbert "establish a store, that he [might] sell goods," it was fruitless to search for other levels of moral significance.[63] More than one critic noted disapprovingly the prophet's rootedness in this-worldliness rather than otherworldliness. Josiah Quincy was one of many to visit the prophet at Nauvoo, one of few who refrained from "advancing any theory respecting this extraordinary man." But he could not resist the comment that "no association with the sacred phrases of Scripture could keep the inspirations of this man from getting down upon the hard pan of practical affairs."[64]

Smith's language could be lofty and sublime at times as well (portions of Doctrine and Covenants sections 76 and 88, for example). But it was the unorthodox Mormon mingling of things spiritual and worldly that generally attracted notice, including that of the editor of the New York Herald. As persecution heated up in Nauvoo in the summer of 1842, James Gordon Bennett reported with amusement: "Jo goes on prophecying [sic], preaching, and building the temple, and regulating his empire, as if nothing had happened. They are busy all the time establishing factories to make saints and crockery ware, also prophets and white paint."[65]

Moroni's golden plates may have vanished from history as surely as the tablets of Moses. But just at that moment when Mormonism's empty tomb invites hearty skepticism, and therefore the possibility of faith, just at that moment when Smith seems to nudge material foundations into mystical indeterminacy, he moves decisively in the other direction. Smith's inclusion in the preface to the Book of Mormon of affidavits signed by eleven witnesses to those plates reaffirmed his stubborn insistence on a facticity behind his religion-making that was not just real, but material, palpable. "We did handle [the leaves] with our hands," report eight of the men, thus

defying those within or without the faith who would seek to spiritual-
ize the earthy solidity of the new religion's bases (while at the same time
invoking the tactile testimony of the first-generation apostle Thomas).

Similarly, the angel with whom Smith conversed and who delivered to
him the plates was not enshrouded in the anonymity of heavenly hosts
or drawn from the sanctioned ranks of Israel's murky, distant past, as
were so many of William Blake's contacts. Instead, Moroni turns out to
be a historical figure from the American continent itself, whose story is
told in the Book of Mormon, and who thus serves as yet one more agent
by which heavenly manifestations and divine dealings are grounded in
a fixed moment and place in history. Sacred text blurs into local, secular
history; divine personage acquires a military biography. The collapsing of
such categories could not go without comment among the contemporary
audience. The author of an Illinois gazetteer remarked in 1834:

> Those who are particularly desirous of information concerning the millions of
> warriors, and the bloody battles in which more were slain than ever fell in all
> the wars of Alexander, Caesar, or Napoleon, with a particular description of
> their military works, would do well to read the *"Book of Mormon,"* made out of
> the "golden plates" of that distinguished antiquarian Joe Smith! It is far supe-
> rior to some modern productions on western antiquities, because it furnishes
> us with the names and biography of the principal men who were concerned in
> these enterprises, with many of the particulars of their wars for several centu-
> ries. But seriously...[66]

"Names," "biographies," "particulars"—in such words of reproach
Mormonism's critics vividly highlight the religious taboos Smith
violated.

Even as Smith wrote, preached, and testified of the reintegration of
things heavenly and earthly, the notion that heaven had ever been correctly envisioned as a realm exempt from rational law was increasingly
vulnerable. The rise of geology in the mid-nineteenth century tended to
discredit creationism (as John Ruskin complained, "If only the Geologists
would leave me alone, I could do very well, but those dreadful hammers! I
hear the clink of them at the end of every cadence of the Bible verses").[67]
Charles Lyell published his revolutionary *Principles of Geology* in 1830,
which was the first work, as one scholar has noted, "to treat the origin
and history of the Earth on the assumption that all its phenomena could
be explained naturally and discussed scientifically."[68] Higher Criticism
filtered the biblical text through the sieve of scientific credibility, and
reduced sacred revelation to the status of just another literary text.

Utilitarianism, Scientism, and other contemporary developments and attitudes combined to make incredible a supernatural paradigm imposed on the present *or* the past.

One ingenious rebuttal to the growing scientism came from Thomas Carlyle. In true Romantic fashion, he argued that not only was the miraculous viable as an element of religious experience, but that the miraculous pervaded the very fabric of daily experience as well. The problem is that "Custom" and "Time," the "grand anti-magician, and universal wonder-hider," convince us "that the Miraculous, by simple repetition, ceases to be Miraculous."[69] From icicles to tollbooths, the right perspective illuminated a hidden wonder and showed up the insufficiencies of a mechanical rationalism as the master key by which to understand the cosmos. "Through every grass-blade...the glory of a present God still beams."[70]

But while Carlyle was alerting mankind to the divinity behind the mundane, "the wonder everywhere lying close on us,"[71] Smith was busy insisting on the terrestrial origins of the divine. At every turn, but increasingly toward the end of his life, it seemed he was intent on demystifying traditional categories of the sacred, on deconstructing the otherworldly into its this-worldly bases. There seems to be little other motive behind his claim that "there is no angel ministers to this earth only what either does belong or has belonged to this earth."[72] The fullest implications of this "heresy" were not unfolded until the spring of his last year, at which point he was publicly teaching that "God Himself who sits enthroned in yonder heavens [was] a Man like unto one of yourselves—that is the great secret!"[73]

Smith's worldview was the obverse of Carlyle's "natural supernaturalism." It was not that the world was always ablaze with the glory of God, and science had merely overlooked this truth; that, in M. H. Abrams's words, "an unassisted transaction between the ordinary object and the dishabituated eye, effects authentic miracles."[74] Rather, Smith alleged that the divine had always been more immediately accessible to human understanding and experience than apostate Christianity had acknowledged. Priest-craft had conspired to conceal this fact. The divine, in other words, was not characterized by the radical otherness that religious tradition equated with the sacred. For this reason, his religious innovation was more the naturalizing of the supernatural than the other way around.

Astonishingly, then, Mormonism's response to the secularist impulse seen in the growth of uniformitarianism, materialism, and positivism is not to challenge or defy these critiques of supernaturalism, to insist on a cosmic dualism, but to produce a religious system consonant with a monistic worldview. In one of the last revelations published by Smith, he would affirm that "there is no such thing as immaterial matter. All spirit is matter, but it is more fine or pure, and can only be discerned by purer eyes; We cannot see it; but when our bodies are purified we shall see that it is all matter."[75]

The protest against Mormonism turns out to be, in the final analysis, much the same as the Enlightenment's protest against Christianity itself. As Gotthold Lessing phrased it, "Accidental truths of history can never become the proof of necessary truths of reason."[76] The historical situatedness of any church's birth—Christian or Mormon—impedes its claim to universal validity. But Mormonism did not merely insert itself conspicuously into historical time; it resisted any attempt to allegorize its origins, its forms, its scriptural canon, or its claims to spiritual gifts and offices.

Why should this tendency be so universally construed as crossing the divide separating heterodoxy from heresy? Clearly, Mormonism's tendencies denied the very basis and conditions of traditional Christian belief, the experience of the sacred as the *mysterium tremendum et fascinosum*. But in addition, one could say that heresy in its simplest terms must be understood as a condition that is not merely repugnant or incomprehensible to orthodoxy, but threatening as well. This threat, in the case of Mormonism, appears to take the form of reflecting back upon Christianity itself in a particularly disconcerting way. Brigham Young's observation on the life of Joseph Smith might therefore not be as simplistic or self-serving as it at first appears: "Again, why was he persecuted? Because he revealed to all mankind a religion so plain and easily understood, consistent with the Bible, and so true. *It is now as it was in the days of the Savior*" (emphasis in original).[77] With all the enthusiasm a disinterested sociologist can muster, Rodney Stark lends emphatic agreement to this assessment, but while completely bracketing the particular religious truth-claims involved: "It is possible today to study that incredibly rare event: the rise of a new world religion"[78] So whether it is seen as sacrilegious parody by outraged skeptics, as reenactment of Christian origins that is a sociologist's dream, or as divine restoration heralded by the faithful, Mormonism stands as a defiant reminder that, much as it tries to, orthodoxy cannot escape the fact of its own construction.

PART TWO

Mormonism and Fiction

CHAPTER 6

"Ground in the Presbyterian Smut Machine": The Popular Press, Fiction, and Moral Crusading

In fact, the idea of the paranoid style would have little contemporary relevance or historical value if it were applied only to people with profoundly disturbed minds. It is the use of paranoid modes of expression by more or less normal people that makes the phenomenon significant.

Richard Hofstadter, "The Paranoid Style in American Politics," 1965

Then I asked: does a firm perswasion [sic] that a thing is so, make it so?
He replied, All poets believe that it does. . . .

William Blake, "The Marriage of Heaven and Hell," 1790

Given the fact that newspapers, novelists, preachers, politicians, and humorists united in heaping contempt upon Mormonism—and upon other heterodoxies as well—in the nineteenth century, it is natural enough to ask what provoked such opposition. In chapter 5, I discussed some of the religious dimensions to the provocation. But there is an additional question one might ask, and which I propose to address in this chapter: what circumstances might have contributed to an atmosphere in which it was possible to galvanize, exacerbate, and express public opinion in a way that created a symphony of censure out of disparate and often unrelated protests? Anti-Mormon expression—at least its most violent manifestations—has abated somewhat in recent years. It may be tempting to suggest that this more harmonious coexistence is the result of Mormonism's accommodation to the American mainstream. (Church members no longer gather, practice polygamy, or flout federal authority, for example.) However, fundamental principles of the faith remain essentially unchanged. And, presumably, human nature has not changed a great deal in the last several decades. Perhaps, therefore, it is worth considering what factors external to Mormonism have affected reactions to Mormonism—and govern expressions of intolerance and hostility generally. I am not referring to the shift away from that Jacksonian ideology that made majority opinion a sufficient justification for outrages against a minority, as lamented by Gustave de Beaumont. Less remarked, but perhaps equally relevant, were the rapidly changing conditions of public discourse in the nineteenth century. Recurring revolutions in technology and literacy, as well as a general upheaval in conceptions and practices regarding narrative authority, authorship, and the delineation of literary categories, were essentially related to the intensity and shape of religious propaganda wars of the nineteenth century.

Fawn Brodie's psychobiography of Joseph Smith opens with the remark that Smith was rash enough "to found a new religion in the age of printing."[1] Most revolutionary advances in science and technology tend really to be evolutionary developments. Not so with the birth of an information-based and image-conscious society. The discrepancy between the rate at which facts, opinions, and misinformation were disseminated at the time of Joseph Smith's birth and at his death less than four decades later is gigantic. "Until the last two decades of the eighteenth century," Nathan Hatch writes, "Americans were still severely limited in the amount and type of information they could receive, and much of its dispersal was still hierarchical."[2] It was out of the experience of the Revolution that newspaper reading became a habit for many Americans.[3] Whereas at the beginning of the War for Independence only thirty-seven newspapers were published in the colonies, by the 1840s, the golden age of journalism, the number was fourteen hundred.[4]

As was true of the boom in publishing generally, the proliferation of the printed word meant a corresponding proliferation of types, categories, and genres. For example, as the secular press grew at a prodigious rate, so did the religious. Gaylord Albaugh estimates that the forty years from 1790 to 1830, the year of Mormonism's founding, saw religious journals multiply from 14 to 605. Readership for the same general period grew from five thousand to four hundred thousand.[5] Religion, culture, and politics became increasingly volatile not only because the mass of information mushroomed, but also because the increase in volume was accompanied by a breakdown of more hierarchical information structures and the proliferation of shifting, nebulous, overlapping sets of genre conventions. The result was a widespread dispersal of discursive authority, and an increasing democratization of ideas. While this might suggest that opinion-making was no longer solely vested in the hands of the elite, it also explains why a few years hence, Senate debates on important policy decisions featured testimony that included such "authoritative" sources as Artemus Ward and pulp novelists.

MORMONISM AND POPULAR JOURNALISM

If Smith was foolish enough to found a religion in the age of printing, he was also canny enough to court the goodwill of James Gordon Bennett, publisher of the *New York Herald* and "founder of a new school of writing."[6] Bennett did not invent the penny press, but he joined the emerging new industry early enough to reshape the face of popular journalism. Coinciding with the first thirty years of Mormonism's history, the new regime of journalism emphasized popular appeal, energetic writing and reporting, and a price that would put newspapers in the hands of every American citizen (the average cost of newspapers was six cents). But it was the *role* of journalism that was the real focus of the revolution. Bennett described his vision in fairly grandiose terms: "My ambition is to make the newspaper Press the great organ and pivot of government, society, commerce, finance, religion, and all human civilization."[7] Equally accurate as a description of his aim, but perhaps a good deal more illuminating when it comes to explaining the shifting role of the media and its influence on the Mormon problem in particular, was his belief that it is a newspaper's function not to instruct, but to startle.

In December 1841, the Nauvoo City Council published a declaration thanking Bennett "for his very liberal and unprejudiced course towards us as a people, in giving us a fair hearing in his paper, thus enabling us to reach the ears of a portion of the community who otherwise would have remained ignorant of our principles and practices." The proclamation also urged their fellow citizens to subscribe.[8] The citizens of Nauvoo further expressed their appreciation in April 1842, by conferring upon Bennett "the freedom of the City" and, through the University of Nauvoo, awarding him the honorary degree of LLD.[9] About the same time, Smith heaped yet another distinction upon him, naming him a brigadier general and aide-de-camp in the Nauvoo Legion. Governor Carlin confirmed the appointment. Bennett was not exactly humbled by this single distinction accorded a mere "gentile." As he trumpeted facetiously in his own *Herald* of August 13, 1842:

> There's honor—there's distinction—there's salt and greens for a modest, simple, calm, patient, industrious editor. We now take legitimate rank, far above Colonel Webb, Major Noah, Colonel Stone, General George P. Morris, or all the military editors around and about the country. We are only inferior in rank—and that but half a step—to good old General Jackson—he being Major-General and LL.D.— we being Brigadier and LL.D. also.... It will be seen, therefore, that I am *Aid-de-Camp* [sic], with the rank of Brigadier-General, to the Major-General of the famous Nauvoo Legion. *This Major-General is no less a man than the* Prophet Joe Smith, *who is very busy establishing an* original religious empire *in the west, that may swallow up all the other different sects and* cliques, as the rod of Moses, turned into a serpent, swallowed up, without salt, the rods of Jannes and Jambres, and the other magicians of Egypt. Heavens! how we apples swim, as the sprat said to the whale, Mount Etna bawling out at the same time, "Let's have another segar." Wonders never cease. Hereafter, I am James Gordon Bennett, Freeman of the Holy City of Nauvoo, LL.D. of the University of Nauvoo, and Aid-de-Camp to the Major-General, and Brigadier General to the Nauvoo Legion, with the fair prospect of being a prophet soon, and a saint in Heaven hereafter [emphases in original].[10]

The prophet's establishment of warm relations with one of the most powerful journalists of his age could be construed as simple political savvy. Doubtless there was much of genuine gratitude as well. Certainly, in the example above and in other treatments of the Mormons, Bennett could be facetious and often sarcastic. In fact, as a consequence of his 1842 columns on the church, Bennett's biographer credits him with having "awakened the people to the dangers inseparable from an adhesion to the faith upon which this remarkable and delusive system of religion is founded."[11]

That was clearly wishful thinking on the part of his biographer, who apparently imputed to the 1842 series of published attacks on the Mormon prophet by disaffected member John Cook Bennett (no relation to the editor) more truth than the editor did. While he ran the scathing denunciations, and conceded that "No doubt Joe Smith and the Mormons are sad sinners," Bennett, the editor, also wrote in the same breath that "we don't believe one half of John Cook Bennett's stories."[12] At times, he could in fact be unabashedly admiring of the prophet and his followers, if sometimes mischievously so. Some months before the Nauvoo honors, he had editorialized that "this Joseph Smith is undoubtedly one of the greatest characters of the age. He indicates as much talent, originality, and moral courage as Mahomet, Odin, or any of the great spirits of past ages."[13] More emphatic was the endorsement the Mormons received in the same issue that trumpeted Nauvoo's endorsement of Bennett. In that January 1842 column he had enthused that Mormonism represented

> a germ of religious civilization, novel, affecting, inviting, wonderful, and extraordinary. How far superior, practical, and comprehensive these movements are, than those of the many other sects around us.... All the priests and philosophers of the day may take a lesson from Joe Smith, who seems to have hit the nail exactly on the head by uniting faith and practice—fancy and fact—religion and philosophy—heaven and earth, so as to form the germ of a new religious civilization, bound together in love and temperance—in industry and energy—that may revolutionize the whole earth one of these days.[14]

Elsewhere Bennett defended the Mormons against charges of complicity in the assassination attempt on Lilburn Boggs. "We can hardly believe the rumor," Bennett wrote. "The Mormons were dreadfully persecuted in Missouri; yet they are a more peaceable, quiet, and moral people than many of those sects—some with and some without piety—that live around them."[15] Given the field day other presses were having with the prophet "Joe" and his "Golden Bible," Smith was undoubtedly grateful for the mixed reviews of the *Herald*. The editorials of "that excellent and useful paper" were, he proclaimed to the Nauvoo City Council, "free from the prejudices and superstitions of the age." In addition, he went on to add, Bennett provided an invaluable service to the missionary-oriented church in reprinting, in their unedited entirety, numerous articles and revelations from the LDS newspaper, *The Times and Seasons*.[16] Given the *Herald*'s 1844 circulation of nearly twenty thousand copies,[17] this was no small boost to the Mormon message. Later, Smith reflected bitterly on what he saw as the more general treatment he had received at the hands of the press: "The pagans, Roman Catholics, Methodists, and Baptist[s] shall have peace in Nauvoo only they must be ground in Joe Smith's mill. I have been in their mill. I was ground in Ohio and [New] York States—a Presbyterian smut machine—and [the] last machine was in Missouri and last of all I have been through [the] Illinois smut machine."[18]

Smith's complaint was not self-indulgent paranoia. The same journalist who credited Bennett with unmasking the Mormon menace was so confident of the power of the press to enforce religious purity that he saw the Mormon exodus to the West not as the flight of a persecuted people, but as a cunning maneuver to evade the media. Writing in 1855, Isaac

Pray opined that it was because "of the sect having craftily removed to regions on the outer borders of civilization, where the power of the Press cannot be felt, [that] the progress of this strange community has been wonderfully rapid."[19] Given the role of the newspaper in shaping public sentiment regarding Mormonism, Pray's comment is almost believable. As we saw in chapter 5, the first printed salvo in the anti-Mormon crusade was launched by a local newspaper in New York before the church was organized or the Book of Mormon was yet in print. Journalistic opposition continued unabated through the Ohio and Missouri periods, and was a prime factor in the tragedy in Nauvoo. Following the Saints' destruction of the hostile *Nauvoo Expositor*, the nearby *Warsaw (Ill.) Signal* echoed the words that led to the Haun's Mill massacre, and with similar results. "We hold ourselves at all times in readiness," editor Thomas Sharp wrote, "to co-operate with our fellow citizens...to exterminate, utterly exterminate, the wicked and abominable Mormon leaders."[20] A few days later, the prophet and his brother Hyrum were dead. The newspaper campaign would go on for years to come before the novelists finally took up the battle in the decade before the Civil War.

Another literary form of particular importance in shaping public perceptions of Mormonism was the illustrated magazine, which rose to prominence in the 1850s. Gary Bunker and Davis Bitton claim that "there had been other important vehicles of expression before—books, pamphlets, broadsides, almanacs, separately published prints—but none of these had as much power to shape attitudes among large numbers of people as did the illustrated periodical." They point out that *Harper's, Leslie's, Vanity Fair, Yankee Notions*, and several others were spawned in this decade, and many soon reached circulations surpassing one hundred thousand. All of them featured articles and illustrations about Mormonism.[21]

TECHNOLOGY, READERS, AND LITERARY TRANSFORMATIONS

The underlying roots of the newspaper revolution had broader than strictly journalistic implications, and we must examine them in more detail if we are to understand the role of fiction in shaping the terms of the anti-Mormon debates. The Industrial Revolution had the immediate consequence of transforming social and economic life in England and then abroad. But it had equally powerful repercussions on political and cultural life as well, though rather indirectly. With the application of the burgeoning technologies to the textile industry, the cost of producing cloth plummeted. Naturally, when apparel became cheaper and more readily available, so did discarded clothing. Rags, the source material for papermaking, had previously been so scarce that paper mills were frequently plagued by shortages; but rags were soon to become as plentiful for recycling as aluminum cans are today. Then, in 1807, the English brothers Henry and Sealy Fourdrinier, improving upon a French design, built a paper machine capable of mass-producing the commodity that until then had been handmade, one sheet at a time. These developments revolutionized the publishing industry. Books were suddenly available in massively increased numbers to a population whose literacy rate was likewise soaring. Once the domain of the cultural elite, literature fast became the property of a new readership. "This is the age of reading," proclaimed Joseph Story in a Phi Beta Kappa speech at Cambridge, Massachusetts, in 1826. In fact, he continued, so advanced had the power and love of reading become, that it was "no wonder that reading should cease to be a mere luxury, and should be classed among the necessaries of life."[22] Recent studies confirm that this fact was as true for rural, isolated areas of America as it was for Boston.[23] Within a few years, wood pulp would replace rags as the principal raw material for paper, adding to the growing affordability and pervasiveness of the printed word.

As Morse Peckham points out in his study of the nineteenth century, these economic developments in publishing are inseparable from drastic shifts in literary standards as well. Peckham refers to the process as reflecting a "kind of cultural Gresham's law...: inferior culture drives out superior."[24] Some of these transformations are evident in publishing data from the period: William Wordsworth inaugurated a new era in English literary history with the publication of his *Lyrical Ballads* in 1798, though its print run was a mere five hundred copies (the poems "have not sold ill," remarked the publisher), and the second edition of 1800 only one thousand.[25] Although these were still not sold out five months after publication, Wordsworth was thrilled that with such numbers, he could soon "command my price with the Booksellers."[26] By the time Byron dominated the English scene a scant fifteen years later, his *Corsair* would sell ten thousand copies on the day of publication and twenty-five thousand within a month.[27]

It is tempting to claim that as mass publishing makes possible that phenomenon known as the best-seller, there is a corresponding shift in the kind of book capturing the public spotlight. In 1788, for example, the two best-selling books in America were Robert Burns's *Poems* and Hamilton, Madison, and Jay's *The Federalist*. Ten years later, the top titles were Hannah Foster's *Coquette* and Regina Roche's *Children of the Abbey*.[28]

But such a conclusion would be premature. "Literary" figures like Scott, Byron, Cooper, and Dickens would continue to dominate the list for the next decades, though increasingly they were in the company of authors like Maria Monk (*Awful Disclosures*). The most dramatic changes were inaugurated when the same technology of fast newspaper cylinder presses that had made the penny press possible in the thirties was applied to the book industry. From 1842 to 1845, a number of printers published books in newspaper format, sending prices plunging from a dollar or two per volume to as low as 6¼ cents.[29] Cutthroat competition, cheap production costs, and the proliferation of players in the new field led one of the innovators to complain by 1843 that "literature is now a drug. All the markets are overstocked."[30] Then in 1860, with the advent of the dime novel, the best-seller lists were almost completely taken over by the likes of Edward Ellis's *Seth Jones* and Mrs. Stephens's *Malaeska*, an adventurous romantic melodrama, each selling in the neighborhood of half a million copies.

These increasing numbers and declining standards are not entirely explained by the decline in the retail price of books. True enough, the economics of publishing created a new audience, and authors adapted to this new audience. If the bawdy author of *The Corsair* and *Don Juan* was more appealing to an increasingly proletarian audience than the staid and sexless Wordsworth, this was true *a fortiori* of Maria Monk. But other powerful, though more subtle, dynamics were also at work here. For as prices plunged, the lower cost of production meant that a different *kind* of work was effectively being created. The dramatically shifting standards of taste did not—or did not only—reflect the dominance of a new readership, to which mercenary authors increasingly paid dutiful homage. They may actually also have reflected the way high culture could become popular culture as a result of the change technology produced on the cultural objects themselves.

An understanding of this correlation between the material facts of a book's production (its appearance, price, format) and its *meaning* (its cultural significance, its aesthetic value, even its genre designation) had been at times consciously exploited from a publishing standpoint. In the case of *Don Juan*, for example, Jerome McGann points out how Byron's publisher Murray aimed to circumvent moral objections to the inflammatory work by pricing it out of the range of the social class that would misinterpret it. Pirated editions rendered his strategy ineffective, but the principles involved were only validated more emphatically as a result. The first limited print run was quietly priced and distributed at £1 11s. 6d. to mildly favorable reviews. Only after thousands of cheaper, unauthorized copies followed did the book elicit a scandal. As a contemporary reviewer put the case: "'Don Juan' in quarto and on hot-pressed paper would have been almost innocent—in a whity-brown duodecimo it was one of the worst of the mischievous publications that have made the press a snare."[31] Cheaper editions had effectively engendered a new work. The development was perfectly on a par with the contemporaneous change from a six-cent newspaper to the penny press, with its corresponding redefinition of the medium from one that instructed to one that startled.

NEW WINE IN OLD BOTTLES

The example of *Don Juan* is especially apropos of the anti-Mormon crusade in popular fiction. Obviously, publishing has long been an instrument in religious propaganda wars, and marginalized groups have long provided fodder for literary caricature, such as Shakespeare's Shylock or Spenser's Archimago in his priestly garb. But the nineteenth century saw the development of a literary tradition that blended the worst of both practices, propaganda and caricature, in large part by appropriating literary genres and conventions that the publishing revolution was already investing with new functions and values.

The gothic novel, for example, had been introduced to Europe by Horace Walpole (*Castle of Otranto*) in 1765. The genre's dark supernaturalism, its trademark castles, labyrinths, and subterranean prisons, are at one level clear effluences of eighteenth-century antirationalism and neo-medievalism. But as the type became popularized and imitations flourished, it became more and more apparent that the books were written and read out of prurient fascination with sexual taboos, female bondage, and as a perverse celebration of religious betrayal and ever more creative versions of transgression. Writers were themselves aware of this slippery passage. Harriet Beecher Stowe, in her introduction to anti-Catholic writer Charlotte Elizabeth Tonna's works, praises her for descriptions that are "sufficiently graphic and minute to produce a full impression of the horror and vice that she is describing, [without being] so minute as to become themselves corrupting."[32] In the case of Tonna, whose works appeared in the 1840s, that may well have been true. Readers seeking to satisfy their prurient interest would have a hard time wading through the severe sermonizing she organized around the thinnest of plots.

Gothic and Protestant polemics are, however, already merged by the 1834 publication of Mary Martha Sherwood's *The Nun*. This is not to say the union is seamless. Sherwood's characters are still mere instruments for the clichéd critiques of Catholic doctrines: "'From whence,' returned

Pauline, with that air of arch simplicity which her features so easily assumed, 'do you derive these principles, Sister Annunciata? Are they found in the Holy Scriptures?' Annunciata gave her a searching look, and seemed to me to be more disconcerted and embarrassed than I had often seen her."[33] Subtleties of doctrinal disputation are soon overwhelmed, however, by blatant intrusions of gothic horror. "'Solitary confinement and a diet of the most meager description has overcome more obstinate cases than this has yet appeared to be; and you know an instance, daughter,' he added, addressing the Abbess, 'in which an individual has been gathered back again into the bosom of the church, after thirty years' resistance.... There are few minds which can stand years of solitary confinement.'"[34] The place of confinement is, of course, soon revealed to be "some subterraneous dungeon," and we next hear of a "sister so bad that they were forced to chain her to a stone pillar in a cell under the house."[35] From underground dungeons, chains, and "a secret spring in the wainscot," it is a matter of very few pages before thinly veiled eroticism makes its appearance as well: "The priests believed themselves to be alone; and whilst the Jesuit carefully closed the trap-door, Father Joachim, having laid the sister on the pavement, supposing her to be insensible...proceeded to draw the altar, which was of wood, over the door in the pavement.... He was proceeding, when she as it were slid through his arms upon her knees, wildly shrieking for mercy; and pleading rather for an instant death than the fate which was prepared for her."[36]

She is saved, of course, as in the background, "oh! horrible, affecting sight! vivid flames [rise] up amid the dark masses of Gothic masonry."[37] It is the peculiar way in which this salvation is effected, however, that most transparently reveals motives other than religious ones. Imputing to Catholicism an evil that deforms both body and soul, Sherwood has Mr. Beaumont rescue his teenage twin sister, but she is so altered by her months of suffering that during the few days of their flight, Beaumont continues to mistake her for a fifty-year-old woman who had been missing as well. When interrogated, she replies, "I have no name,...they made me nameless; they wiped away all memory of me."[38] Yet on one level, at least, it is clear that not oppression, but the particular *form* of oppression is what the nameless one and sympathetic audiences must eschew. For while the place of her bondage bursts into flames in the distance, "a demur had occurred [among her liberators] how the rescued sister could be conveyed, as it was evident that she could not support herself on a horse; this was, however, soon settled by Mr. Beaumont, who caused her to be lifted behind him, his horse being powerful, whilst he bound her to himself with her veil."[39] Apparently, salvation means substituting the proper kind of bondage for the wrong one. In this case, that means effectively replacing a Catholic captor with a Protestant one.

Maria Monk's *Awful Disclosures of the Hotel Dieu Nunnery of Montreal* (1836), most popular of all the convent novels, pushed the genre to its limits.[40] Rampant sexual bondage of nuns, routine infanticide, and other horrors were duly chronicled in this personal account of her awful travails. The frontispiece even folded out to reveal a plan of the convent complete with locations of trap doors, "secret apartments," "Priests' gaming and feasting room," "Purgatory room," and "chamber where St. Frances was murdered" and where "Infanta [was] smothered."

The tradition continued seamlessly into the Mormon realm. In 1881, Mrs. Paddock would describe a burial pit with the remains of small children, and, in 1917, a "New York Detective" working for the Secret Service would describe secret passages and trap doors common to "nearly all Mormon houses."[41]

The transition from Walpole through "Monk" Lewis to Maria Monk was not simply a matter of probing the sensationalistic limits of a new form. What made it possible to people the ranks of gothic villains and victims with real names must not be reduced to nativism and the no-popery crusade alone. As Walpole's audience of a few hundred literary elite was supplanted by the mass audience of Maria Monk's and Ann Radcliffe's best-selling thrillers, the overall significance of the genre, its narrative authority and impact, were increasingly tied to radically changing conditions that govern public discourse in general, and to which we will soon turn.

The experience of American readers with yet another popular genre also paved the way for the representations of Catholics and Mormons soon to be written. Indian captivity narratives began as a form of seventeenth-century religious expression, in which a benevolent God redeemed the individual from the clutches of the unbeliever, as the children of Israel were brought out of Egypt. The form was adapted for eighteenth-century anti-French or anti-British propaganda, and ended up as the nineteenth-century penny dreadful.[42] Correspondingly, the emphasis shifted from an edifying focus on providential deliverance to sensationalistic and prurient exploitation of bondage itself as a salacious theme. The famous series of "Dime Novels" published by Erastus Beadle began with Edward Ellis's 1860 *Seth Jones; or, the Captives of the Frontier*, one of the most popular of all tales in the series, selling over four hundred thousand copies in half a year.[43] The American wilderness does not lend itself to medieval settings and labyrinthine abbeys and castles,[44] but the zeitgeist readily accommodated supernaturalism, perverse evil, and lots and lots of bondage. Thus, the Mormons with their closed communities and allegedly unorthodox sexual practices, like the Shakers and Catholic orders, invited exploitation by two ready literary genres.

These prurient features of popular fiction were seldom absent from even the most reform-minded works of the period. Especially in the years 1790 to 1860, writes Jane Tompkins, authors were engaged in a particular kind of "cultural work." Her famous study seeks to combat the elitist literary tradition in the West, which she feels is founded upon the myth of timeless classics, according to which such "ineffable products of genius" transcend the particular moment of their conception and escape "national, social, economic, institutional, and professional interests."[45] In discussing the works of popular fiction that are her subject (and mine), she resorts instead to a model of literary works as "attempts to redefine the social order," ways of "articulating and proposing solutions for the problems that shape a particular historical moment."[46]

Obviously, anti-Mormon novels, like anti-Catholic ones, are trying to *do* something besides merely entertain. They are trying to eradicate heresy and popery—two examples of cultural work at its most blatant. But there are problems with any theory of literature that attempts to universalize in the way Tompkins does. "To have political ideas, to express them in literary form, and to attempt thereby to influence 'the men who now govern the world'…was the raison d'être of an American author," she asserts.[47] Clearly this is the case with a Harriet Beecher Stowe, or a Charles Brockden Brown, who sent to Thomas Jefferson a copy of *Wieland* together with a letter proclaiming a role for fiction in "the operations of government."[48]

If Tompkins's study had extended to popular works of fiction in the anti-heresy crusade, with their heavy-handed polemics and militant prefaces, her observations would have been even more self-evident. The problem, of course, is that such an approach would ignore the very tensions and hypocrisies so evident in so many of the salacious treatments of Catholics and nuns. As W. D. Taylor writes, "The favorite subject of the dark reformers was sexual transgression.… Despite its legitimacy as a social issue, it was ideally suited for the 'moralist' whose hidden agenda was prurient titillation."[49] In his look "Beneath the American Renaissance," David S. Reynolds gives the name of "subversive reformers" to a vast group of writers (including the early Walt Whitman) who "de-emphasized the remedies for vice while probing the grisly, sometimes perverse results of vice." "To influence 'the men who now govern the world'" is too dignified a description for a novelistic enterprise that so often, in Reynolds's phrase, relied upon the "pretense of reform [while it] manufactured sex and violence to titillate the masses"—all in the service of economic rather than political motives.[50]

GENRE AND DISCURSIVE AUTHORITY

Another problem with analyses like Tompkins's is their tendency to reify categories that may not have functioned in the nineteenth century as they do for us. By opposing what she calls her "heuristic and didactic" corpus of popular works to the canon of "mimetic" high art, Tompkins skirts the question of how such categories and literary distinctions worked historically. For it was the tentative evolution of popular fiction as a new form, the very imprecision of its emerging generic boundaries, that may have contributed to its considerable political power in nineteenth-century society—and to reshaping public attitudes toward Catholics, Mormons, and others. Taylor quotes Edgar Allen Poe's remark that the influence of penny dailies upon the life of the nation was "probably beyond all calculation," and then adds, "the same might be said of the brand of fiction they spawned."[51] This is certainly because, to a large extent, the two forms were so interconnected, exploited similar audiences, and relied upon similarly ill-defined narrative authority.

To understand the role of fiction in the moral crusades of the nineteenth century, then, it may be useful to focus less on the competing merits or struggles of the literary modes that Tompkins refers to and more on the ways these categories were confused—the ways in which new mediums, subjects, and audiences outstripped the containment and organization of public discourse in the early nineteenth century. The economic, educational, and technological transformations of the period not only produced a new reading public, but also, and equally significantly, created new literary forms. Truth claims, credibility, legitimacy, influence—all are shaped and conditioned by perceived rules governing those particular literary forms in which statements are made. And seldom has the world witnessed the proliferation of genre and media of communication that characterized the early and middle nineteenth century. As a consequence, narrative authority, or the degree of assent demanded by a given text, became increasingly unclear. So, rather than conceive of the rise of the popular press and popular literature as merely new literary forms for a new public, it may be fruitful to consider such developments as complicating the authority of the printed word in general, and facilitating a kind of unpoliced rhetorical violence.

The increasingly literate audiences; the plummeting costs of publishing; the proliferation of journals, newspapers, penny dailies, nickel weeklies, and dime novels—these developments, as I have argued, not only made possible a new literary audience, but also militated against the rigid aloofness of literature as an autonomous realm of elite discourse. Writing in 1857, Boston publisher Samuel Goodrich metaphorically characterized the consequences. As Nathan Hatch writes,

> Goodrich recalled that for the previous generation books and newspapers "had been scarce, and were read respectfully, as if they were grave matters, demanding thought and attention." Spectacles, he noted, were made and used differently then: "These instruments were not as now, little tortoise-shell hooks, attached to a ribbon, and put off and on with a jerk; but they were of silver or steel, substantially made, and calculated to hold on with a firm and steady grasp, showing the gravity of the uses to which they were devoted. Even the young approached a book with reverence, and a newspaper with awe. How the world has changed."[52]

Goodrich may have been lamenting what he saw as a decline in the gravity of those works falling under public scrutiny, a shift that is perhaps suggested by the displacement of *The Federalist* as best seller in 1788 by Hannah Foster's *Coquette* in 1798. Increasingly, however, the proliferation of the printed word, and of the discursive forms it assumed, occurred in the absence of normative guidelines for how those works were to be read and interpreted. At the level of elite culture, British Romanticism of the early nineteenth century had promulgated an (alleged) flight from the constraints of genre. Impassioned moral fervor, sincerity, and poetic subjectivity had become any expression's raison d'être. Neoclassical obsession with formal categories and systems was replaced by the posture, at least, of spontaneity and freedom. Authentic sentiment, not decorum, became the supreme ground of moral authority. Out of this critical stance, Rousseau published his *Reveries*; the Schlegels in Germany published the *Athenaeum Fragments*; Coleridge published "Kubla Khan" as a "Dream *Fragment*," and "Religious Musings"; the British essayists published their informal essays and conversation pieces. Wordsworth even argued in his appendix to *Lyrical Ballads* that authenticity of the poet's voice, and not the form of expression, was the ultimate criterion of literary value.[53] Meanwhile, at the level of popular culture, language was even more dramatically freed from the constraints of genre conventions. Perhaps nowhere was this phenomenon more evident than in that forum where religious hostilities met developing forms of popular fiction.

The year 1823 saw the publication of what is generally considered the first of hundreds of anti-Catholic novels, Grace Kennedy's *Father Clement*. The next year, the first fictionalized attack on the Shakers came out, Catharine Maria Sedgwick's *Redwood*. After a few decades of journalistic and religious invective, the first full-length American novel about Mormonism appeared in 1853, John Russell's *The Mormoness; or, the Trials of Mary Maverick*. Some fifty more anti-Mormon tales followed before the turn of the century. In preface after preface, the authors of these tales show a great deal of self-conscious bewilderment as they struggle to situate their new creations, these novelistic religious critiques, relative to contemporary genres. In 1854, Orestes Brownson published *The Spirit-Rapper*, his Faustian morality tale against spiritualism. He remarks, "If the critics undertake to determine, by any recognized rules of art, to what class of literary productions the following unpretending work belongs, I think they will be sorely puzzled....I am puzzled myself to say what it is. It is not a novel; it is not a romance; it is not a biography of a real individual; it is not a dissertation, an essay, or a regular treatise."[54]

Anti-Catholic and anti-Mormon writers more commonly—but spuriously—claimed the genre of "memoirs," as did Maria Monk and Maria Ward, to name but two of the most successful. One might assume such claims were mere marketing gimmicks, the cynical exploitation of a gullible public, if not for the very real problem confronting a writer like Brownson. The historical novel, born with Walter Scott's *Waverly* series in 1814 and soon adopted by James Fenimore Cooper in America, was still in its infancy. The two popular forms of narrative I have mentioned, the gothic novel and the captivity tale, helped shape the form and elements of the new genre, but, apart from their adaptation, the memoir was the closest available form that allowed the presentation of detailed, lurid description with the force and credibility of the personal account. That is why, at least in the case of a Brownson, an author could subtitle his work "An Autobiography," while simultaneously disclaiming it as "a biography of a real individual."

George Lippard was another who chose the popular "memoir" label, even though his *Memoirs of a Preacher* (1864) was not even written in the first person, nor did it feature the depraved preacher, Edmund Jervis, as the protagonist. The work features a variety of denominations, including the kindly Millerite preacher Mervyn, revivalists, and charitable priests. The villain is a popular evangelical, but a closet spiritualist, who uses "Magnetism" to mesmerize and sexually exploit young women.

Lippard has been called the most combative American novelist of his age,[55] but he was also one of the most confused and divided against himself. He fervently berated intolerance, as when he sarcastically digresses for a moment in *Memoirs*:

> Yes, it is our duty, first of all, to hate the Catholics, hate them heartily, with all our
> might, hate them in our Papers, in our Churches, in our Prayers....And next to

hating the Catholics, it is our duty to hate every Protestant sect which may differ from our own, either in the fashion of its steeple or its creed. As Presbyterians, we hate the Methodists; as Methodists, we hate the Presbyterians. As Episcopalians we hate them both. As Orthodox we hate the Heterodox.[56]

Nevertheless, such high-minded tolerance is not exactly uniform in his novels. As the title of his earlier *Quaker City; or, the Monks of Monk Hall* (1844–1845) suggests, elements of lurid anti-Catholic literature (torture chambers and depraved priests) fill his own novels; similarly, it is hard to take seriously his claim that *Memoirs* is *not* "an argument against [magnetism's] reality and its benefits to mankind,"[57] when he paints in such exquisite detail the consequences of such a power for innocents like the young Fanny. As he says almost in the same breath, "Magnetism thoroughly destroys...all consciousness through the senses. It is the operation of one Will over another, and can never be accomplished in its important phases, unless the *subject* yields his will captive to the will of the operator."[58] The view we are given of the lecherous Jervis, as "he gently parted the folds of [Fanny's] cloak,"[59] can hardly be intended to portray an unfortunate aberration of the system.

Spiritualism featured prominently in other novels, as well, for decades to come, such as in William Dean Howells's *The Undiscovered Country* (1880) and Henry James's *The Bostonians* (1886). The former features Dr. Boynton, an earnest but deluded spiritualist seeking in the movement consolation and reassurance of immortality after his wife's death. It is a sober and searching study of the potential for self-deception and exploitation that result when religious skepticism, personal grief, and religious longings collide. *The Bostonians* is set against a background of séances and spiritualist hucksters, while taking seriously the complex psychology and sexuality of charismatic, Mesmeric figures.

Far more common than such sober treatments of spiritualism were the numerous satires that began appearing within three years of the movement's founding. Anticipating the frequent clumsy frauds that would soon plague the more earnest practitioners, James Russell Lowell published his humorous poem "The Unhappy Lot of Mr. Knott" in *Graham's Magazine* in April 1851. Months later, Samuel Clemens would include humorous anecdotes about the "rappers" in the column he wrote for his brother's Hannibal newspaper.[60] As Clemens became "Mark Twain," his comic references to mediums, poltergeists, and spiritualists multiplied.[61]

One of the first treatments of the Shakers in literature was Catharine Sedgwick's *Redwood*, published in 1824. Its moral was, in the words of its reviewer William Cullen Bryant, "properly a religious one."[62] In critiquing what she saw as the faulty idealism of utopian thought, Sedgwick shows Shakerism to be a fertile bed for hypocrisy and exploitation. The corrupt and venal leader Harrington, failing equally to intimidate and to seduce the vulnerable Emily, resorts in the end to abduction.

Before a tradition of negative portrayals could establish itself, a contrary depiction appeared in 1833 with the publication of Nathaniel Hawthorne's "The Canterbury Pilgrims," a tale of the Shakers. One could hardly overemphasize the importance of one of their first literary treatments—and by a figure of Hawthorne's talent, at that—being a positive one, full of admiration and envy. A Shaker couple falls in love and, consistent with the rules of their order, makes preparations to leave the society. A succession of outsiders then attempts to dissuade the lovers from their plan, insisting that the world they long to enter is a miserable one, that true love is a transitory illusion, and that they are forsaking Eden. Of course, young love is heedless of such advice, and they leave paradise behind.

By the time Hawthorne wrote "The Shaker Bridal," in 1837, his views of the Shaker utopia were displaced by the opinion that it subverted "precious human instincts."[63] Still, his respect for the sect continued to be evident in this later story, in which he describes the Shakers as a "strange people" but pious, dignified, and "hospitable." In this brief tale, a devoted Martha follows her destitute lover, Adam Colburn, to a Shaker village. Never able to fully repress her carnal love for him, she dies of a broken heart while they are being installed as the community's presiding "brother and sister."

The next several Shaker treatments were also short stories, similarly sympathetic to the tragedy of young feminine beauty cloistered in a celibate community. "The Shaker Girl," by Caroline Lee Hentz, appeared in *The Lady's Book* in February 1839. Then came Joseph Holt Ingraham's "The Southern Bell; or, the Shaker Girl of Lebanon" (1847), followed by the anonymous "The Shakeress" and Daniel Pierce Thompson's "Shaker Lovers" in 1848.

The ambivalence of Hawthorne's treatment was reflected by the dozens of fictive representations that followed. Genuine admiration for the society's asceticism, industriousness, and communal spirituality alternated with censure of the society's prohibitions against sexual or even romantic intimacy, to create a poignancy and exoticism ripe for literary treatment. So side by side with indignant portrayals of mortally wounded hearts were admiring depictions of a people who had actually succeeded in finding heaven on earth. In her study of Shakers in fiction, Ruth McAdams claims that the figure of the happy Shaker was so common as to constitute a major character type in literature written by non-Shakers.

William Dean Howells, who had lived next to the Shaker community in Shirley, Massachusetts, published two works particularly favorable to its society, *Three Villages* (1884) and the aforementioned, more successful *The Undiscovered Country*. In the latter work, the Shakers offer healing to the spiritual damage done to Dr. Boynton's daughter Egeria by his dabbling in spiritualism. Although the marriage prohibition of the Shakers was unorthodox, celibacy at least is readily construable as restraint rather than excess, as deprivation rather than indulgence. A sense of loss rather than a sense of outrage therefore characterizes even the negative portrayals of Shaker social life.

By far the largest share of religious propaganda was directed against the Catholics. Virtually an entire industry, and several careers, were supported by a veritable tidal wave of published invective. Ray Allen Billington lists over five hundred books and pamphlets as well as forty-five newspapers and periodicals devoted to the anti-Catholic crusade in the first six decades of the nineteenth century. As we have seen, anti-Catholicism in nineteenth-century America is not decipherable apart from the history of nativism responsible for much of it. Billington goes so far as to say that "until the middle of the 1830s American nativism was directed almost entirely against Catholicism."[64] Anti-Catholic propaganda has a lengthy history and a series of fluctuating motives and functions. Martin Luther gave impetus to its early forms, when he claimed that "all who have the spirit of Christ know well that they can bring no higher or more acceptable praise offering to God than all they can say or write against this bloodthirsty, unclean, blasphemic whore of the devil."[65]

Many of the anti-Catholic novels that began to appear in America with Grace Kennedy's *Father Clement* were merely watered-down versions of the theological propaganda wars that originated with Luther. Kennedy's Catholics are no child-murdering villains, only misguided Christians who, with the proper scriptural direction, are often quite happy to embrace the true Protestant path. There is little plot, with most of the text given over to detailed theological critiques of Catholic dogma, all duly footnoted with appropriate scriptural references. We have already seen how another category of anti-Catholic fiction assimilated the forms and paraphernalia of gothic melodrama. Besides paving the way for anti-Mormon writers who would similarly exploit prurient fascination with bondage and sexuality under a cloak of righteous indignation, anti-Catholic writers themselves reflect this ongoing genre confusion as well. The allure and transferability of gothic forms so aptly demonstrated with the Maria Monks and Mary Sherwoods of the nineteenth century foreshadow and explain the treatment in store for the Mormons.

The vulgarization of standards we see in this fiction (influenced in large measure by the popular press) may reveal less about the virulence of anti-Mormonism than it does about a rampant anarchy of discursive forms and literary categories. Assumptions about the uses and claims of historical fiction are not clearly defined, and religious propaganda, political polemics, and prurient sensationalism mingle freely in this new and developing novelistic form. These conditions made it possible to achieve a pitch of literary virulence that may be misleading if viewed by today's standards of public discourse. This is not to downplay the reality of hostile intentions and the very real inflammatory impact such writings had, especially among the credulous. Many writers and readers alike clearly did want to see Catholics, Mormons, and others not only vilified but exterminated. But my observation *is* meant to suggest that the demonization of the Other is a process governed both by the real or perceived malignance of a foreign entity when viewed in the context of prevailing values and ideals, *and* by the mechanisms of representation that are available to those doing the constructing. That is why any accurate picture of intolerance as a historical phenomenon must go beyond the social, political, cultural, or religious aspects of conflict, to examine the means by which difference can be invoked, constructed, and disseminated at given times in history.

For example, Charlotte Elizabeth Tonna was another popular—and rather prolific—author who specialized in novels addressing "the Catholic question." Harriet Beecher Stowe praised her works, and even defended Tonna's decision, "however [shocking to] the fastidious," to publish her autobiography ("of a lady" at that!) during her lifetime.[66] Conceding that Tonna is something of an ultraist, Stowe considers it "however pleasant to observe that this bitterness is directed against the *system* [of Roman Catholicism] and not against those who profess it."[67] Clearly, Stowe is engaged in an apologia that both reflects the intensity of the debate already raging, and bodes ill for its increasing ferocity. But in addition, Stowe's self-consciousness about the disturbing qualities of Tonna's work presents us with a wonderful case study of some of the anxieties and the rationalizations that surround much polemical fiction of the period and which are the consequence of a unique convergence of historical and literary developments.

Lacking, in a most striking way, from any number of the novelists of this period is a sense of oneself *as* a novelist, or of one's task as being novel writing. Just as Brownson was "puzzled" about the classification of his own work, only content with indicating that it was *not* "a novel; it is not a romance; it is not a biography of a real individual; it is not a dissertation, an essay, or a regular treatise," so is Stowe more concerned with what her protégé's work does than with what it is, and she frames her defense of Tonna in terms of politics rather than art. Acknowledging that Tonna "may to some ears sound harsh and intolerant," she assails the basis of the complaint, tolerance, rather than claim exemption in the name of her craft: "There has appeared to be in the [public] community an extreme and fastidious delicacy with regard to the Roman Catholic religion, which in its great fear of bigotry and intolerance has scarcely allowed the common liberty of speech on the subject." Not only is such delicacy misdirected— it is unnecessary: "After all, time has shown that all this circumspection is extremely unnecessary since the [Catholic] system has developed a most abundant ability and disposition to take care of itself, and to help itself."[68]

Frequently, the ground for narrative authority is neither literary (the license of the poet to invent) nor political (the imperative to defend national interests). It is simply confessional: the "this is a faithful account of the facts of my life" mode. "Mrs. Sherwood," author of *The Nun*, is one further example of an author whose uncertainties about her narrative positioning show both rhetorical and structural confusion, and she ultimately falls back upon autobiographical form as the easiest solution to the dilemma. The title page of Sherwood's book gives no hint of the genre to which it pertains: just *"The Nun,"* with no explanatory subtitle so typical of the period. Her opening sentence is a claim that "no form of religion on earth...has supplied so many scenes for romance, as that of the great Roman Catholic Apostasy."[69] She nevertheless insists that her story is unprecedented. One assumes at this point that perhaps she has invoked "romance" and "the many works of fancy" in order to oppose them to her "true account" that is to follow. She disappoints such expectations, however, by putting forward a different claim to her work's uniqueness. With the exception of one minor contemporary dramatic piece, she says, "I hardly know where else to find any thing like a representation of the interior of a convent."[70] Is her story's uniqueness, then, based on its subject, on its being a view of "the interior"? Or is it rather the case that her story is not "romance," but autobiography? Given the outrageously— and highly conventional—gothic elements of her story, and her refusal to make a passionate claim to truth and appeal to our belief after laying the groundwork to do so, one is tempted to conclude that her "representation" is but another in a series of fictional accounts. After all, it is almost inconceivable that she would consider the inclusion of a convent description more noteworthy—more essential to the work's rhetorical power and persuasive force—than its truthfulness, if the latter were a legitimate claim available to her as well.

On the other hand, if one considers that the very next year Maria Monk's infinitely more fanciful *Awful Disclosures* came out, followed by a flurry of substantiating accounts, public endorsements, public debates, and a positive verdict by the New York Protestant Association,[71] it becomes impossible to dismiss the truth claim of a book like Sherwood's on the basis of its incredibility alone. Furthermore, she coyly refuses to tell us her name (although she gives us her husband's), or "the true name of the town, near to which the events took place of which I am about to speak."[72] Finally, her concluding lines to the narrative affirm that "those things respecting the Roman Catholic Church" have been "faithfully recorded."[73] So it would appear to be a documentary account after all. Apparently, Mrs. Sherwood does not feel that clearly affirming the work's autobiographical status is essential to its rhetorical impact. This failure to reify the work's distinctness from the genre of romance exemplifies in a particularly acute way the confusing of rhetorical categories so common to this period. It may also suggest the difficulty nineteenth-century writers had constructing a first-person narrative outside the conventions of romance.

The ambivalence about Sherwood's narrative positioning is further aggravated by the curious structure of her work itself. Normally, one would, as we have, seek in an introduction clues to the truth value of an autobiographical account, since it is presumably *about* the narrative that an introduction speaks. In Sherwood's case, she does indeed begin with a discussion of her project. She eschews any rhetorical device signaling the beginning of romance or autobiography, and comments on fiction and Catholicism generally, and refers to the work she is "about to bring forward," making hints as to its veracity, already cited. Next, she tells us that she will "not trouble my reader with a very particular account of my early life. I am a native of Turin."[74] We learn of the author's orphaning and early religious inclinations. But rather than reaching the identifiable point of her narrative's commencement, which juncture would clarify the distinction between the author's voice and that of the story's narrator, separating the introduction from the memoir, the reader gradually comes to realize that we have already slipped imperceptibly into the narrative itself. No rhetorical markers indicate a shift in the narrative position. A glance at the page confirms that we are still in the "Introduction." Nevertheless, characters appear and take shape, dialogue is added to reflection, and the author's biographical self-introduction has become the story we are reading. So it is all a rhetorical tautology, in which the author speaking for the truthfulness of her character turns out to be that character, in a narrative already under way. But the slippery quality of this narrative authority, while it might be a serious flaw in one age and a postmodern gimmick in our own, has a negligible value in its contemporary context.

A similar twist occurs in the introduction to Maria Monk's work. Sensitive to the complaint that her story may be "too monstrous to be believed," she makes an offer that is not as compelling as she apparently believes. Regarding her claims of bondage and suffering at the hands of sinister priests, she states, "I have offered, in case I should be proved an impostor, to submit to any punishment which may be proposed—even to a redelivery into the hands of my bitterest enemies, to suffer what they may please to inflict."[75] In other words, "You think I'm crazy to believe this cup of coffee is poison. If it turns out you're right, I'll drink it!" The claim to rhetorical authority is revealed, again, to be tautological. Her credibility is based upon a conclusion that is itself in dispute, and her threat is the mere intransigence of a paranoid (as later events confirm). The force of her argument relies upon the same odd insistence that flesh-and-blood villains and fictional characters are equally daunting specters.

Orvilla Belisle, who wrote against Mormons and Catholics both, used a similarly mongrelized narrative form. In the introduction to *The Arch Bishop*, she expresses her doubt that "a tale related of events so recent…would find a welcome in the hearts of the people, as free and warm as that accorded to its mystery-clouded, but perhaps less truthful contemporaries."[76] So it is a "truthful tale." But its opening line epitomizes all that is clumsy and confused about these attempts at narrative authority: "During an evening of October, 1843, a high Dignitary of the Romish Church, in one of our large cities, sat alone in his library." The date suggests historical veracity, the coy refusal to divulge too many details enhances her aura of authority, but the absence of spectators to this scene forces her to assume a position of omniscient narration. Or almost omniscient, since she admits that "what his thoughts were that night, none but his God ever knew."[77] And then to resist her narrative's slide into stock historical fiction, she sprinkles her narrative with over two hundred footnotes, further spinning her web of incongruous appeals to authority: when the monologues she imputes to the fiendish prelate strain credibility to the breaking point, she cites, among others, a scathing history of Romanism, the *Harrisburg Telegraph*, and "a letter from a mother."

Some of the most dramatic instances of genre anarchy and the vagrant character of narrative authority are to be found in the arena of anti-Mormonism. We will turn in the next chapter to anti-Mormon fiction in detail, but for the present it may be useful to cite a few examples. As late as 1888, the author of the harshly anti-Mormon *Father Solon; or the Helper Helped* attempted in his preface to forestall criticism that his account was clearly fictitious. "Why term such books 'novels'? Are they merely light and strange? Are they love and passion pictures, designed only to please and entertain?...Should not such works be designated according to their intention and effects? Are they not dramatic parables—life lessons in portrayal? Certainly they are not novels."[78]

A little earlier, and firmly in the tradition of Sherwood's *The Nun*, was the novelette *Bessie Baine* (1876), about a young Quaker girl who resists the advances of the overzealous Elder Russell. The subsequent bondage theme that is developed, including humiliation, torture, and indefinite incarceration, is concluded with the narrator's assurance that this punishment lasts until the inmates "promise obedience or [are] driven insane" and is "still used by the Mormon leaders as a prison for refractory women."[79]

This author's insistence on the veracity of her story's horrors is typical of most of those novelizing the Mormon theme. That they were taken at their word is evident from the fact that such important debate as that surrounding the Cummins Bill (legislation designed to strip the Utah Territory of self-governance) was largely informed by "facts" garnered from "reliable sources" that turn out, on inspection, to be the novels and "exposés" we will examine. In his testimony of May 18, 1870, Senator Aaron Harrison Cragin quotes liberally from works by John Hyde (*Mormonism: Its Leaders and Designs*, 1857), Catherine Waite (*The Mormon Prophet and His Harem*, 1866), and numerous others he does not name ("I have read of some women...") to impute to the Mormons corruption, licentiousness, and "hundreds and thousands of murders." Some of the charges he recites (human sacrifice, for example) appear to have been too bizarre for novelists even to attempt adapting.[80]

In a reciprocal way, many of the undocumented themes he introduces into his testimony are to become mainstays of anti-Mormon fiction for the next generation, if they weren't current already. He alleges that women were driven insane by the "plurality" and that others were "hunted" down for rebelling; that Brigham Young's apartments contained private passageways and secret subterranean torture chambers (where he "punishes his refractory wives"); that there was a white slave trade; and other unimaginable depravities. All these scenarios will serve as the plots for scores of pulp novels. In one curious example of how this influence can run in both directions, Cragin's comparison of Mormon infamy with the Hindu car of Juggernaut, infant sacrifice, and suttee[81] will resurface in Jennie Bartlett Switzer's *Elder Northfield's Home* (1882).

Even literary satire became repurposed as political argument. In February 1867, the House of Representatives was debating woman suffrage. Some critics of Mormonism felt that the vote would give the women of Utah Territory a weapon with which to free themselves from the burden of polygamy. In lending his support to the bill, Representative T. E. Noell represented a humorous anecdote about Mormon polygamy from Artemus Ward's *Travels* as having been an actual experience of Ward's while in Utah (a group of polygamous widows propose en masse to a wealthy bachelor). The point of Noell's reference is more comic relief ("they were pretty enough, ... it was the muchness of the thing that he objected to") than persuasive evidence of the "base prostitution" he thinks the story reflects.[82] But the use to which he puts the story is beside the point. It is the *status* accorded the account that is striking. "When Artemus Ward was in Utah..." may serve to introduce a tall tale or a deadly serious episode, and perhaps politicians are especially vulnerable to confusing the two. But the pervasiveness of this disregard for distinctions between fiction and fact gives a universalizing quality to anti-Mormon rhetoric that is especially resistant to rebuttal. How does one refute a joke? What discourse is appropriate to challenge evidence authors admit is novelistic?

No wonder, then, that "documented" case histories found credible audiences, such as happened with *The Fate of Madame La Tour*. Though it was a novelized account of life in Utah, its impressive format included an appendix with affidavits alleging the discovery of the burial pit mentioned earlier containing "rawhide thongs" and the battered skulls of several children.[83] Other affidavits imputed to the Mormons a variety of equally grisly crimes and atrocities perpetrated against rebellious members.

Such legalistic accoutrements might win popular belief even today. But as we have seen, frequently these "affidavits" have a rather dubious twist to them. In 1872, for instance, citizens opposed to Utah's petition for statehood filed with Congress a "Memorial...Against the admission of that Territory as a State." Dozens of affidavits were included, alleging all manner of crime and criminality to the Mormons. But the following phraseology is typical of the line before the signature:

> About the endowment house oaths and the rest she sincerely believes to be true.[84]

> Affiant further says that he has read Bill Hickman's book about murders and other crimes, and he believes it true, ... Affiant believes that Brigham Young and the leaders commanded murders and robbery.[85]

> Affiant further says that he has read the affidavits of Abraham Taylor, James Ashman, and John P. Lloyd, on Mormon matters, and he knows the contents thereof, and he believes each one to be true.[86]

> Affiant further says that he has read "Bill Hickman, the Danite Chief's Book," and he believes it true; also, Beadle's book, and he believes that true: also Mrs. Ward's book, and he believes that true.[87]

We may wonder if such a reading list has the effect of substantiating or discrediting the force of the complaint, if the testimony is buttressed by or extracted from such accounts. Affidavits cite affidavits, memoirs cite affidavits, and affidavits cite memoirs.

I am not suggesting there is something new in the appropriation of literary forms of discourse to political or moral crusades. I am suggesting that a dispersal of narrative authority occasioned by economic, educational, and technological trends created an ambiance in which narrative boundaries themselves were unusually fluid and ineffectual. In other words, the very distinction between literary and nonliterary, or elitist and popular forms of literature, depends upon distinctions that popular writers of the period by and large did not recognize. In fact, this may turn out to be a key in understanding why the campaigns waged against unpopular groups like Mormons were carried off not just with a savage intensity typical of Jacksonian politicking in general, but with a pervasiveness, with a plethora of vehicles and forms, made possible by the absence of well-established literary boundaries.

The importance of this claim for our present study is that it suggests we should not assume, in an analysis of rampant opposition to Mormonism in the nineteenth century, that the pervasiveness of the hostility (pulpit, media, dime novels, and U.S. Congress) is a simple index of the disrepute of the object of scorn. Rather, we may begin to appreciate that the remarkably unified chorus of angry voices protesting any number of menaces to cultural orthodoxy may have been made possible by the shifting rules governing public discourse. As long as the onslaught of the printed word and the rapid rise of literacy overwhelm genre demarcations, creating a forum in which persuasiveness rather than authority rules discourse, the moral crusade against slavery, Catholicism, Mormonism, or any other social institution can be carried on by any writer using any discursive vehicle at his disposal. The collapse of literary boundaries makes it possible to galvanize and unite public opinion in a way that is no longer possible. (As I will show at greater length in chapter 7, any moral crusade waged in the contemporary political forum will be at least partially constrained according to those literary categories that operate as governing principles of public discourse.)

At the same time, if the religious heresy that is the source of an outraged public sensibility can be reconfigured in secular terms, moral indignation and intolerance can be made to serve, rather than threaten, political values (as in the case of "patriotic" anti-Catholicism). Mormonism, as we saw, did not lend itself to this solution as readily as did Catholicism. At least, the secularizing of the Mormon heresy would require the resources of fiction for such artful recasting. The key to understanding the fictional response to Mormonism is to remember that the religion's marginal status contained within itself the corrective to the peculiar anxiety it fostered. Such marginal categories, whether cannibals, heretics, or Mormons, provide at one and the same time the occasion for dread, and the opportunity for the elaboration of difference into distinctions that are comforting and self-affirming. Nineteenth-century writers of fiction were well equipped to effect just such a transformation, one that was sensationalistic, exploitative, and ultimately reassuring.

Thompson Dunbar elopes with Mrs. Ballygag's entire boarding school. Such comic portrayals of Mormonism were overshadowed, in popular fiction at least, by more malignant portrayals that combined the lurid and the melodramatic. (Charles Heber Clark [Max Adeler], *Tragedy of Thompson Dunbar, A Tale of Salt Lake*, Philadelphia: Stoddart, 1879)

A common theme of anti-Mormon novels had the polygamous husband introducing a younger wife into his home, taking both old wives and new bride by surprise. Resulting tensions fueled many a fictional domestic tragedy. (Orvilla S. Belisle, *The Prophets; or, Mormonism Unveiled*, Philadelphia: William White Smith, 1855)

In Alfreda Bell's version of life in Utah, women are both victimized and corrupted by Mormonism. Exposure to the evils of sadism, wife-swapping, and other horrors leads Cephysia to murder her rival's infant, descend into raving lunacy, then commit suicide. (Alfreda Eva Bell, *Boadicea, the Mormon Wife*, Baltimore: Arthur R. Orton, 1855)

Anti-Mormon novels moved beyond the perverse eroticism of convent thrillers to portray both men and women as subject to Mormon Mesmerism, bondage, and violence. Here a Quaker who refuses to relinquish his wife to a polygamous elder receives a dose of Mormon justice. (M. Quad [Charles Bertrand Lewis], *Bessie Baine: Or, the Mormon's Victim*, 1876, in the *Novelette* no. 5, Boston: G. W. Studley, 1898)

Writers from England's Sir Arthur Conan Doyle to the relatively
obscure Orvilla Belisle described how loyal Mormons worked diligently
to supply fresh wives for the "harems" of the prophets. Women who
resisted the arrangement were tortured, killed, or given to the Indians
as "squaws." (Orvilla S. Belisle, *The Prophets; or, Mormonism Unveiled*,
Philadelphia: William White Smith, 1855)

[set together]: Whether invoking the secret of "magnetic influence" taught to
Joseph Smith by a German peddler, mysterious sexual dynamism, or simple
brute force, anti-Mormon novels relied heavily upon the erasure of will.
Such loss of autonomy was one fictional response to the
peculiar anxiety of seduction Mormonism occasioned.
(Alfreda Eva Bell, *Boadicea, the Mormon Wife*,
Baltimore: Arthur R. Orton, 1855; and William Loring Spencer,
Salt-Lake Fruit: A Latter-Day Romance, Boston: Rand, Avery, 1884)

The Novelette.

NUMBER 4.

CONTAINING THE STORY COMPLETE OF

BESSIE BAINE:
—OR,—

THE MORMON'S VICTIM.

A TALE OF UTAH.

BY M. QUAD, OF THE DETROIT FREE PRESS.

ILLUSTRATED.

"I AM COME TO LEAD YOU TO TRIAL!"

[WRITTEN EXPRESSLY FOR THIS ESTABLISHMENT, AND COPYRIGHT SECURED ACCORDING TO LAW.]

BOSTON:
OFFICE AMERICAN UNION AND BALLOU'S MONTHLY MAGAZINE.
No. 23 HAWLEY STREET.

Narrative descriptions of Mormons frequently alluded to their "foreign looks."
Such nativist strategies of representation worked more credibly against
certain immigrant populations than against the heterogeneous Mormons,
but illustrators persisted in the practice nonetheless.
(M. Quad [Charles Bertrand Lewis], *Bessie Baine:*
Or, the Mormon's Victim, 1876, in the *Novelette* no. 5,
Boston: G. W. Studley, 1898)

Both Mormon speech and Mormon dress in this Frank Merriwell adventure serve to heighten the sense of radical difference. Such discernible otherness was an essential feature of the construction of Mormonism into a manageable heresy. (Burt L. Standish, "Frank Merriwell among the Mormons: Or, the Lost Tribes of Israel," *Tip Top Weekly*, June 19, 1897)

Masks and cloaks appear in this "New York Detective" adventure, in the Frank Merriwell story, in *Bessie Baine*, and many others. In addition to sensationalizing Mormon secretiveness and mysteriousness, such devices preserved the illusion of a Mormon identity that was radically alien. ("The Bradys among the Mormons—or—Secret Work in Salt Lake City," *Secret Service; Old and Young King Brady, Detectives*, no. 964, July 13, 1917)

CHAPTER 7

"They Ain't Whites . . . They're Mormons": Fictive Responses to the Anxiety of Seduction

Fresh women appeared in the harems of the elders—
women who pined and wept, and bore upon their faces
the traces of an unextinguishable horror.

Sir Arthur Conan Doyle, *A Study in Scarlet*, 1888

"While the feelings of the non-rational and numinous constitute a vital factor in every form religion may take," asserts Rudolf Otto, "they are pre-eminently in evidence . . . in the religion of the Bible."[1] If such a quality is, in fact, a constant in Christian orthodoxy, then we now understand how Kenneth Winn's judgment about the causes of the Missouri persecutions ("the Missourians displayed a relative indifference to the content of Mormon theology") may be true in an ironic way. Since Mormonism threatened the very conceptualizing of religion in traditional terms, what it offered in place of the nonrational and numinous was indeed slightly beside the point. Still, to ignore the religious roots of anti-Mormonism because the militia who murdered Joseph Smith was not attuned to theological subtleties makes as much sense as believing that Samuel Morse was not anti-Catholic, just pro-American. It is precisely to miss the point that public discourse in America has been constrained by a myth of religious pluralism that conditions the presentation of all but the most irrepressible religious bigotry.

REWRITING ANTI-MORMONISM

In the nineteenth century, then, whenever possible, Mormonism was written as a political threat rather than a religious one. This recasting was easily enough accomplished in the case of anti-Catholicism, as we have seen. From Morse's rhetoric of Jesuit agents and foreign powers to Mrs. Sherwood's and Maria Monk's romances that portray the convent as a castle of the infidel, occasioning the chivalric rescue of its female victims by the great American hero, there was a progressive de-emphasis on the purely religious dimensions of the menace. As was the case with anti-Mormon fiction, a frequent purpose of the anti-Catholic fiction of the nineteenth century was to portray Catholicism as an institution inimical to the ideals of the American political tradition. This much is obvious from a mere perusal of titles: *Popery Subversive of American Institutions* (Thomas Bayne, 1856) and *Americanism versus Romanism; or, the Cis-Atlantic Battle between Sam and the Pope* (J. L. Chapman, 1856); and so on. One spectacularly successful writer, Charles Frothingham,[2] produced several accounts centered on the Charlestown nunnery that was burned to the ground in 1834, all with the express purpose of convincing the audience that the fire was a just punishment and blessing to Americans everywhere. One such story begins, "On Bunker Hill my grandfather shed his blood....My father...became a sworn foe to all oppression and tyranny."[3] Another tale, *The Haunted Convent* (1854), takes place in Boston, in the shadow of the Old North Church.

When we meet priests in these novels, they are usually gloating about the enormous power they already have over America and her politics. In *The Haunted Convent*, the opportunistic Mr. Abbot is running for governor, and trades his daughter to Father McFaley's convent in exchange for the Catholic vote of Massachusetts ("I will instruct every Catholic voter in the city to cast his vote for you").[4] The priest knows, based on Catholic espionage, that Abbot once belonged to the Native American Party, but Abbot repudiates "the native cause" and gives his daughter as security, so the deal is closed.

In *The Convent's Doom*, we are warned by a priest that "because America is new, you must not think we have neglected her. Our society can count its thousands here."[5] In fact, we learn the Jesuit headquarters are shortly to move from Rome to the United States. A conspiracy to aid in just this objective is the plot in Orvilla Belisle's *The Arch Bishop: or, Romanism in the United States* (1854). The author informs us in her preface that Vatican officials "are looking to our own happy country for a place of refuge— in which they design, at no distant day, if successful, to set up the Papal See—locate the chair of St. Peter—and establish the Popish throne!"[6]

Clearly, the purpose of Frothingham and his colleagues was to justify a campaign of hysteria about a religion that posed a challenge to American ideals of independent thought and democratic theology. This was in addition to the more mundane hostilities engendered by Irish immigrants and other foreigners whose influx put pressure on an already shaky economic situation. Nativism in one form or another is clearly one ideological rationale behind a whole line of convent thrillers.

However, in spite of the appealing novelistic posture of a patriotic high ground in defense of American values and interests, nativist strategies were simply not very effective against the Mormons. Depictions of American Jesuits taking their orders from headquarters in Rome at least had a basis in historical truth. Claiming that the Mormon city of Nauvoo was secretly owned by an Englishman intent on imperialist aims in America, as did Robert Richards, was nothing short of silly. Mormonism was simply not as accommodating to nativist paranoias as was Catholicism. Unlike Catholicism, Mormonism was not readily reducible to foreign roots or control, its priests were not readily parodied as French- or Italian-speaking foreigners, and wave upon wave of potato-blighted Mormons had not recently immigrated to this country, threatening to further destabilize a precarious economy. (In Mormonism's Nauvoo period, immigrant members averaged a mere six hundred a year. Even in the decade previous to the Civil War, the numbers averaged around twenty-one hundred yearly, most of the converts coming from England.[7])

True enough, fears of ethnic immigrants fed into the anti-Mormon crusade, but the direction it took with Mormonism was *of necessity* a strange one. For ultimately, Mormons *were* Americans, and in a most vexing way, at that. In the case of Mormonism there was a body of religious, social, economic, and political beliefs and practices that were perceived to be out of sync with mainstream American values. But the group holding them was, historically and ethnically, American to the core (or at least Anglo-Saxon, in the case of a later flood of British converts). The Amish, to mention another example of heterodoxy, manifested a similar degree of group solidarity. But they were bounded both by distinctive, visible markers and by a self-imposed isolation. The spiritualists, to pose a much larger example, numbered in the hundreds of thousands by the Civil War and were well outside Christian orthodoxy, but they were not characterized by anything approaching the group cohesion of the Mormons. Consequently, the strategies of nativism would not work in their case, either.

So the representational challenge facing opponents of Mormonism was more daunting than it was for Samuel Morse. While both Roman Catholicism and Mormonism were viewed as inimical to American institutions, Mormonism's indigenous ethnicity, its emergence from native soil into a distinctive subculture, is central to understanding that group's resistance to facile, exotic caricature. Opponents were motivated to exaggerate Mormon deviance and invent a more comprehensive difference than really existed, but this construction was complicated by Mormonism's marginal position. Mormon authoritarianism, communalism, and defiance of Protestant orthodoxy may have been inimical to American values, but Mormon converts were to all appearances unexceptional. Compounding this problem, as we saw earlier, was the difficulty of attacking Mormonism's most consistently displayed religious doctrines, blatantly reminiscent as they were of primitive Christianity. As mentioned before, author John Russell was leery of employing religious attacks on the Mormons "that bore equally hard upon the miracles of Scriptures."[8] All these imperatives, of political expediency as well as ideological and theological consistency, presented opponents of Mormonism with an insistent problem: how to reconstruct heresy—an especially slippery category in a religiously pluralistic society where such categories are virtually untenable—into a nonreligious identity, one that Americans could attack with the same self-righteous fervor they directed against Irish papists for threatening American jobs and democratic institutions. But how to do it in the case of a home-grown religion that resisted the kind of ethnic demonization that worked with Catholics? Fiction offered a solution, as the resulting depictions from the era make clear.

My purpose in turning to fiction, then, is to better understand some of the mechanisms by which religious animosities may acquire the veneer of legitimacy. Specifically, numerous examples will show how literary representations can preserve the socio-religious function of heresy in a secular context. In the case of anti-Mormonism, literary treatments serve as the means by which the heretically suspect becomes recast as the ethnically distinct, demarcated as Other, transgressive, and dangerous.

Though the Mormon church came into existence in 1830, decades passed before poets and novelists routinely made it the subject of their parodies, potboilers, and romances. During the church's history in the eastern United States, as we have seen, it was primarily ministers and disaffected Mormons who sought to discredit Joseph Smith through a publishing crusade. By 1850, more than two hundred articles and "exposés" had appeared, effectively preempting the novelists and poets.[9] Then too, America's Walter Scott, James Fenimore Cooper, did not develop the historical novel (most anti-Mormons' medium of choice) as a major literary form until the approach of midcentury. Whatever the combination of factors, the 1850s saw the first flowering of anti-Mormonism in fiction. By the turn of the twentieth century, fifty-six anti-Mormon novels and tales would be published.[10] Initially, the plots usually revolved around polygamy as female sexual bondage, and the "Avenging Angels"[11] as terrorist minions of a despotic Brigham Young. Exploiting these subjects provided all the eroticism and violence a voracious public appetite could demand.

The Danite or Avenging Angel theme first appears in an English novel by Frederick Marryat (*Monsieur Violet: His Travels and Adventures among the Snake Indians*, 1843). And although the first American anti-Mormon novel, *The Mormoness* (1853), does not mention polygamy, its public announcement in 1852 would lend impetus to the first spate of novels, many of which exploited the harem theme, as in *Boadicea, the Mormon Wife* and *Mormon Wives*, both published in 1855. But such themes and their historical parallels do little to explain the variety and complexity of Mormon depictions in fiction. What is particularly surprising about the Mormon caricature as it develops are the ways in which it goes well beyond depictions of lustful elders and prurient lifestyles. Not the catalog of crimes imputed to the Mormons, but the particular ways in which the Mormons are demonized, is the key to illuminating public anxieties and how fiction exploited—while it alleviated—them.

It has been pointed out that in popular fiction especially, stock villains are in constant demand, and a group like the Mormons, both relatively obscure and culturally objectionable, was ready grist for the mill. Certainly little theorizing is necessary to unmask the sensationalism of anti-Mormon literature and reveal the crass commercialism so often behind it. An *Illustrated Christian Weekly* of 1876, for example, advertised for "a Lady Agent" for "every city and Town in the United States" to sell an exposé on the Mormons written by "Brigham Young's 'Wife Number Nineteen.'" The Philadelphia publisher claimed salespersons could expect to make a minimum of seventy-five dollars a month peddling the salacious account.[12] But while Mormons lent themselves readily to public appetite for the sensational and villainous, the intersection of genre requirements and peculiar historical circumstances produced a large body of writing with remarkably consistent patterns. Such patterns suggest that beyond the stock formulas and mere animosity, a particular kind of psychological conciliation on the part of a non-Mormon audience was at stake. The patterns of representation that resulted, though scattered over several decades and against diverse historical backgrounds, repeatedly suggest certain constant features of the peculiar threat to which they were a response.

In fictive treatments of Mormonism, two recurrent patterns of representation emerge: the prevalence of "Oriental" images,[13] and themes of coercion and bondage. These strategies serve to establish a kind of psychic distance between the represented object and the audience, disarming popular anxiety while pretending to exacerbate it.

The case is perhaps best put forth by one of the first of the anti-Mormon novels to appear, *The Mormoness; or, the Trials of Mary Maverick*, by John Russell (1853). This novel, which purports to be "a Narrative of Real Events," is fraught with a highly ambiguous voice, as if the author can't decide whether to vilify or justify Mormonism. Ostensibly, the work is a generous-hearted condemnation of anti-Mormon intolerance. The action unfolds in a small community known as Sixteen Mile Prairie. There, religious liberty is the order of the day, except when it comes to Mormonism. The narrator is appalled that the "state of public opinion" concerning this "deluded" religion is such that "hundreds...would gladly have exterminated the whole sect."[14] In fact, Russell does chronicle an actual massacre perpetrated against the Mormons in Missouri, the one at Haun's Mill, of which he apparently learned from Mormon refugees themselves.[15] Narrating the gruesome details, Russell laments with lofty moral indignation that "our institutions, which guarantee the freedom of religious opinion to the Jew, the Mahometan, the Pagan, and even to the *Atheist*, afforded no protection to the Mormon."[16] After her husband and child are brutally murdered by the mob, the Mormoness goes on to become a sister of charity. The Missourian who made her a widow falls in love with her years later, and goes mad when he learns her true identity. She dies in saintly service.

The generous voice of indignation that constitutes the ostensible narrative is inconsonant, however, with a profoundly disturbing, counterpoint narrative unfolding at the level of psychological drama. The hero of the story is the good gentile James Maverick, whose worthiness "no phrenologist accustomed to the study of human character would have doubted."[17] He is "deadly hostile" to the Mormons, but with good reason—the casualties of the Mormon missionary effort are striking closer and closer to home. "Men whom he had known from childhood at the East—had known at the vanguard of the sacramental host—had fallen into the fatal snare of Joe Smith."[18] His parents, learning of the incursions of the "odious sect," express both fear and threats lest he, too, fall under its sway. When a Mormon preacher comes to town, James, bristling with righteous indignation, steadfastly refuses to attend his sermons. His wife, on the other hand, as we are informed with chilling suggestiveness, has "too much of gentleness and goodness in her heart to find room for such emotions, even against the vilest of the human race."[19] Her innocence is, of course, her downfall. She attends the meetings and is gradually swayed by the preacher's "ingenious sophistry."[20] It appears that James alone remains a steadfast holdout against what has by now assumed the character of a fearsome, spreading malignancy. At the critical moment, welcome respite from James's anxiety and isolation seemingly appears in the form of a stranger who calls unexpectedly one day:

> For an instant Maverick gazed upon him with speechless surprise, then, uttering the exclamation, "*Why! Mr. Wilmer!*" sprang from his seat, seized the hand of the stranger, and shook it with the most cordial gratification. He was in the act of introducing the new-comer to his wife, when he learned, to his overwhelming astonishment, that this was no other than the Mormon preacher who had held forth to the people of the settlement the night before, at the school house. . . . The thought had not once struck him as possible that Mr. Wilmer, of all others, could be deluded into a belief of Mormonism.[21]

At this point, the horror of the inevitable is palpable. James, left without gentile friend, wife, or refuge from the allure of Mormonism, succumbs himself within a matter of pages.

The text is thus a curious blend of, on the one hand, moralistic flag-waving in defense of religious toleration and a spirited condemnation of the "mobs and lynch law," and, on the other, a novel of psychological horror, the drama of a relentlessly encroaching menace that spiritually devours James's neighbors, his wife, an old friend, and, inevitably, himself. Thus, while protesting the injustice of anti-Mormon violence with one voice, Russell is, with another, projecting onto the character of James an anxiety sufficiently disturbing—and warranted—to excuse the most extreme measures imaginable for self-preservation.

The example of this author divided against himself may serve as a paradigm of the peculiar anxiety of seduction provoked by Mormonism, a consequence of factors that distinguish Mormonism and its effects from other social conflicts and their literary treatments. One other example will suffice to introduce most of the themes typical of anti-Mormon literature, while echoing the agonized self-contradictions of *The Mormoness*. In a Frank Merriwell adventure, published in the nickel *Tip Top Weekly* (1897), the cyclist hero from Yale finds himself in "the lost valley of Bethsada," where a band of Mormons "have built up a town that is shut off from the rest of the world—a town of which few outside its boundaries know anything at all."[22]

Once in the valley, the cyclist and his friend, Jack, are called upon by a Mormon youth to save his lover from being forced into plural marriage with an aged lecher. Frank agrees to help out. They are themselves caught, but rescue the couple and make good their escape from the community.

The "author of Frank Merriwell" (Burt Standish) appears torn between the sensationalism to which Mormonism so readily lends itself (polygamy and secret temple rites) and his self-appointment as a moral instructor of youth (he digresses for several paragraphs when his heroes drink at a well, to lecture on the virtues of springwater and the evils of the bottle). So even as the hero's alter ego is proclaiming "I am getting a different opinion of the Mormons than I once had....I believe some of the wild stories told about their religion, and their ways are a mess of lies,"[23] they are on their way to an encounter that dramatically undermines such open-mindedness: "They came to a square chamber, which was lighted by flaring, smoking torches. In a semi-circle at one end of the chamber sat twelve cloaked and cowled figures, their garments of somber black.... Then the figure that wore the bear's head ... stood and read a passage from the ... Mormon Bible."[24]

And while the hero anticipates his and Jack's execution by means of "the pit of fire" (a grisly fate reminiscent of Poe), this same companion is repeatedly insisting that "These men are not Mormons!...At their worst, the Mormons never destroyed their enemies in such a manner."[25] The point, of course, is that such incredulity proves suicidal, and tolerant impulses in the face of Mormonism prove so much foolishness. After Frank and Jack escape, they are warned by a wise old hermit to tell no man their tale, as it will never be believed. We see here an author clearly at cross-purposes with himself. Inclined on the one hand to dismiss fantastical representations of Mormon outrages through the voice of the reasonable Jack, his character ultimately comes to represent naiveté, not reason, as the fantastical has vividly been made actual before our very eyes. Disarming tolerance through the fictive defeat of skepticism, and preempting disbelief through the metafictive warning of the old hermit, the author fulfills the function of the guardians at the gates of Bethsada. As Mormonism remains a foreign realm impenetrable by the railroad or the gentile culture that the railroad represents, so will representations of Mormonism remain forearmed against the assaults of reason or skepticism.

What, then, do these stories reveal about prevalent perceptions and preoccupations regarding Mormonism? They tell us that the hostile imagination can become its own enemy. Mormonism was for many nineteenth-century authors a chimera that was, ironically, useful in proportion to the threat it posed. The bigger the dragon in the fairy tale, the more valor the knight shows in slaying it. But the author must beware lest he create a monster that overwhelms hero and reader alike. The hero of John Russell's story is the American character, and those frequently invoked American "institutions" that establish and preserve freedom, liberty, and toler-ance. Those sacrosanct values are sufficiently generous and entrenched, he writes, to successfully accommodate "the Jew, the Mahometan, the Pagan, and even the *Atheist*." The Mormon, however, represents a threat far beyond these other adversaries of American Protestantism. Mormons are less easily identified than the Jew and Mahometan of popular imagi-nation, and a more insidious challenge to orthodoxy than blatant pagan-ism or non-belief. Standish depicts Mormon perfidy with such earnestness that the prudence and discretion of the typical hero are suddenly inap-propriate; Russell depicts Mormon seductiveness so compellingly that the wisdom of tolerance and forbearance are likewise cast in doubt.

Russell is at times quite explicit about what he believes is at stake in tolerating the intolerable. He who would justify the instigators of anti-Mormon violence, he asserts, "utters a base libel upon our republican government, and is unworthy of the name of an American citizen.... [It] is equivalent to saying that such a government as ours is *utterly worthless*. This is acknowledging the truth of the charges which the despots of Europe bring against our free institutions."[27] But he is simultaneously so appalled by the Mormon menace that he can only equivocate helplessly. "We will return to the narrative of passing events, from which a desire to vindi-cate the republican institutions of our country from slander and abuse has drawn us."[28] But of course, he has acknowledged the dilemma, not resolved it. We are left in the uncomfortable position of feeling both repugnance and anxiety toward the seductive heresy this "narrative of passing events" depicts, and shame for our "republican institutions" and her citizens who responded to it with such violence. Seduction and assimilation, or selling out to mob rule and lynch law, appear as the only options.

The paradox of Mormon quasi-ethnicity is one of the complicating features of the dilemma facing authors of such works as *The Mormoness* and "Frank Merriwell." The anxiety of seduction experienced by James Maverick is peculiar to the unusual circumstances characterizing Mormons as a group. A certain uneasiness with revolutionary religious or social practices being exhibited within the American heartland is itself understandable enough, especially if those practices are deemed abhor-rent and immoral by mainstream Anglo-American Protestants. Such was surely the response to claims of supernatural visitations, a profoundly authoritarian church government, and practices like communalism and, eventually, polygamy. But such practices and beliefs are doubly threat-ening if they cannot be relegated to a foreign culture or "otherness." Potential converts to Mormonism shared with the adherents cultural, political, racial, and geographic backgrounds. It was for this reason that

Mormonism presented a particularly devilish challenge for psychic distancing. Hindus practicing suttee in faraway India may have been but a curiosity to a nineteenth-century American. Watching kinsmen and neighbors fall prey to what was thought to be at a safe remove is downright disturbing.

The cultural, racial, and geographical proximity of Mormonism enhances popular anxieties, even as American traditions of religious tolerance and the rule of law complicate the remedy. But these dilemmas are not without fictive solutions. Through a proliferation of fictional representations of Mormons that begins in the mid-nineteenth century, writers manage to effectively recast religious heresy as a more manageable difference. At the same time, fictional representations of Mormonism often have as their true purpose the defining and safeguarding of American identity.

History, as we said, is indeed written by the victors. But in the same sense, so is "Literature." Consequently, mainstream notions of what it means to be African American, or Jewish, or Chinese have traditionally been shaped not as a result of reading slave narratives, the Talmud, or Chuang Tzu. Rather, the West's traditional canon of ethnic education would more likely include Harriet Beecher Stowe, Shakespeare, and Earl Derr Biggers (creator of the Charlie Chan novels). Caricature, of course, is the exaggeration of particular identifiers, often with comic effect. In literary representations of another culture, an author has the power to choose those characteristics that will be considered as fundamental, as definitive, of that cultural identity. Naturally those characteristics chosen for exaggeration or focus serve the function of emphasizing difference. Racial features, linguistic patterns, dietary identifiers, or other areas of cultural distinctness are seized upon and exploited to secure and solidify a sense of otherness. Studies such as Edward Said's *Orientalism* have emphasized the utility of such strategies as a mechanism of self-empowerment, isolating and domesticating what a society chooses to deem Other. Such caricature often presents an ostensibly benign face, secure in the bubble of identity, of selfhood, that the very exaggeration of the Other has served to cast into relief. This has often been the case, for example, with Orientalism. From Marco Polo to the Impressionists, Asia served the West as the stuff of curiosity and amusement. Oriental motifs were popular in design and architecture, the harem recurs as a realm in which sexual fantasies of various kinds may safely find unbridled expression, and the Muslim is, if anything, useful as a narrative mask through which Western, not Eastern culture, is critiqued (Montesquieu's *Persian Letters* and Goldsmith's *Citizen of the World*, for example).

"ORIENTALISM IN THE EXTREME OCCIDENT"

Proportional with Mormonism's rise as a denomination of significance was a tendency to caricature the new religion. Not coincidentally, one of the most pervasive forms this caricature took was the Orientalization of Mormonism. Superficial parallels provided the basis for a depiction that seemed to relegate Mormonism to the safe realms of the primitive, the pagan—the Oriental. Even a casual perusal of American fiction about Mormons reveals repeated appeals to perceived comparisons with Oriental religion. References to Joseph Smith as a Mohammed, the abundance of allusions to the harems of the elders, and, as late as 1912, a popular text on the religion entitled *Mormonism: The Islam of America* (by Bruce Kinney), bear out this widespread practice. The comic depiction of the Mormon polygamist with his flock of complaisant brides that we saw in Artemus Ward is repeated countless times under the rubric of "Orientalism in the extreme Occident," to use Charles Heber Clark's expression. In his spoof *Thompson Dunbar* (1879), his hero goes "the polygamy of Turkey" one better. "I've eloped with Mrs. Ballygag's boarding school. It loved me, and they wanted to marry it to another man, Arbutus Jones, you know; so it fled with me."[29]

More typical than such comic treatments, however, are the novels and "real life narratives" in which references to the specter of Eastern harems carry more-sinister connotations. In these cases, the pejorative nature of the comparison with Islam bespeaks a sense of outrage that what presents itself as "us" (Mormonism is, after all, a religion laying claim to being quintessentially American and Christian) is in reality more like "them," meaning Oriental in precisely those ways that are un-American and un-Christian.

Writing in 1792, Mary Wollstonecraft expressed her bewilderment at Milton's description of Eve as being formed for "softness and sweet attractive grace": "I cannot comprehend his meaning, unless, in the true Mahometan strain, he meant to deprive us of souls."[30] Almost a hundred years later, as the Cummins Bill, designed to strip the Utah Territory of self-governance, was being debated on the floor of the Senate, Senator Aaron Harrison Cragin similarly invoked Eastern religion as the embodiment of antifeminism: "The Jew thanks his Maker for not having made him a woman. The Moors do not allow women to enter their places of worship; and Mohammed denies that women have souls. The Turk allows women to enter into his heaven, but only to minister to his passions and wants. The heaven born Christian system...elevated a woman to her equal and true dignity." Brigham Young, on the contrary (continues Cragin), "following in the footsteps of Mohammed,...declares that women have no souls."[31]

Of course, neither Brigham Young nor other Mormon leaders ever suggested that women were without souls. Nor, for that matter, did Milton. Wollstonecraft's suggestion was rhetorical: the objectification of a human being is tantamount to the erasure of that individual's soul. In the case of Senator Cragin, the charge is meant more literally. To a man who could report from the Senate floor that Mormons practiced human sacrifice,[32] imputing misogyny to Brigham Young is not merely a rhetorical flourish. Of course, the practice of polygamy by the Mormons, of which Cragin and his audience were aware, suggested to many of that day (and our own) an objectification of women not unlike the kind protested by Wollstonecraft. Given the reputation of Islam in nineteenth-century America, the comparison is therefore understandable. In the case of the Mormons, however, it is not polygamy alone that drives the comparison. Surely the likening of plural wives to Eastern harems was irresistible, and the suggestions of rampant sexuality and exoticism didn't exactly work against the marketability of the popular fiction with which we are dealing. Sir Arthur Conan Doyle's reference to the "harems of the elders" in *A Study in Scarlet* and James Oliver Curwood's "harem of the king" in *The Courage of Captain Plum* are instances of such a use.[33]

Oriental parallels, however, were represented in reference to a variety of Mormon practices. In addition to plural marriage, the office of the prophet was a frequent occasion for Islamic analogies. Before Cragin found the comparison of Brigham Young to Mohammed useful, Joseph Smith had long been referred to as the American Mohammed. Sydney Bell's 1935 account of "Joe Smith" ruling his "tens of thousands like an oriental despot" is only one of the latest in a long line of books that began at least as long ago as E. D. Howe's 1834 comparison of Joseph Smith with "the great prince of deceivers, Mohammed."[34] In those instances, at least, it was not Smith's marital practices, but his claim to prophetic authority and patriarchal rule that occasioned that appellation. Taken as a whole, it would seem that Mormonism was likened to Islam for reasons ranging from its history (post-biblical prophets) to its unconventional scriptures (the Book of Mormon was considered additional revelation) to the alleged fanaticism of its adherents. At least one author, Jennie Switzer, saw in Mormonism evidence of the cruelty and fanaticism she associated with Asian religion: "Is God pleased to see the Hindoo mother throw her innocent babe into the Ganges as a sacrifice to appease His wrath? Does He delight in seeing the men and women of heathen lands throw themselves down for the wheels of Juggernaut to crush them?...Or does He look upon the cruel wickedness in the Mormon Church with any degree of pleasure?"[35]

In perhaps the most transparent example of the obsessive compulsion to cast the Mormons in the role of Asian oddity, Charles Heber Clark gives the following description of Salt Lake City: "America has no other [city] like it. Surveyed from a distance it wears a distinctly Oriental appearance. So we of the Far West who have only dreamed of the East, imagine how Damascus may look. White houses shining amid rich masses of green foliage. A dome, a tower, a spire that may answer for a minaret, . . . a sky of more than Oriental softness overhead."[36] An imagined scarcity of women on the streets is equally explainable under this protean comparison that has already encompassed authoritarianism, revelation, polygamy, zeal, spires, and Utah skies: "But where are the women? Of men there are enough. Now and then a Gentile woman passes, but not often; and the Mormon women appear still less frequently. It is Orientalism in the extreme Occident."[37]

So frequent are the instances of this kind of comparison that it is easy to mistake the intrinsic merits of the analogy (dubious however interesting) as the important issue.[38] Much more significant, literarily and psychologically, are the *purposes* such analogies serve. That a genuine correlation between Islam and Mormonism is *not* the point is apparent in light of the many permutations the Oriental motif may take. What all such representations share is the function of throwing into stark relief the *un*-Christian, *un*-American, *un*-Western nature of the Mormon religion.

In his chapter on the two Orientalists Silvestre de Sacy and Ernest Renan, Edward Said refers to their strategy of reducing "the Orient to a kind of flatness, which exposed its characteristics easily to scrutiny and removed from it its complicating humanity."[39] Such a maneuver suggests how the construction of the Other is often but a prelude to an envisioned relationship of domination or exploitation with that Other; however, the terms of that relationship cannot blatantly contradict the identity or ideology one wishes to present before the world. The first item of business in colonialist discourse is therefore to mitigate the general claims of humanity one person has over any other, since the moral dissonance such claims engender is an obvious impediment to projects that are imperialist or otherwise exploitative.

Dehumanizing is obviously the tried-and-true path to such self-exoneration, and was a prominent feature of Orientalizing, as well as other types of colonial discourse. But such a strategy hits immediate snags in the case of anti-Mormonism. Mormons are resistant to this kind of dehumanizing, because observable markers of a distinct "ethnicity" are lacking. Since the cultural work of dehumanizing or at least demonizing Asians had been well accomplished by the time of Mormonism's advent, exploiting that ready-made category was easier for fiction writers than constituting an alien identity from scratch.

This strategy of employing Orientalizing motifs as a means of distancing the new religion from familiar, acceptable (that is, "civilized") practices and institutions is unmistakable. Because the Mormon religion could not be situated in a distant hemisphere, authors resorted to numerous strategies to invent or exaggerate its physical remoteness. These strategies, though at times carrying no hint of actual ethnic identification, function in the same way as the Orientalizing we have just seen.

James Oliver Curwood, a writer of popular fiction at the turn of the century, exploits a real event in Mormon history—the defection of a convert named Strang who founded a colony in Michigan—to draw an elaborate portrait of an "island kingdom" that is an odd mix of Utopia and Hades, in *The Courage of Captain Plum*. Men enjoy multiple wives, modest skirts are forbidden, and women must wear their hair long. The cultural and social isolation of the colony is accentuated by its geographical boundedness.

When the setting shifts to Utah, that territory comes to assume a position in a kind of mythic space, a mysterious region of darkness and secrecy, or to use Clark's oxymoron, Orientalism in the extreme Occident. Conan Doyle, though an English author, accurately captures in *A Study in Scarlet* the American sense that Utah was an alien world unto itself, with its own laws, its own mysteries and dark secrets: "Not the inquisition of Seville, nor the German Vehmgericht, nor the secret societies of Italy, were ever able to put a more formidable machinery in motion than that which cast a cloud over the Territory of Utah."[40]

Doyle and authors like him effectively portray the Utah frontier as a boundary that separates America from a surreal domain of horror and evil. To escape Utah is to leave behind a world of darkness and blight, as *A Study in Scarlet*'s hero and heroine discover: "Looking back, they could see the solitary watcher leaning upon his gun, and knew that they had passed the outlying post of the Chosen People, and that freedom lay before them."[41]

With the coming of the transcontinental railroad in 1866, novelists had of course lost one important ground for painting Utah as virtually inaccessible to the civilized world at large. The new rail lines only served to heighten novelists' reliance upon other devices to create a sense of Mormonism as a western kingdom, an isolated, impenetrable realm. One such fictive ploy that perpetuated the theme of Mormonism's isolation was to invent hidden domains within the vast Utah wilderness, such as the hidden valley of Bethsada in the Frank Merriwell adventure. Here, as with Doyle's depiction, sentries are even posted to keep gentiles outside—and to keep, as per the usual bondage theme, the Mormon maidens *in*. The attempts of the author to paint a foreign culture result in a people more a curious blend of Amish and Elizabethan than Mormon, but exotic at any rate. At one point, the Mormon elder screams at the young bicyclists, "Remove from my sight these inventions of Satan!" and wanting the youth to move away from his intended, commands, "Cease to defile her with thy polluting touch!"[42]

At times, the otherworldly character of the Mormon realm borrows heavily from the gothic tradition, as its images of the mysterious and the exotic, its themes of confinement and psychological horror, compound the impression of a domain that defies Western access and comprehension. The gentile visitor or new convert, on first surveying the Mormon realm, stands more confounded than Balboa on a peak in Darien. The good Captain Plum, for example, is attracted to the capital of Strang's colony "because the secret of its life, of the misery that it had confessed to him, was hidden somewhere down there among its scattered log homes."[43] When Switzer's heroine, the newly baptized Marion, arrives in the Salt Lake Valley, she scans the settlement and is filled with foreboding: "Now, as I look down there, it seems to me I see sorrow and misery on the faces in those homes."[44] When the veil of mystery is parted, it reveals a realm where the values of civilized society have clearly been overwhelmed:

> "I must tell all. I *must* tell it all for their sakes," as she pointed towards the garden, where her children had gone. "Have you seen a large brick house on the side of one of the mountains, just out of the city?"
> Marion replied affirmatively.
> "Do you know what that building is?"
> "No," said Marion, "I do not."
> "Then I will tell you, for I know. It is where they carry the women when their miseries, and sorrows, and unutterable agony of mind robs them of their reason.... When you come there I will take you into my room, for I shall go there again, I think, before long. You will come, too, though not for many years; but you are a Mormon's wife, you know."[45]

In this realm of moral desolation, brutality and depravity know no bounds. Authors vie with one another to paint evil in the most shocking tones, with results more often melodramatic than disturbing. In Zane Grey's *Riders of the Purple Sage* (1912), the character Lassiter is a renowned Mormon-killer, scourge of the Salt Lake Valley. As we are introduced to him, the heroine is offering to water his horse for him. Noticing that this range-roaming steed is peculiarly handicapped (the horse is blind), she can't help inquiring,

"What blinded him?"

"Some men once roped an' tied him, an' then held white-iron close to his eyes."

"Oh! Men? You mean devils.... Were they your enemies—Mormons?"

"Yes, ma'am."[46]

Not surprisingly, such wickedness evokes comparison with Oriental villains. Curwood, for example, refers to a Mormon heavy as "Croche, chief of sheriffs, scourge of the mainland—the Attila of the Mormon kingdom, whose very name caused the women of the shores to turn white and on whose head the men had secretly set a price in gold!"[47]

Consistent with this drive to render the Mormon radically Other is a refusal to consider Mormons as "white." The Orientalizing establishes not just a cultural but a racial distinctness as well. As early as 1833, Missourians had insisted Mormons were an inferior breed, and evoked racist associations. The Jackson County document claimed they were "elevated...but little above the condition of our blacks, either in regard to property or education; they have become a subject of much anxiety on that part."[48] Fiction writers generally preferred the equally racist but literarily more exotic connotations of the Orient. In a pinch, any hint of foreignness would do. Zachary Tarrant, the hero of Dane Coolidge's *The Fighting Danites* (1934), describes the Mormons he encounters in Utah: "In his buckskin shirt and leggings, his broad hat and well-made boots, he stood out among them like a man of a different race, for they were clad in homespun and hickory shirts. Their cheap wool hats had slouched in the rain and wind and their boots were big and coarse; and in their eyes, or so it seemed, there was a strange, foreign look."[49]

Most authors are more blatant. The hero of Jack London's *Star Rover* (1914) is a condemned man confined to a straitjacket. He develops the ability to escape his bodily constraints by projecting himself back into past incarnations. One life we watch him relive is that of a young boy, slain along with his family by Mormons in the infamous Mountain Meadows massacre. As the tragedy unfolds, the besieged pioneers notice that the attacking Indians are accompanied by what appear to be white men. To this observation the boy replies, "They ain't whites...They're Mormons."[50]

In the Frank Merriwell adventure, how to categorize them is more ambiguous. When called upon by a Mormon youth to save his lover from being forced into plural marriage with a lustful patriarch, the hero agrees to help, telling his friends that "He seems to be a white man and all right, even if he is a Mormon."[51]

"White" obviously had connotations other than the purely racial, as is clear in a novel like Coolidge's. His hero Zachary Tarrant, a government spy, enlists the willing help of a prospector in infiltrating and dismantling the Mormon infrastructure in Utah. The prospector agrees, since "out in this Western country we white men have got to stick together." "White" is here obviously intended to mean non-Indian and non-Mormon—that is, in the code of the West, true American. As the prospector continues, "So if you meet any Navvies [Navajos] you tell 'em you're an American, if you don't want to lose your hair.... They won't kill an American, but Mormons are different."[52]

That fictive representations and popular perceptions of the Mormon "race" overlapped is evident in reading Warren Foote's account of his 1846 trip westward. He received this helpful advice from a woman they passed en route: "If the Mormons would scatter around amongst the white folks, they could live in peace." The next day, he records that a curious family came to examine his party. "After looking at us, [the father] said to the boys 'They havent [*sic*] got any horns have they! and they look like other folks don't they.' This he said laughing as he told us that the boys had thought the 'Mormons' were terrible looking creatures."[53] A few years earlier, a militia officer had expressed surprise as naive as these children's. General Wilson Law said to Joseph Smith in 1842, "Well, from reports, we had reason to think the Mormons were a peculiar people, different from other people, having horns or something of the kind; but I find they look like other people."[54]

Apparently, some of the more "scientifically" inclined were not so easily persuaded. In a meeting of the New Orleans Academy of Sciences in 1861, Dr. Samuel Cartwright and Professor C. G. Forshey gave a paper using parts of a report made by U.S. Army assistant surgeon Roberts Bartholow on the "Effects and Tendencies of Mormon Polygamy in the Territory of Utah."[55] The findings described characteristics of a new racial type, at least as reported by Bartholow. Attached to the army corps sent to Utah from Fort Leavenworth in the expedition known as the Utah War, Bartholow was charged with reporting on diseases and topography incident to their travels. Once in the territory, he turned his attention from local flora and fauna to "the Mormon, of all the human animals now walking this globe,...the most curious in every relation." "Isolated in the narrow valleys of Utah," he observed, "and practising the rites of a religion grossly material, of which polygamy is the main element and cohesive force, the Mormon people have arrived at a physical and mental condition, in a few years of growth, such as densely-populated communities in the older parts of the world, hereditary victims of all the vices of civilization, have been ages in reaching." This condition, he continued, was characterized by what he saw as evidence of general debilitation (high percentage of female births and infant mortality). More surprisingly, perhaps, he insisted that the Mormons shared numerous physiological features, so much so, in fact, as to be constitutive of a "new race":

> This condition is shown by . . . the large proportion of albuminous and gelatinous types of constitution, and by the striking uniformity in facial expression and in physical conformation of the younger portion of the community. . . . Whether owing to the practice of a purely sensual and material religion, to the premature development of the passions, or to isolation, there is, nevertheless, an expression of countenance and a style of feature, which may be styled the Mormon expression and style; an expression compounded of sensuality, cunning, suspicion, and a smirking self-conceit. The yellow, sunken, cadaverous visage; the greenish-colored eyes; the thick, protuberant lips; the low forehead; the light, yellowish hair, and the lank, angular person, constitute an appearance so characteristic of the new race, the production of polygamy, as to distinguish them at a glance. The older men and women present all the physical peculiarities of the nationalities to which they belong; but these peculiarities are not propagated and continued in the new race; they are lost in the prevailing type.[56]

It would be hard to imagine more convincing evidence of the success achieved by a generation of inventive literary ethnography than such "scientific" assent to a fictively constructed racial category. Confirming the verdict of history is that fact that Mormons are currently listed, as we noted in the introduction, in a respected encyclopedia of ethnic groups.[57]

A few years later, the tools of phrenology would be added to those of ethnology in an attempt to settle the question "strictly from a scientific point of view."[58] While admitting that the Mormons "have constituted a more distinct type than any other of modern communities," writers from the *Phrenological Journal*'s "Department of Ethnology" concluded that examination of the heads of "hundreds of representative men and women of the Mormons" demonstrated that, "phrenologically and physiologically, they are about like their class in any part of America."[59] (When it came to the Prophet Joseph Smith himself, phrenologists were apparently divided. An 1874 handbook used a profile of Smith to illustrate a highly developed propensity toward sociability.[60] Years earlier, one of Mormonism's most vociferous defectors and critics published phrenological charts of Smith to support his allegations of Smith's perfidiousness.[61])

In a refreshingly unscientific version of the ethnicity theme, humorists found distinctive physical commonalities of their own to serve the function of distinctive racial characteristics: Mark Twain, for example, claimed that he had been an advocate of reform in Utah. At least he was, until he "saw the Mormon women. Then I was touched, ... and as I turned to hide the generous moisture in my eyes, I said, 'No—the man that marries one of them has done an act of Christian charity ... and the man that marries sixty of them has done a deed of open-handed generosity so sublime that the nations of the earth should stand uncovered in his presence and worship in silence.'"[62] And Oscar Wilde, in a letter to Mrs. Bernard Beere (April 17, 1882), described the Mormons he encountered on a visit to Utah: "They ... are very, very ugly."[63]

SERPENT CHARMERS AND WHITE SLAVERY

As we saw earlier, resentment of foreigners and hostility toward Roman Catholicism were easily allied by emphasizing the Roman power base and the large Irish-immigrant population. If the same nativist hostility to a threatening Other is to be directed against a truly indigenous population, then fiction must construct an alien identity, whether it be Oriental, nonwhite, or, as for humorists Twain and Wilde, just plain ugly. In fiction as in politics, caricature becomes the ground on which difference, and the authority to censure it, is built. The reification of difference itself, not its particulars, is the essential thing.

Granting the ideological usefulness of caricature, the dread of assimilation expressed by James Maverick is nonetheless genuine. A revulsion for Mormonism strong enough to provoke a history of violence, persecution, and voluminous literary output was easily converted into anxiety when such a shunned and excoriated institution found wider and wider acceptance by peers and relatives. As the narrator of *The Mormoness* expressed it, there was no person "who would not have resented, as a gross insult, the bare suggestion that he might one day become a friend of the Mormons."[64] Nonetheless, in the brief span from 1830 to 1857 (when *The Mormoness* was published), not only friendship, but membership, had grown from a handful to tens of thousands—fifty-five thousand, in fact.[65] In addition to justifying political exorcism, then, presentation of Mormonism as an alien presence clearly serves to create the illusion of a comforting distance and distinctness. For arguably similar reasons, insistence on ethnic perimeters is often accompanied by fictional geographic boundaries as well, as we have seen.

By themselves, however, such strategies of caricature and physical containment proved insufficient to resolve the dread of assimilation pervading so much anti-Mormon representation. Situating the Mormons behind imaginary walls or depicting them as Oriental villains invited either passive acquiescence or rabid intolerance, both solutions that failed to satisfy at least some writers, as we saw with Russell and Standish. One alternative—or supplement—to the construction of a comforting distance through Orientalizing and fictional boundedness turned out to be the insistence that participation in the alien system could never be the result of conscious choice. Conversion, in other words, was rewritten as coercion. On this point, virtually all versions of the Mormon menace converge to employ a literary structure that resolves this anxiety of conversion. Magnetic attraction, compulsion, captivity, enslavement, kidnapping—these words and images pervade virtually the entire gamut of works in which Mormons figure as characters.

The psychology appears fairly transparent. The distance suggested by Orientalizing the "Other" is not, ultimately, a convincing one in the case of a group that continues to subvert or seduce its members from among the "Us." So, if neither ethnic nor geographic markers actually exist to safeguard one from contamination by what is anathema, one's sense of a stable, uncontaminated self can at least be assured by denying the function of personal will in whatever seduction by the Other does occur. There is some consolation, and psychological refuge, in the belief that no one has ever *chosen* to become Mormon. From creating the illusion of visible difference and separation from that threatening Other by fictionally created ethnicity, then, fiction writers at times progress to the insistence that what masquerades as conversion is in reality coercion. Absorption into the Mormon fold, in other words, is never depicted as the result of conscious choice.

The resulting representation of Mormonism in popular American fiction functions rather like the lawyer's argument by alternative: "Don't worry about Mormonism—it's too exotic to touch us. If it does get close, you will readily recognize its alien features. And even if it succeeds in claiming a few victims, at least they don't go willingly." We thus see a persistent erasure of agency, the elimination of effectual choice, in representations of the Mormon experience. Only in the absence of free will was the phenomenon of conversion to such otherness thinkable. Into the vacuum thus created, two literary types of the Mormon experience emerged recurrently to provide the engine for action where will was lacking: Mesmerism and bondage.[66]

Those in *The Mormoness* who adopt the Mormon faith are referred to repeatedly as innocents "falling directly into the snare of Mormonism."

Seduction is the mode, and choice has nothing to do with the process. Subsequent novels quickly incorporated themes of occult powers and agencies typical of the gothic novel in order to explain Mormonism's influence in terms of mystical compulsion. The compelling attraction, often part and parcel of romantic novels generally, became transformed into something a bit more unsettling, a bit more *unheimlich*. For example, in explaining her sister's departure for Utah with a Mormon husband, a character in Switzer's *Elder Northfield's Home* asserts, "I knew that man had bewitched our Flora, or she never would have left us."[67] But the bewitching is not a mere metaphor for the power of sexual attraction. In another case of Mormon attraction, the narrator in Zane Grey's *Riders of the Purple Sage* explains how the gentile Frank Erne came to lose his wife: "Another preacher came to the little town. . . . He preached some other kind of religion, and he was quick an' passionate where Frank was slow an' mild. He went after people, women specially. In looks he couldn't compare to Frank Erne, but he had power over women."[68]

Frequently, the women acknowledge this force they are powerless to resist, as in the case of one of Maria Ward's heroines. Explaining her "seduction" by the Mormon leader Joseph Smith, the innocent Ellen complains that "he exerted a mystical magical influence over me—a sort of sorcery that deprived me of the unrestricted exercise of free will."[69] Since Ward's account of *Female Life among the Mormons* (1855) purports to be a "narrative of many years' personal experiences," the stakes are especially high when she comes to explain the reasons for her own long involvement with Mormonism. Though always knowing the sect to be full of "absurdities," she marries a Mormon she meets on a stagecoach only days after he first fixes on her "one of his piercing looks. I became immediately sensible of some unaccountable influence drawing my sympathies towards him. In vain I struggled to break the spell. I was like a fluttering bird before the gaze of the serpent-charmer."[70] Only at the end of her "captivity" in Utah does she learn the secret of her own, and countless others', seduction. As a repentant Mormon, she confesses,

> "The early Mormon leaders possessed a singular and fascinating power, which they practised on all that came within their influence, by which they pretended to cure diseases and work miracles, and which"—
>
>   "Is now popularly known by the name of Mesmerism," I said, interrupting her.
>
>   "Even so," she answered; "and that mysterious influence, so little known at that time, contributed, in no small degree, to his success, and that of those engaged with him."

"The mystery of it is, how Smith came to possess the knowledge of that magnetic influence, several years anterior to its general circulation throughout the
country."

"That is no mystery to me," she replied. "Smith obtained his information, and
learned all the strokes, and passes, and manipulations, from a German peddler,
who, notwithstanding his reduced circumstances, was a man of distinguished
intellect and extensive erudition. Smith paid him handsomely, and the German
promised to keep the secret."[71]

Ward's story about the German peddler connection may have strained
even nineteenth-century credulity, but at least one influential newspaper
suggested a similar source of influence. Under the heading of "Mormonism
and Mesmerism," the *New York Herald* reported that the "celebrated Mons.
L. De Bonneville, formerly Professor of French in Harvard College, since
then professor of Magnetism all over the country," had given up his "lucrative situation" to join the Mormons and give lectures "on the extraordinary connection between Mormonism and Mesmerism, to the salvation
of sinners."[72]

There was certainly nothing inherently dubious about the phenomenal powers ascribed to Mesmerism. Spiritualism attracted thousands
on the basis of its psychic demonstrations, and even the cynical found in
Mesmerism a more palatable explanation for certain religious phenomena than the alternatives available. James Gordon Bennett, the sometime
champion of Joseph Smith, is a perfect example of such a believer. After
praising the prophet's "moral courage," the editor of the *Herald* offered
this account of his ministry: "He believes himself divinely inspired and
a worker of miracles. He cures the sick of diseases—so it is said—and
although Smith is not aware of the fact, we have been informed by a medical man that his influence over nervous disorders, arises from a powerful
magnetic influence."[73]

In fiction, this mesmeric phenomenon often creates a dilemma for
the story's hero who endeavors to rescue the wronged woman—but simply can't come to terms with the nature of the bondage, as in the case
of Captain Plum: "'As there is a God in Heaven I would give ten years of
my life for the secret of the prophet's power over Marion!' he groaned.
'Three months ago her hatred of him was terrible. She loathed the sight
of him.'"[74] Now she has promised to be his wife, leaving Plum to marvel at
"the terrible power that chained this girl to the Mormon king."[75]

In Coolidge's *Fighting Danites*, an army officer goes undercover to break
the back of the Mormon resistance to government control of the Utah
Territory. He falls in love with an orphan, Deseret. But she is claimed

by the head of the Danite terrorist organization. And, strangely, she does not resist the malevolent Lot Drake's demands, even though she knows him to be the killer of her own parents. That which appears to her would-be savior Zachary as incomprehensible, he ultimately ascribes to the same *je ne sais quoi* of the Mormon mystique: "Not for nothing had he dominated the lives of his people during thirty years of strife—he swayed her against her will by the touch of his hands and the power of his masterful eyes."[76]

One clear distinction between this Mormon magnetism and the mere stuff of romance is that the former's victims are not only women. In the boy's weekly *Frank Merriwell*, the captive heroine writes to her lover how her abductor "Elder Holdfast had demanded her as an addition to his wives, and how the man seemed to exercise a hypnotic influence over her father, who had agreed to all his demands."[77] This is particularly horrifying, considering that those demands entail a father's handing over his virgin daughter to a lascivious demon of a man. In fact, whole groups of Mormons respond to the hypnotic power of the leaders. When a wagon train is annihilated by Mormons in Coolidge's novel, the atrocity is attributed to this same power: "When the priests had ordered the massacre the people had responded, doing their bidding like men in a dream."[78]

Curwood's courageous Captain Plum similarly feels the mysterious power exuded by Mormon leaders:

> As the warm hand of the king clasped his own Captain Plum knew that he was in the presence of a master of human destinies, a man whose ponderous red-visaged body was simply the crude instrument through which spoke the marvelous spirit that had enslaved thousands to him, that had enthralled a state legislature and that had hypnotized a federal jury into giving him back his freedom when evidence smothered him in crime. He felt himself sinking in the presence of this man and struggled fiercely to regain himself.[79]

The narrator of Theodore Winthrop's *John Brent* (1862) likewise complains that "the recollection of the [Mormon leader] disgusts me! And yet he had an unwholesome fascination, which compelled us to listen."[80]

Even Zane Grey's hardy heroes have a difficult time fighting a force that they can't identify. Lassiter's romantic interest is Jane Withersteen, Mormon by birth but not by inclination. For most of the novel he can only helplessly watch as "that secret, intangible power closed its coils round her again, [as] that great invisible hand moved here and there and everywhere, slowly paralyzing her with its mystery and its inconceivable sway over her affairs."[81]

From the allure of sexual charisma to the use of naked force is but a small step, since in both instances what is denied to the represented victims is the power of choice. In both cases, these mythologies of mental and physical coercion avoid the unsettling specter of countrymen voluntarily affiliating themselves with Mormonism. What would seemingly be Mormonism's vindication thus turns out to be its condemnation—its reliance on converts to the system. In such a case, containment is clearly impossible and contagion an ever-present danger. And the irony is that the possibility of willing affiliation that conversion implies is actually more threatening than coercion to that very identity that conversion undermines. This is why the query "Why would anyone *choose* to participate in such a system?" must be precluded from the very start. Choice must be entirely written out of the equation.

In the literary treatments surveyed above, choice is overwhelmed in the presence of sexual charisma, hypnotic trance, or other psychic powers that defy rational or merely romantic explanation. More commonly, representations of Mormonism have recourse to more unambiguous solutions: kidnapping, captivity, bondage, and brutal servitude. The imperative to depict some kind of coercion in relationship to Mormomism is typified by Jennie Switzer's formulation. At the beginning of *Elder Northfield's Home*, the young hero and his bride, recent converts to Mormonism, hear of the doctrine of plural marriage with disapproval, but believe their union need not be disturbed by the practice. The anxious bride seeks reassurance from her new husband: "'Henry, is there any danger of our being forced into polygamy...?' 'No, there is no danger of my ever being forced into polygamy.'"[82] Given the pervasive mood of foreboding characterizing this novel, the dramatic irony is clear. The exchange can only be understood as addressing a more frightening possibility, which Switzer is concerned to dispel: "Is there any danger of our willingly choosing to practice polygamy? No, dear reader, there is no danger of our ever *choosing* polygamy (i.e., Mormonism)." *Coercion* into polygamy is an assault on our sacred institutions (democracy, monogamy, Christianity). But *conversion* to polygamy challenges the reader's sense of self.

Given a choice, the writer of anti-Mormon fiction does not hesitate. Captivity, not conversion, will always define the narrative structure. A number of precedents existed for combining captivity themes with anti-Mormon fiction. Eight years before Mormonism's organization, and before Hawthorne had a chance to write his impressions of Shaker life, Mary Dyer had already published her *Portraiture of Shakerism* (1822), in which she claimed to have been held captive in a Shaker community against her will. Adding fuel to the fires of popular perceptions was the

Shaker practice of controlling contact by visitors, assigning elders to chaperone and respond to questions that might arise. The sect's reclusiveness and guardedness could only exacerbate rumors of sexual repression run amok.

The convent system had been a constant source for prurient treatment as far back as Chaucer, Boccaccio, and Aretino. Decades before the no-popery crusade in America, Matthew Lewis had held Europe spellbound with the most famous of gothic thrillers, *The Monk* (1796), whose title villain commits abduction, rape, and murder. Unlike many of the anti-Catholic works to follow, whose villains escape to perpetuate and exacerbate readers' anxiety, Lewis's evil Ambrosio at least meets a satisfyingly gruesome doom of his own.

By virtue of their exclusivist, tightly knit communities, Mormons invited similar treatment as destroyers of feminine freedom and virtue. Once polygamy was publicized, the literary possibilities were too good to miss. Novel writing could suddenly be salacious, lucrative, pious, chivalrous, and patriotic all at once. Throughout a variety of genres, the theme of Mormon abduction plays itself out with virtually perfect consistency, from the nickel novel series *Buffalo Bill*, in which Brigham Young dispatches (or countenances) raiding expeditions on wagon trains for the purpose of bringing back young virgins, to Doyle's Sherlock Holmes, who tracks his first murder to Mormon kidnappers of gentile women. In *Buffalo Bill and the Danite Kidnappers* (1902), a wagon train is completely massacred by Mormon "Danites," save for the two young maidens who, their mysterious savior tells them, "were their intended victims."[83] Shortly thereafter, the raiders track them down with bloodhounds (a motif we shall see again) and make off with them to their Salt Lake stronghold. Only with the aid of Buffalo Bill are they spared the fate that was planned for them. Brigham Young himself gives the heroines the choice of betrothing themselves to him, or being handed over "to the Ute chief for squaws."[84]

A full eighty years after the first burst of anti-Mormon fiction, the literary patterns formed generations earlier persist. Deseret, the heroine of *The Fighting Danites*, does not even have the options afforded the victims of the "Danite kidnappers." Her gentile parents are murdered when she is a child, and she spends the next twenty years a captive of "these Mormons who . . . kept her as a bound-slave."[85] She is eventually rescued by an army officer.

Similarly, in Grey's *Riders* women from time to time mysteriously disappear at the same time that Mormon elders appear in the vicinity. One of the women, Millie Erne, is rather resistant to the proselytizing. "She had been bound an' gagged an' dragged away from her home by three men"[86] Then she is imprisoned. When her brother tries to rescue her, she writes him "to give up the search because if he didn't she would suffer in a way too horrible to tell."[87] *Harper's* ran a three-part fictional series (July–August 1896) entitled "Mormons from Muddlety," in which we follow the thwarted efforts of missionaries to secure their "converts" by means ranging from seduction to physical intimidation. In Doyle's *Study in Scarlet*, women mysteriously appear from time to time "in the harems of the elders." The sleuth's first mystery is set in motion when a woman makes the error of fleeing the Utah Territory. She is tracked down, her father killed by way of reprisal, and a cycle of vengeance begins. Similarly, Robert Louis Stevenson has his heroine of *The Dynamiter* (1925) escape the threat of polygamous union, only to be pursued by a Danite "Destroying Angel."[88]

Depictions of polygamy were also, and as predictably, wildly distorted. But then, the actual practice of plural marriage was seldom the stuff of steamy fiction. Writers of pulp fiction were unanimous in their claim that, in one author's words, "what was planned by Young for man's paradise proved woman's hell."[89] But from Brigham Young's pronouncement that he would rather be the corpse in a funeral procession than have to accept the doctrine of polygamy,[90] to the dozens of elders incarcerated in territorial prison for their devotion to the practice, to a generation of uniquely stressful marital relations for men and women alike, polygamy was far removed from the male paradise of fiction. Plural marriage was in practice a painful struggle against consciences shaped by Puritan values that most members, converts from Protestant faiths, shared. Domestic arrangements were inconvenient, fraught with jealousies, and, after the first wave of anti-polygamy legislation, hampered by flight, concealment, and frequent relocations. The observation of George Tanner, son of a polygamous marriage, would surprise no one: "I doubt there was a woman in the church who was in any way connected with Polygamy who was not heartsick."[91] (Not that men were much happier with the arrangement, which is why the great majority of Mormon men never took a plural wife.)

Also at odds with the fictional portrayal of the practice is the fact that in 1852, the same year that polygamy was publicly announced as a principle, Utah passed a divorce statute "that provided women much more control over their lives than was given by any other divorce statute of the nineteenth century, save only that of Indiana."[92] In an 1861 address, Brigham Young stated that "when a woman becomes alienated in her feelings and affections from her husband, it is his duty to give her a bill [of divorce] and set her free." Even more surprisingly, he claimed that for a husband to continue cohabiting with such a wife was tantamount to fornication.[93] Such opinions were clearly not meant merely for show. During his presidency, Young granted 1,645 divorces.[94]

Polygamy, then, proved to be a male utopia only in the conceptions of some indignant—but apparently envious—novelistic fantasizers. Why the ferocious response by both the secular and the religious press? Such an egregious affront to Western standards of moral propriety may seem self-evidently offensive, but more than moral indignation is at work here. That such sensationalizing took place in the context of the most vehement moral outrage is neither surprising nor disingenuous. For it is precisely the transgressive nature of polygamy that excites both envy and rejection. The supposed virtue of exposing "the moral leprosy" of Utah gives at the same time opportunity to luxuriate in all the seamy details one is excoriating. As Louis Kern, himself a harsh critic of Mormonism, observes, "That polygamy endured for over half a century...suggests that Gentile critics were both repelled and attracted by the 'twin relic of barbarism' and that it was but a distorted mirror of the imperfections inherent in their own sexual relationships."[95]

The rubric of "utopia" under which Kern and others consider Mormonism is a category fraught with this ambivalence by very definition. To imaginatively figure forth a wondrous "no place" is to cast into relief the inadequacies of "this place." But it is the imaginative distance between our own and other worldly realms that makes an imperfect existence bearable. To shrink that distance, to attempt such a heavenly city on earth, is to imperil not only the existing social order, but more immediately, one's own sense of self-denial as a necessary and valuable offering. If that self-denial takes the form of monogamy, the discovery that such a burden was never a moral necessity would not be a happy one. The natural response to such a threatening fantasy would be to explore the possibility of such freedom, while demonizing its actualization.

Ralph Waldo Emerson was no psychologist, but he knew psychic turmoil when he saw it. As he scathingly remarked, "Nothing is so hypocritical as the abuse in all the journals,—& at the South, especially,—of Mormonism & Free-Love Socialism. These men who write the paragraphs in the 'Herald' & 'Observer,' have just come from their brothel, or, in Carolina, from their Mulattoes."[96]

Perhaps the most grotesque depictions of the bondage motif are those in which women are imprisoned in asylums that double as torture chambers for recalcitrant wives. As already noted, Switzer refers in her novel to the ominous "brick house on the hill," where women driven mad by the Mormon system end up; her heroine is eventually imprisoned there. Similarly, the novelette *Bessie Baine* (1876) is about a young Quaker girl whom Elder Russell desires as his fifth wife. When she declines, she is kidnapped, drugged, and dragged to Utah, with the "husband" explaining to curious witnesses that he is returning his daughter to an asylum. The horror eventually weakens her mind, and by the time she arrives at the institution, she is trying to convince herself she is not insane.[97] Still resistant to Elder Russell's advances, she is subjected to head shavings, whippings and beatings, and torture. Through it all, she hears other screams and cries echo through the labyrinthine passages.

Salt Lake Fruit (1884), by "An American," repeats the theme of Mormon atrocities against women. In this novel, Patience refuses a bishop's advances, her family (her mother, a crippled little brother, along with an aged friend) is massacred in revenge, and she is held in an insane asylum—though in this case, her experiences push her over the brink of sanity and nearly qualify her to be an inmate. The virulence of the alleged Mormon vengeance is equaled only by that of the author. In her preface, she claims that "the incidents written within this book are not exaggerated" and, unlike her contemporaries, insists anti-Mormon legislation is not the answer. Hope will only come if, "in her might, Liberty puts her heel on the serpent's head, and crushes it. No intermediate legislation will avail. Exterminate, or be exterminated."[98] This, we have seen, was Governor Lilburn Boggs's exact prescription.

The bondage at times is depicted as captivity within the Mormon territory. In several accounts (such as *Riders*, and the Merriwell adventure), this captivity is geographically defined, with actual guards being posted at the frontiers to prevent both invasion by gentiles and egress of Mormons. The captivity often assumes a more oppressive aspect in the shape of polygamy itself. Perhaps the most familiar image in fiction of Mormonism is the sight of the young woman pleading in vain to be spared, while a lascivious, towering hulk of an aged man forces her to the altar. The "author of Frank Merriwell" paints this picture in typical colors: "'No!' she cried again. 'I will not go!' The good elder folded his hands, and a sinister, mirthless smile curled his withered lips.... 'If thou wilt not go willingly, thou shalt be carried by force.... What is your power against mine?'... She crept to his feet, begging for mercy."[99]

Curwood's is perhaps the most exaggerated version of force as the mode of Mormon conversion. Not only the women, but the men too are subject to a tyrannical ruler who enforces his decrees savagely, as Nathaniel Plum soon learns:

"That is MacDougall with the lash—official whipper and caretaker of the slave hounds," explained Obadiah in a whisper.

Nathaniel gave a start of horror.

"Slave hounds!" he breathed.

The councilor grinned and twisted his hands in enjoyment of his companion's surprise.

"We have the finest pack of bloodhounds north of Louisiana," he continued so low that only Nathaniel could hear. "See! Isn't the earth worn smooth and hard about that post?"[100]

The suggested comparison with slavery is not fortuitous. As we saw, the association had become entrenched by the time that the first Republican Party platform stipulated the eradication of "the twin relics of barbarism—slavery and polygamy." Most authors were quick to point out the similarities, and Charles Pidgin's anti-Mormon *House of Shame* (1912) is dedicated to Harriet Beecher Stowe. Stowe herself had dramatically linked the two crusades by turning from abolition to anti-Mormonism, in a preface she contributed to Mrs. Stenhouse's *"Tell It All": The Story of a Life's Experience in Mormonism* (1874). Now that "the slave-pens of the South have become a nightmare of the past," she writes, "the hour is come to loose the bonds of a cruel slavery whose chains have cut into the very hearts of thousands of our sisters."[101] (Elsewhere, as we have seen, her stature as a foe of slavery and oppression made her especially valuable as a presenter of anti-Catholic narratives.)

Indeed, no analogy could be as immediately relevant and powerful to late nineteenth-century readers as likening membership in the Mormon church to enslavement in a prewar South. The horrors Curwood evokes, though sensationalistic from a modern perspective, have a familiar resonance in the antislavery rhetoric of the period. Describing what is in store for intransigent and recaptured Mormons, he writes,

"Your hands are tied to the post very loosely, with a slack of say six inches," continued Neil with an appalling precision. "There is a rawhide thong about your neck, wet, and so tight that it chafes your skin when you move your head. But the very uncomfortable thing just at this moment is the way your feet are fastened. Isn't that so? Your legs are drawn back, so that you are half resting on your toes, and I'm pretty sure that your knees are aching right now. Eh? Well, it won't be very long before your legs will give way under you and the slack about your wrists will keep you from helping yourself. Do you know what will happen then? . . . You will hang upon the thong about your neck until you choke to death," finished Neil. "That's the 'Straight Death.' If the end doesn't come by morning the sun will finish the job. It will dry out the wet rawhide until it grips your throat like a hand. Poetically we call it the hand of Strang."[102]

Pidgin makes the comparison of Mormonism with slavery explicit in his preface, and has his non-Mormon characters quote from Stowe's *Uncle Tom's Cabin* at least three times in describing what they see in Utah. In what claims to be a faithful representation of the facts, Switzer gives the enslavement motif one of its more elaborate treatments. The mother of Marion, having long since renounced Mormonism but still held to her husband by inexplicable bonds, plans for years for her daughter's escape from Utah. The daring plot is carried off successfully, but Marion is enticed to return. Her family pleads with her to again flee the growing danger:

> "But, mother, you do not fear that any personal harm will come to me, if I now remain quietly at home, do you?"
>
> "My child,...I have never told you of the 'Death Society,' 'Avenging Angels,' or 'Band of Danites,' as they were called, which the old Mormon women have told me used to exist in full force, and even now exists in secret...."
>
> "Tell me about them now, mother!" and Marion's eyes dilated with horror.
>
> "...To apostatize then, during that reign of terror, was to have the throat cut from ear to ear, or to suffer some other ignominious death,...and though murder in the Church was a terrible crime, yet the killing of the Gentile was no murder....Polygamy was established,...and the revival of the old Jewish sacrifices was even contemplated." Thus she showed [Marion] that the most terrible crimes of all descriptions had been the dark results of Mormonism's teachings. [Marion] was now almost trembling with terror.[103]

That same night, Marion is brutalized and shot. She tries to leave, but is followed for two days and nights on the train, and then finally kidnapped and handcuffed by two men who allege to bystanders that she has escaped from an asylum. And that is, in fact, where they take her, in a horrific sequence, as she pleads to be believed but can barely repress her growing hysteria.

With slavery the analogue, it was inevitable that some writer would see an Underground Railroad as the temporary solution to the white slavery of polygamy, and here again fiction and history come together only to immediately veer apart. The heroine of Switzer's *Elder Northfield's Home*, after being lured back to Utah, makes the best of her situation and begins a covert operation to rescue fellow wives through an underground network of safe houses. She is successful only briefly, and retribution (imprisonment in an insane asylum) follows swiftly. But the point has forcefully been made. Bondage in the Mormon religion is not to be taken metaphorically.

In reality, an attempt *was* made to offer sanctuary to female escapees from Mormonism, in the form of the Woman's Industrial Home. Originally founded in Salt Lake as a private institution in 1886, the organization was soon awarded federal appropriations to "aid in the emigration of those who should come to the 'Home' and desire to remove permanently from the territory to escape polygamy."[104] The program was a dismal failure, and after ten years of existence, even its advocates could claim no more than a total of ten polygamous women who had sought shelter at the home.[105]

When it came to the practice of polygamy, the novelists, like the feminist activists who intended the freeing of their Utah sisters, absolutely depended for their moral zeal upon the equation of plural marriage with slavery. Even if such a comparison was initially sincere, it could not bear up under the weight of the Mormon women's response to their would-be liberators. The English journalist Phil Robinson observed the rather unanticipated response to the Harriet Beecher Stowes of polygamy, in 1883:

> Instead of being thanked for helping to strike the fetters of plurality off their suffering sisters, they are met with the retort that they ought to try being wives and mothers themselves, before they come worrying about those who have tried it and are content! . . . But even more staggering is the fact that Mormon women base their indignation against their persecuting saviours on *women's rights*, the very ground upon which their saviours have based their crusade!
>
> . . . [But] the plural wives of Salt Lake City are not by any means "waiting for salvation" at the hands of men and women of the East. Unconscious of having fetters on, they evince no enthusiasm for their noisy deliverers.[106]

As early as 1870, three thousand Mormon women had rallied in Salt Lake to protest government attempts to interfere with the practice of plural marriage.[107] Mormon wives frequently invoked the argument made by a non-Mormon visitor to Utah: "The one lesson to be learned from the morals of Salt Lake City is that polygamy and immorality are quite incompatible. The man with five wives behaves himself with exemplary propriety. It is the man with only one who spends all his spare hours looking for the five he has not."[108]

Perhaps the most crippling blow to the popular stereotype of Mormon gender relations as master/slave is the fact that the right of all adult women to vote was first exercised in this country in, of all places, Utah—and during the height of the polygamous period (on February 12, 1870). Utah women did not use the vote to abolish polygamy, presumably a factor in Congress's decision to rescind their suffrage in 1887.

The reality was that Switzer's crusading heroine was wasting her effort, as Switzer herself confesses in an apparently forgetful moment, when she admits that Mormon marriage was not without its remedies. Her heroine

ultimately finds a rather pedestrian solution to the dilemma of polygamous bondage: "The man upon whose help the wives counted did not fail
them, and the result was, as they hoped, a divorce, which could always be
obtained by paying Brigham Young ten dollars."[109]

Equating Mormonism with white slavery was of course not the only way
to avoid the unpalatable specter of voluntary affiliation with the system.
The erasure of will may be effected by other, subtler means. Ignorance of
alternatives is equally destructive of agency, and that is the tactic Jennie
Switzer imputes to Mormonism in her preface to *Elder Northfield's Home*.
Switzer, writing in 1882, expresses in a highly self-conscious way the anxiety with which so many writers in her genre contended. She asks herself,

> Why are [the Mormon women] so simple-minded as to receive, and submit to
> such teachings? the answer is apparent. They know no other life.... They have
> been kept ignorant by the authorities lest a cultivation of the intellect stir up
> rebellion against their oppressors. For a successful reign of tyranny and oppres-
> sion, ignorance in the subjects is a necessity ... so the Mormons look upon educa-
> tion in their subjects as destructive to their institutions.[110]

In a church that had grown from six members in 1830 to almost
150,000 by the year Switzer was writing,[111] the number of converts meant
few members would have known "no other life"—and women in the Utah
Territory experienced a degree of educational opportunity unknown in
the other states.[112] Perhaps because her assertions are embarrassingly
groundless, Switzer found recourse in the familiar—and less easily dismissed (or verified)—charges of physical compulsion:

> There have always been men and women in the Mormon Church who did not be-
> lieve in the religion they professed to accept. But though broken-hearted, though
> stung to madness, though plunged into the deepest despair by their wrongs, yet
> the possibility of liberating themselves from their bondage scarcely occurred to
> the women, and indeed has not existed many years. If a desperate soul sought
> relief from her troubles in flight from the Territory, she was pursued, not by the
> blood-hound that scented the African refugee, but by the blood-hound in hu-
> man form, who sought to capture her and return her to the miseries of Mormon
> life.[113]

Certainly these models of coercion were pervasive long before and independent of Mormon representations. The captivity narrative, the gothic,
the sensation novel—all employed similar themes. Naturally, the writers
of anti-Mormon fiction made use of materials available to them to respond

to ideological and psychological imperatives particular to that historical moment.

One important variant to the bondage motif does surface from time to time in nineteenth-century fiction. Perhaps sensitive to the absurdity of portraying Mormonism as mass Mesmerism or kidnapping on a global scale, some authors portray Mormon women as needing liberation *in spite of* their choice. The western novel, especially, resurrects the chivalric ideal as one in which men need to be liberators at all costs. Thus, in Winthrop's *John Brent*, the two male heroes are stymied when they learn the Mormoness, whom, along with her father, they wish to free, is not seeking a liberator: "These two souls [Ellen and her aged father] were clutched by this foul ogre [the church], and locked up in an impregnable prison. And we two were baffled. Of what use was our loyalty to woman? What vain words those unuttered words of our knightly vow to succor all distressed damsels.... Did [they] wish to escape? No."[114]

So they respond in a way that echoes the efforts of nineteenth-century women's rights crusaders trying to galvanize the uninterested Utah women: "She must be saved, sooner or later, whether she will or no."[115] The scene is hauntingly reminiscent of Mary Sherwood's Mr. Beaumont, who rescued his sister Clarice from the evil Jesuits, only to "b[i]nd her to himself with her veil" even as the gothic edifice burns in the background. Salvation in these circumstances does not, apparently, occur because the *woman's* welfare demands it. Winthrop makes clear what is at stake— what in fact has been at stake all along in these renderings of the Mormon as alien: It is America—that is, the American male—that has given to the "Old World...tobacco, woman's rights, the potato."[116]

In both cases, then, whether Mormon by deception or by choice, the victim is depicted in a way that foregrounds supposed essential constituents of *American* identity: Americans are *not* willful heretics, being neither polygamous, communalistic, nor "Mahometan"; and Americans— American men, at any rate—*are* nineteenth-century knights-errant, dispensers and defenders of woman's prerogatives. Self-fashioning is still the emphatic, and in Winthrop's case, explicit, motivation behind these representational forms.

Mormonism burst upon the scene in a time when the struggle for American independence was still vivid memory for many. It is hard to say by what time—if ever—the notion of what it meant to be American was a relatively fixed concept. Surely the contemporaries of Joseph Smith were in the first stages of that laborious self-definition. As the Latter-day Saints struggled to find a niche in Missouri in 1837, Emerson, in his "American Scholar" speech, was exhorting the students at Harvard to throw off the shackles of European culture and inaugurate a native cultural identity. While the Mormons retrenched in Nauvoo, it was still possible, but barely, for James Fenimore Cooper to write a trilogy like the *Littlepage Manuscripts*, wherein he argued the virtue of a landed gentry class as a friend to domestic stability. America had yet to break with its Anglo-European heritage, let alone establish a distinctive American identity. Stephen Greenblatt has pointed out that such "self-fashioning is achieved in relation to something perceived as alien, strange, or hostile. This threatening Other—heretic, savage, witch, adulteress, traitor, Antichrist—must be discovered or invented in order to be attacked and destroyed."[117]

Without question, Mormonism was perceived as representing values and practices antithetical to the evolving image of America. Exaggerating these conflicts, emphasizing or inventing Mormonism's alien character, strange beliefs, and hostile intents toward American institutions, could only facilitate the self-definition of a people who chose to see themselves as theologically Protestant, morally Puritan, and politically Jacksonian. Just as anti-Mormon fiction is informed by politics, reflecting and exploiting deep-seated anxieties and interests, so does politics in this case construct itself as fiction, appropriating exaggerated villains and heroes, moral absolutes and devilish scenarios, in order to create both character and plot, shaping its own national identity and portraying its own idealized destiny.

Insofar as Mormonism was merely Other, its appropriation as a stock source of villainy was shaped by the literary genres into which the characters were written, the stereotypes their peculiar practices and beliefs generated, and the ideological investment that purveyors of popular fiction had as self-fashioning Americans. In this regard, the case of Mormons in fiction shares much with representations of the Other generally. But unlike the subjects usually chosen for exemplary otherness, Mormons represented a unique case of an Other that was, ultimately with profoundly disturbing implications, a community not subject to the same means of exorcism as communities ethnically, racially, culturally, or geographically distinctive. For once Mormons were constructed, for whatever variety of reasons, into a demonized Other, their lack of self-manifesting characteristics, their lack of a racially distinct appearance, the ordinariness of their cultural and intellectual composition—these features, in combination with a burgeoning convert pool that knew no boundaries, produced an anxiety of seduction perhaps unique in the American experience of otherness. The literary consequences—construction of a distinct ethnic identity and erasure of the will—represent a two-pronged strategy to contain a threatening Other that proves resistant to both extermination and assimilation.

CHAPTER 8

"Murder and Mystery—*Mormon Style*": The Mormon Image in the Twentieth Century—and Beyond

There are twin Gates of Sleep, of which one is said to be of horn, allowing an easy exit for shadows which are true. The other is all of shining white ivory, perfectly made; but the Spirits send visions which are false in the light of day.

Aeneid, book 6

This novel is a work of fiction. Names, characters, places and incidents are either the product of the author's imagination or are used fictitiously. Any resemblance to actual events or locales or persons, living or dead, is entirely coincidental.

Standard disclaimer for contemporary novels

In the nineteenth century, literature could be deliberately and irresponsibly inflammatory and provocative. Under the pressure of important ideals of pluralism and religious liberty, authors found in the case of Mormonism a means of enacting violence in such a way as to effectively mediate irreconcilable difference. Images of coercion and Mesmerism served as devices by which the infiltration of American religion by the Mormon heresy was made palatable. The Mormon conversion narrative was by such means transformed into the orthodox captivity narrative. Radical difference was thus accounted for in a way consistent with American self-definition. The Mormons, artfully constructed as Oriental, racially atavistic, or otherwise Other, were seen to have imposed an alien value system on Americans by fraud or by force.

NEW VARIATIONS ON OLD THEMES

Although depictions of the Mormons as Mesmerists and abductors have for the most part disappeared, similar strategies are commonly at work today, fulfilling a familiar function with other religious groups that fall outside the mainstream. As these more recent religious movements have come to be seen as utterly inharmonious with mainstream Protestant models, or more important, with the social class from which many of their converts are drawn, there is a virtually identical tendency to rewrite those institutions as coercive. Often, the charge is that dubious mystical agencies are at work. The federal confrontation with Branch Davidian "cultist" David Koresh spawned news coverage that referred to his "wizardry," the "mystic spell" he cast over members, his "magnetism," and the "victims" who "came under his spell, sexually as well as spiritually."[1] The impulse to accuse such groups of mental or physical coercion is understandable, given that some of them have emerged with sinister agendas and horrific outcomes. (Koresh's group, including twenty-one children, suffered alleged sexual abuse and met a fiery death in 1993; over nine hundred disciples of Jim Jones, leader of the Peoples Temple, committed mass suicide in 1978.) But the danger of imputing coercion is twofold: First, although simplistic mind-control explanations may satisfy our need to make sense of the inexplicable, our own peace of mind is a poor substitute for real understanding of the complex mechanisms of group attraction. Second, such explanations can too easily be wielded promiscuously to target any group we happen to find objectionable.

This strategy has also been invoked with other sects that acquired "cult" status in the late twentieth century, such as the Unification Church and Scientology. Opponents of both groups have charged that coercive persuasion deprives members of any choice in their conversions. The Supreme Court of California, in a case involving the Unification Church (*Molko v. Holy Spirit Association for the Unification of World Christianity*), went so far as to validate one such allegation that "brainwashing" rendered its members "incapable of exercising their own will."[2] In a similar 1984 case, a plaintiff alleged that the Unification Church conspired to "take control" over one Charles Meroni, through "a form of hypnotic control." The Supreme Court of New York ruled there was sufficient evidence for the case to go to trial.[3] Brainwashing might seem a more respectable term than Mesmerism or the evil eye. In reality, the idea emerged during the Korean War to explain how patriotic young American servicemen could transform, in captivity, into communist sympathizers or collaborators. The concept thus served purposes identical to allegations about German peddlers teaching mind-control to Mormons: to emotionally insulate us from the distressing possibility that people we know and love might *willingly* choose to embrace a system we find deplorable.[4] The allegation of brainwashing emphasized the innocence and helplessness of the victims in the face of an overpowering, sinister entity, even as it reassured observers that they and their value systems were impervious to genuine conversion.

Deceptive and manipulative proselytizing practices certainly deserve condemnation. But one cannot escape the strong impression that what is at stake in these cases is a conception of self that, in retrospect, cannot tolerate willing affiliation with the culturally designated "cult." This interpretation is suggested by the way plaintiffs build their case upon their proven "respectability" (the two plaintiffs in *Molko*, for example, were pointedly introduced as a member of the Pennsylvania bar with numerous "educational successes," and a college student, respectively) and by the transparent reasoning behind such legal verdicts. As the dissenting justice argued in *Molko*, all such attempts fall into one of two constitutional (not to say logical) errors: (1) they fail to regard the religious experience as potentially outside of legalistic, rationalistic comprehension, by presuming to ascertain the impetus behind conversion in a courtroom setting; or (2) they fail to successfully distinguish "coercive persuasion" in churches like the Unification Church from traditional, orthodox modes of religious conversion that rely on more historically sanctioned, but essentially similar modes of conversion. In fact, the court in *Molko* enumerated the characteristics of "brainwashing" in such a way as to again reveal the capricious nature of heretical categories: "fasting, chanting, physical exercises, cloistered living, confessions, lectures, and a highly structured work and study schedule."[5] These eerily familiar practices are supposed to constitute the basis of a judgment of religious fraud? As Meredith McGuire notes, it is not difficult to unmask such facile construction of religious practices into ersatz heresies: "Two researchers compared conversion and commitment processes of the Unification Church of Sun Myung Moon and similar contemporary sects with the nineteenth- and early twentieth-century practices of the now socially acceptable Tnevnoc 'cult.' The Tnevnoc practices were essentially comparable and seem bizarre until we discover that the authors were actually referring to life in the convent—which, spelled backwards, is Tnevnoc."[6] The moral seems to be that invoking the specter of psychological coercion is a tempting but dangerous strategy by which to rewrite conversion narratives as captivity narratives, religion as heresy.

Occasionally the momentum of decades-old representations produces unexpected eruptions of the old Mormon stereotypes, sometimes clothed in the garb of academic respectability. Harold Bloom, for example, reads at times like a parody of nineteenth-century phrenologists when he maintains with apparent sobriety that "the visitor to Salt Lake City, after just four days, has learned to tell the difference between certain Mormons and most Gentiles at first sight. There is something *organized* about the expressions on many Mormon faces as they go by in the street."[7]

The Jackson County, Missouri, mob document that referred half facetiously and half fearfully to the invading swarms of Mormons who threatened to appropriate the county to their theocratic kingdom also finds a distinct echo in Bloom's assessment of Mormonism. On the one hand, Bloom is effusive in his praise of Mormon leaders Joseph Smith and Brigham Young, putting the first on a par with Ralph Waldo Emerson as one of America's premier visionaries and thinkers. The proclamation of polygamy in 1852 he finds the "most courageous act of spiritual defiance in all of American history."[8] On the other hand, Bloom also notes with great interest current growth patterns of the church ("one American out of eight [by] 2020") and increasing LDS involvement in politics, from the MX missile controversy to the Equal Rights Amendment to the abortion issue. Considering that the Missouri War took place in a decade that saw the early church explode in membership from its six founders to thirty thousand, and given that the atrocities of Haun's Mill and their aftermath were most immediately precipitated by election violence at Gallatin, one can see the familiarity of Bloom's concerns. In light of the admiration for Mormonism he has already and so profusely expressed, he is at pains to "stress that this is not a viewing-with-alarm, since I am wholly sympathetic [to the Mormons] ... and am not particularly exercised by politics."[9] But on the same page he refers to Mormons' "spiritual audacity," "titanic designs," and their "sublime insanity." His epilogue is undeniably the clarion call of an alarmist, as he invokes the specter of "the burgeoning, soon-to-be Established Church of the West, the Mormons" and expresses horror at "the parodistic American Religion's militancy in the concluding decade of the twentieth century," in which "we are on the verge of being governed (with the complicity of the Mormons and Baptists) by a nationally established religion."[10]

If the Missourians had grounds to fear that an influx of thousands could alter a precarious political balance, what are we to say of Bloom's concerns when they are buttressed by speculations like those of the sociologist Rodney Stark? Speaking in terms of tens of millions rather than thousands, Stark predicts that the Mormons will soon transcend denominational status to achieve a "worldwide following comparable to that of Islam, Buddhism, Christianity, Hinduism, and the other dominant world faiths." With no small irony, Stark, like Bloom a respectful observer, inevitably slips into a rhetoric that evokes old stereotypes and anxieties: "Today they stand on the threshold of becoming the first major faith to appear on earth since the Prophet Mohammed rode out of the desert."[11] Joel Kotkin's references to Mormonism as an emerging "global tribe," and recent studies of Mormonism as a "corporate empire,"[12] repeat the pattern of observations that mingle admiration with the gravest misgivings— or outright alarm. Anson Shupe's and John Heinerman's comments are fairly typical: "The LDS Church empire, in terms of its economic, political, and media influence, is enormous, dwarfing the Moral Majority, the 'electronic church,' and even the entire New Christian Right."[13] How the Mormons can be larger than a coalition they are presumably a part of is never explained.

Until recently, more blatant, frontal assaults on Mormonism are, compared to those of the nineteenth century, rare. The most obvious explanation for the shifting winds of representation would be changes in Mormonism itself. Beginning in the 1950s, Mormonism entered a new era of respectability. Klaus Hansen has made a case for the "bourgeoisification" of Mormon culture,[14] evidence of which might be alleged in a variety of examples: Howard Hughes's choice of Mormons as his personal aides, because they exemplify clean living and trustworthiness; the tendency of the FBI and the CIA to recruit heavily among the LDS population, exploiting their reputation for moral standards, patriotism, and family values; J. Willard Marriott's exemplification of the successful Mormon business ethic; and Mormon apostle Ezra Taft Benson's position as one of the most popular cabinet members of President Eisenhower's administration. In 1992, two of George H. W. Bush's most visible aides were prominent Mormons.[15]

The basis of the Mormon heresy, however, has not changed. Accordingly, animosity toward the church as a deviant cult can be as vociferous as ever. A recent study by three sociologists of religion revealed the startling finding that in spite of "a high degree of value consensus" between the two groups, "just under 20 percent of the Conservative Christians would deny Mormons residence in their country."[16] A look at a recent critique of the Mormons produced by a Christian group, and the response it elicited, suggests a number of reasons for the changing scope and form of Mormon representations in the present day.

NARRATIVE AUTHORITY AND THE CONTROL
OF PUBLIC DISCOURSE

One of the most widely distributed anti-Mormon works of the late twentieth century was the film *The God Makers*. It has aired in churches, in rented public halls, and on cable television channels in a large number of American communities. The fifty-nine-minute film has been characterized by the Anti-Defamation League (ADL) of B'nai B'rith as invoking "one of the longest-standing canards of religious defamation—that one religion (or its adherents) control a disproportionate share of our nation's resources" and intend to use such power "for evil ends."[17] The National Council of Christians and Jews (NCCJ) similarly criticized the film for its emphasis on Mormonism as "some sort of subversive plot—a danger to the community, a threat to the institution of marriage, and…destructive to the mental health of teenagers."[18] Some of the original fears that moved the Missourians to violence in the nineteenth century once again make their appearance. These charges have changed remarkably little since Harriet Beecher Stowe and Robert Richards exploited nativist fears of papist conspiracies and transformed them into popular alarm about Mormon theocratic conspiracies; concern for "mental health" evokes ghosts of Mesmerism and kindred evils of the nineteenth century.

In spite of such familiar echoes, the twentieth century saw dramatic changes in the discourse of what the NCCJ calls "anti-ism." One was the relegation of frontal attacks like this film to ad hoc committees (like the "Concerned Christians, Inc.," airers of *The God Makers*) and fundamentalist Christian publishers. The arena within which such hostile representations are played out has narrowed for a number of reasons. Mormonism itself has undergone substantial changes in the last century and a half. It is possible that religious toleration had greater currency as a value in the twentieth century than previously. But it is also possible that, whereas the nineteenth-century proliferation of popular fiction combined with the delayed development of rules of genre to exacerbate public intolerance for deviance, today the more general compliance with literary categories has helped to mediate cultural conflict. Simply put, rhetoric and representation are increasingly constrained by the way in which culture has come to divide up discourse generally.

That the ADL would label this film "invidious and defamatory" and the NCCJ condemn it as a mélange of "half-truth, faulty generalizations, erroneous interpretations and sensationalism" can be seen, it is true, as evidence of modern intolerance of intolerance—at least in some quarters. And no one disputes that—socially, at least—mainstreaming of Mormonism has been fairly thoroughly accomplished. Not just social norms, but rules of discourse militate against the literature of the hostile imagination today. The reaction of the ADL to this film, in particular, typifies the extent to which genre categories have come to function as instruments of discursive control. For example, the ADL faults the producers of *The God Makers* for using "a documentary format with a factual tone [in] a clever ploy to convey a high degree of believability to what is in fact merely an anti-Mormon work." This kind of sleight of hand, as we have seen time and again, was acceptable in nineteenth-century polemical fiction; the demand that such a documentary presentation deliver on its implicit contract is far more pronounced in public discourse today. The "high production values" and "sophistication" of the film, also cited in the ADL document, similarly emerge as grounds for serious moral concern, since they suggest a reliability and seriousness of purpose wholly out of sync with the filmmakers' ulterior motives, not to mention the actual content of the film.

The issue of toleration aside, the industry of "anti-isms" operates under a burden of greater rhetorical scrutiny, of more sophisticated genre conventions, than prevailed during much of the nineteenth century. With the exceptions noted above, changing values and also changing rhetorical norms mean that familiar patterns of Mormon representation will necessarily be assimilated to new narrative strategies. In 1890, Zane Grey could get in his shots against the Mormons, newspapers from New York to California could call for their extermination, and Representative T. E. Noell could cite Artemus Ward in congressional testimony to the same end, without this strange mélange of sources and forums devoted to a common political end jarring anyone's sensibilities. It may be no easier today than in the nineteenth century to sort out hysterical hate-mongering from objective reporting of the facts when a new and threatening presence appears on the American cultural or religious scene. But if fact and fiction are still slippery labels, we find a kind of intellectual refuge in genre distinctions, and at least attempt to control discourse that way.

There are, of course, exceptions. Contemporary satire, for example, certainly blurs the gates of ivory and of horn, but like the roman à clef, this very obfuscation is its raison d'être, not an incidental blemish. Historical fiction forewarns by its very label that the poet "nothing affirmeth." When fiction presumes to claim the authority of history, as when Hollywood increasingly usurps the role of journalism, a category like "docu-drama" immediately emerges to contain the new area of transgression. When a filmmaker like Oliver Stone pairs sensational speculation with historical subjects, the boundaries again seem to blur. But the widespread criticism that this practice engenders is again proof of its outrage against literary propriety.

We have seen how in the nineteenth century affidavits were appended to novels, novels were used as evidence in affidavits, Senate testimony cited humorists, and a general disregard for genre distinctions facilitated moral crusades against Mormons and other unpopular groups. The contrast with today's respect for rules of genre is striking. It is not merely that genres have proliferated. For old forms fade out (satyr plays, epic poetry, sonnets) as new forms develop (sitcoms, sound bites, the academic novel). Perhaps what *has* changed is the extent to which genre distinctions have come to pervade public discourse, and not in such a way as to demarcate *how* an object is represented, but rather to constrain the claim such a representation makes upon us. (Hence the rebranding of James Frey's memoir, *A Million Little Pieces* [Doubleday, 2003] as a "semi-fictional" memoir, after public outcry at the discovery of its abundant fabrications.) These literary labels are more important for what they tell us about the authority the words carry, than what form those words take. Thus authority and legitimacy displace nineteenth-century persuasiveness and moral fervor as the privileged rhetorical criteria. Credentials are more important than eloquence; a kind of propriety in the author/audience and author/subject-matter relationships assumes an importance not known since Horace.

This is part of the reason literature of intolerance currently finds its institutional forum almost uniquely in sectarian publishing houses and fringe hate-groups. Newspapers have become elaborate reports on crime and economic indicators and relegate blatant editorializing to a clearly demarcated section. As for the degree to which editorializing pervades even the front page, precisely because it does not pass unnoticed but is constantly subject to scrutiny and negotiation, it further affirms the reliance we place on genre boundaries to define and circumscribe narrative authority.

So pulp fiction is quite happy to occupy its niche of profitability and intellectual disrespectability, with neither the inclination nor the credibility to engage in social polemics. (And the omnipresent formulaic disclaimer about persons and events being strictly fictitious would be necessary even in a less legalistic milieu.) Far from diminishing, the appetite for Mormon villains has only intensified in recent years. One bibliography lists, from the last two decades of the twentieth century alone, almost one hundred works (novels or "true crime" narratives with fictional elements) in which Mormons figure prominently.[19]

Some of the old Mormon caricatures *appear* to resurface in fairly generic ways. Popular romance writer Jennifer Blake, for example, invokes the foil of a "fanatic Elder Greer, who called his wanton desires the 'will of God,'" to contrast with her slightly more monogamous hero Ward Dunbar.[20] Mystery writer Tony Hillerman exploits the Mormon figure in equally melodramatic ways. The mysterious entity behind strange happenings in *The Thief of Time* turns out to be Brigham (!) Houk, a schizophrenic triple murderer (of his mother and siblings) who tortures frogs and babbles about the devil and the angel Moroni.[21]

In spite of the old specters of violence and perversion raised by such caricatures, however, contemporary depictions of Mormonism are invariably domesticated, defanged as it were, by strategies of one kind or another. In the popular romance genre, the malignance of the depiction is generally mediated by historical distance. (Blake's novel and Cleo Jones's *Sister Wives*, to name another, are set in an almost mythic pioneer past.) In crime fiction like Hillerman's, the same effect is achieved by including extenuating circumstances—in this case, the Mormon's insanity.

It is perhaps surprising, then, that in the academic world selective bigotry continues to find intellectual respectability if the target is Mormons, fundamentalists, or other groups not yet beneficiaries of the "new tolerance." As noted in chapter 3, for example, Paul Fussell suggests in his *Bad: Or, the Dumbing of America* that "the creeping nincompoopism" that threatens to engulf our culture had its origins in the rise of Mormonism. Religious historian Martin Marty offers one explanation for such persistent bigotry. "Fundamentalists," he notes, "seem to be one of the few groups that have no effective anti-defamation lobby."[22] (Ironically, Marty himself had been cited as an example of "the blatant prejudice against fundamentalists in American academe."[23])

"THE CENTRE CANNOT HOLD"

Other developments have complicated the picture with respect to Mormonism. Through the nineteenth century, Mormonism lent itself readily to a political discourse largely preoccupied with questions of American identity. What values made the Union worth preserving? What criteria were relevant in the admission of a territory to statehood? How would the new Republican Party define itself? Likening polygamy to slavery, as the first Republican Party platform did, comparing Brigham Young to an Asian despot, representing Mormon women as victims and frontier heroes from Captain Plum to Buffalo Bill as their saviors, accounting for the prophet Joseph Smith's martyrdom as the penalty for his violation of the right to a free press—in these and many other scenarios Mormonism made available to the playwrights of the Great American Saga the heroes and antiheroes, the virtues and vices, of that dramatic self-creation.

Today the Mormon caricature has changed considerably, and so has the plot. A perusal of contemporary novels reveals that the Mormon image in fiction has evolved accordingly. Two writers in particular reflect the new ambiguities and dilemmas facing modern caricaturists of Mormonism. Like that of many of his nineteenth-century predecessors, Edgar Award nominee Robert Irvine's perspective is shaped by past affiliation with the church ("he comes from a pioneer Mormon family," the book jacket advertises). Indeed, the most salient—and salacious—features of early anti-Mormon fiction are also present in his works; he has written several successful "Moroni Traveler" mysteries set in contemporary Utah, which purportedly "give the reader a very compelling glimpse into this fascinating subculture" and reveal "telling details of its church-dominated region."[24] And what a subculture it is!

Church security is Orwellian, involving spies as young as twelve years old. Even public pay phones are monitored by the church, hidden TV cameras are everywhere, and computers keep detailed records on all aspects of members' lives. And when Mormons aren't glutting their lust in polygamy, they are joining celibate male cults: "fifteen or twenty men dressed in black trousers and white home-spun shirts. All wore straggly beards that made them look like Orthodox Jews." They don't wear zippered pants, since "they're an invention of the devil."[25] They are anti-women and anti-sex, and engage in bizarre "touching" rituals.

Like Hillerman and Blake, Irvine makes a token gesture at distancing himself from anti-Mormonism by imputing the evils in his fiction to fringe groups. Ultimately, however, he ignores his own disclaimers. Not only do the fundamentalist cults practice polygamy, but in fact "a lot of Mormons around here, Mormons in good standing, have more wives than the law allows."[26] When heinous murders occur, the distinction between cultists and mainstream Mormons again evaporates: "She'd been strung up by her feet and butchered. The Mormon way..."[27] As in the novels of Zane Grey and Sir Arthur Conan Doyle, the Danites, a secret Mormon terrorist organization with alleged ties to the church hierarchy, are suggested as likely suspects ("whatever their present-day duties, membership was a closely guarded secret").[28]

In the fiction of Cleo Jones, also self-advertised as the work of "an ex-Mormon," the situation is equally horrific. In addition to deranged fanatics, totalitarian church government, intrusive surveillance, and pervasive polygamy, we find a cover-up of church involvement in Watergate, the Bay of Pigs, and President Kennedy's assassination.[29] To top it off,

Mormons have "five times the child murder rate!" and rampant child abuse ("Her stomach was all puffed up and yellow and trembling").[30] For Jones, Mormon obsessiveness with sex reaches as far as their famous icon, which she calls "the great phallic tabernacle organ."[31]

So far, these novelists sound like hatemongers dredged up from the Jacksonian period, writing in the familiar paranoid style. But these modern caricatures of Mormonism have some surprising permutations. In the nineteenth century, difference, especially radical difference, carried with it its own taint of transgression. In contemporary representations, difference and evil are not at all synonymous; homogeneity, not difference, is devalued. Also, given Mormonism's movement toward the political mainstream, the mechanically employed old stereotypes ring jarringly false. Novels like Irvine's and Jones's are riddled with traces of this dissonance. Thus, we have Traveler's flash of insight: "For the first time, he truly understood…why Mormons still swore temple oaths against the federal government."[32] But the old depictions of political disloyalty and subversion so effective against nineteenth-century Catholics and Mormons collide with the image of a Mormon people that Irvine has already characterized as patriotic to a fault. The Mormons, he reminds us in every one of his novels, have taken over the once Catholic-dominated FBI. Jones is at pains to point out that Brigham Young University is the third-largest supplier of army officers,[33] and in one of her novels a recent prophet was dismissed as that "John Birch Society President."[34] These writers could not have foreseen that their dated depictions would keep the old stereotypes fresh enough to be readily invoked against a Mormon presidential candidate in 2008 and 2012.

Even more revealingly, both Jones and Irvine run into difficulties when they revive the single most ubiquitous charge against Mormonism. Both are fond of depicting polygamy in the traditional way—a thinly veiled "justification for [Mormon] lust."[35] Mormon villainy in another of Irvine's novels (*Called Home*) takes the form of a conspiracy between two men to drug and systematically rape virtually every woman in an entire community. But when it comes to explaining the causes of Mormon depravity, Irvine and Jones fall into similar contradiction. Rigidly conservative notions about sexual morality turn out to be the root of the problem. Thus in Irvine's *Angel's Share*, we have the case of Heber Armstrong, the head Mormon apostle's son who thinks he is the reincarnation of Jack the Ripper. He hunts down and sexually mutilates his young victims. The trigger for his insanity is discovered by the non-Mormon detective: "It's all my fault," confesses the fiancée of the murderer's friend. "I wouldn't sleep with Heber before he left for England.…But I now see that I was wrong."[36] Sexual deprivation makes Heber and his companion easy prey to a prostitute seductress, and the ensuing guilt drives one to celibacy and the other to madness.

In *Prophet Motive* ("Murder and Mystery—*Mormon Style*," the dust jacket proclaims), Cleo Jones depicts another deranged Mormon missionary, apparently pushed over the brink by strict sexual standards and resultant sexual paranoia. The "gentile" chief of police listens sympathetically to the lunatic's ravings: "I remember those missionary days when you weren't allowed to think of women."[37] By contrast, this same healthy, neurosis-free non-Mormon knows enough to get out of a sexually repressed relationship. He leaves his Mormon wife because "you can sure get tired of being on top of a praying woman."[38] Mormon polygamy, then, is the institutionalization of unbridled lust, while at the same time the church is equated with the institutionalization of repressed sexuality. So it is sometimes hard to tell if it is Mormon inspired lust or repression that ruins marriages, unhinges missionaries, and creates serial killers.

Most telling of all is Jones's explicit assessment of Mormonism's corruptive power. Her hero finally confronts the crazed killer (not the deranged missionary, but a bishop's wife who has, with fairly transparent symbolism, murdered her husband and concealed his body in a Mormon food storage bin): "This is the true face of evil, I thought. But I knew immediately that that wasn't true either—that she was just a pudgy housewife before the high shelves of canned raspberries that told of her valiant effort to do right and strive for perfection."[39] This book is marketed as an examination of "the extremes to which guilt and the quest for purity can drive ordinary people."[40] And there we have the irony of such contemporary caricatures. If such people are meant to be taken as "ordinary," then obviously it is the norm itself that is in need of a vigorous reexamination. And that is precisely the point. In the nineteenth century, any transgression of the sexual morality inherited from the Puritans was unquestionably evil. The depiction of Mormons as sexually voracious carries little or none of the original moral taint in an era that has made homophobia rather than homosexuality the suspect category, and replaced the stigma of sexually transmitted disease and of single motherhood with the stigma of rigid moralizing. In 2012, a national political candidate could even try to win points by contrasting his "more normal" serial adultery with the committed monogamy of a Mormon rival "who wanders around seeming perfect."[41]

More enterprising in his Mormon caricature is the science fiction novelist L. E. Modesitt Jr. He manages to update nineteenth-century precursors without dissonance, by the simple expedient of recasting the "Oriental" label in a way that plays upon contemporary Islamophobia. In this future universe, Mormon "Deseretists" merge with neo-Muslim "Mahmetists" to threaten galactic peace. They follow a fanatical prophet, read the Book of Toren, take up to six wives, and, in a terraforming version of Utah settlement, aspire to "make that island bloom" as a rose.[42]

The persistence of the Mormon stereotype shows the tenacity of literary paternity, but (apart from Modesitt's version) the contradictions entailed in modern treatments reveal a simple truth about caricature. The malleable features of any caricature must be reconfigured as value systems change, if they are to elicit the same derision as the original formulations. Irvine and Jones are clear examples of caricature caught in anachronism. A funny hat and unorthodox living arrangements no longer a villain make. But, as the two authors also suggest, albeit in a confused fashion, the wrong kind of conformity may. And thus a new paradigm of caricature is now possible, in which too much, rather than too little, accommodation becomes a negative value. The basis of Mormon caricature thus undergoes a 180-degree reversal.

It was once a simple matter to assume a norm for American culture and situate the Mormon well outside it. But today, the Mormon businessman has not only been assimilated into American society, but has *become* American society—"American to the core," in Harold Bloom's words. "It is weirdly true," he continues, "in 1991, that the Mormons are as mainstream as you are, whoever you are."[43] To borrow from Jones herself again, "BYU is the third largest supplier of army officers. Mormons were Howard Hughes's right-hand men. And so on."[44] The stereotypical Mormon is successful, Anglo-Saxon, middle-class, suburban, in a traditional family with one working parent and a stay-at-home mother and five children. If Tom Clancy wants a shorthand way of creating a young, clean-cut, patriotic guy-next-door, he may simply make him LDS, like *Hunt for Red October*'s Randall Tait. (The fact that the Russians consider him "a religious fanatic"[45] is presumably to his credit.) Similarly, Clancy's hero in *Clear and Present Danger* says that Mormons are "honest and hardworking, and fiercely loyal to their country, because they believed in what America stood for."[46] Once the target of a federal expeditionary force under President Buchanan, charged with rebellion and sedition, the Mormons are now seen as the embodiment of public-spiritedness and "traditional values." In film, the reversal is captured perfectly by the Coen brothers in their quirky comedy *Raising Arizona* (1987). The movie ends with Nicolas Cage's vivid dream of domestic bliss in a utopian place "where all parents are strong and wise and capable and all children are happy and beloved." It has all the earmarks of heaven. But then again, he concludes, "maybe it was Utah."

The meaning of this new role, however, is especially dubious in today's intellectual and political climate (not to mention in a world that now has more Mormons in foreign countries than in America[47]). It is now because Mormons occupy what used to be the center that they fall into contempt. Their embrace of ultraconservative values, not their flagrant rejection, is now construed as the source of Mormon perfidy. For, since Vietnam at least, employment in covert activities can suggest criminality as readily as it can be read by others as loyalty (as the case of Oliver North demonstrated). The nuclear family seems a distant relic, as Murphy Brown and the Gilmore Girls replace Ozzie and Harriet and the Waltons. Then *Modern Family*, with its gay white adoptive parents of an Asian baby and a cross-cultural second marriage, celebrates the definitive end of hegemonic family models.[48] Multiculturalism rather than melting pot is now the ruling paradigm. The repercussions of these developments for the Mormons were suggested as early as a 1971 *Ramparts* article by Frances Lang that faulted the church for providing the FBI and CIA with a steady supply of reliably conservative defenders of capitalist interests.[49] In his novel *The Russia House*, John le Carré captures the irony, the simultaneous gain and loss, of Mormonism's new place in American society. Two agents sent by the CIA to assist in a British operation are described as faceless twins, "Americans, so slight, so trim, so characterless," whose "Mormon cleanliness I found slightly revolting."[50]

More recently, *Angels in America*, Tony Kushner's Pulitzer and Tony award-winning "gay phantasia," reprises nineteenth-century anti-Mormonism, but from the opposite end of the political spectrum. The culprit in this case is not sexual deviance but rather its opposite: sanctimonious sexual piety. And its human icon is one "Joe Pitt, Utah Mormon"—and closet homosexual. As a Mormon, his wife, Harper Pitt, doesn't drink tea or coffee but is a Valium addict, reinforcing Kushner's personal vision of Mormonism as not just "horrible," but "disingenuous."[51] In the play, Mormonism's function as the embodiment of repressive conservatism is reinforced by scenes set in the Mormon Visitors Center, repeated references to Harper's religious affiliation, and depiction of the eponymous Angel as a parodic version of Mormonism's Angel Moroni.[52] Harper's decision at play's end to abandon Mormonism for the "heaven" of San Francisco suggests a twofold hope, for America's cultural future and Mormonism's oppressed victims. One scholar has noted that in spite of its Mormon angels, characters, setting, and history, of almost four hundred reviews of this celebrated play, the vast majority fail to mention the religious component.[53] This may be a reflection of the unsettling moral dissonance at the play's core: religion is mercilessly caricatured to promote "acceptance, not just tolerance, [as] the only legitimate principle guiding human behavior."[54]

A flurry of books and articles on "white male paranoia," along with Hollywood films that exploited that fear of diminishing hegemony, like Joel Schumacher's *Falling Down*, starring Michael Douglas, and the 1993 Whitney Biennial Exhibition, which "showcased gay, female and nonwhite artists who, as associate curator Thelma Golden wrote in the catalog, 'work consciously to deconstruct and de-center the politically constructed site of whiteness,'"[55]—these were a few late twentieth-century indices of the changeable value associated with status as "mainstream." Mormonism had seemingly effaced all traces of otherness, only to find the model of "Americanism" it appears to have embraced fast becoming the new anti-hero of the Great American Saga. We have reached a point in contemporary culture where the politics of the periphery have devalued the center. Indeed, in the politics of marginalization and collective guilt as they operate today, status as an oppressed group is not without its political advantages.[56] The furious storm of opposition to E. D. Hirsch's 1988 "Cultural Literacy" project, in which he attempted to establish a baseline for a common national culture, like the desperation and rejection of Pat Buchanan's 1992 Republican convention speech in which a beleaguered, fading majority sought to consolidate its stewardship of cultural values, suggests that the word "mainstream" had by the century's turn become almost as obsolete as it was already becoming opprobrious, though the culture wars continue unabated into the new millennium.

In this climate where the center seems to be fading and the margins are imbued with new vitality and worth, difference acquires new value. If we return to John Russell's account of Mormonism, we see that he framed his plot within an explicitly rendered set of values. Russell, torn between hostility and toleration, showed signs of this tension when he peppered his critique of Mormonism with repeated references to "our institutions," and to the themes of American toleration and pluralism. Yet toleration can only be demonstrated in the face of acutely felt difference: "the Jew, the Mahometan, the Pagan, and even...the *Atheist*" are its beneficiaries.[57] In order to lay claim to such tolerance, in other words, one must first define the Other as sufficiently different or threatening to make tolerance necessary. The precondition for one's claim to this American virtue is therefore the identification of an unorthodoxy situated outside it. Therefore, it is necessary to exaggerate difference, to demonize the Other, and to the same degree valorize one's tolerance as generous enough to embrace even such difference. This is the root of the tension characteristic of nineteenth-century literature of the hostile imagination that does not entirely succumb to the paranoid style, caught between xenophobia and the need for self-presentation as a tolerant, law-respecting American.

As diversity becomes more valued than conformity, the ideological investment in exaggerating difference becomes even more important than it was for Russell. This shifting paradigm is clearly illustrated in the case of a *Picket Fences* television episode in which Mormonism featured prominently. A young girl is observed engaging in an apparently incestuous liaison with her father.[58] The case is prosecuted over the girl's objections, and in a startling courtroom revelation we learn that what appeared to be incest is actually clandestine polygamy. Sexual aberration, of course, is still the issue. As one horror is substituted for another, the dramatic interest is heightened by the fictive transgression of not one but two societal taboos. With shock and repugnance at an appropriately high level, the ensuing courtroom scene plumbs the complexities of this conflict of religious conscience and law. There appears to be no victim; any constraints on loving, sexual relationships are made to appear outdated and hypocritical; and the viewer is challenged to reconsider this sympathetically portrayed "difference."

Two Mormon-affiliated stations, in Utah and Washington State, pulled the series in protest, even though the writers had incorporated a disclaimer that made clear the Mormon church no longer officially sanctions polygamy. So the piece could not be accused of misrepresenting the church, and the Mormons were in fact fairly likable characters; what was the problem? The point, of course, is not merely that juxtaposing Mormonism and polygamy has a power of association that no disclaimer can really temper. Neither is the show's thematizing of perverse deviance exactly subtle. Concurrently running subplots include a case of psychic twins who enjoy vicarious orgasms and a religious cult that engages in the theft and ritual sacrifice of domestic animals. More seriously, the network, like Russell, was clearly engaged in the use of deviance as a mirror in which the viewer's tolerance and generosity of spirit may be reflected—or at least interrogated. The outrageousness of the transgression becomes the measure of the liberalism of spirit that can accommodate it. Difference has not been embraced—it has been prostituted to the parading of pluralism.

The same logic was again at work in the series *Big Love*, demonstrating that prurience sells as well in the twenty-first as in the nineteenth century, even if it is now marketed under the banner of intriguing diversity rather than moral indignation. The blockbuster drama of a modern family with a twist—three wives for one husband—ran for five years (2006–2011). As with the *Picket Fences* episode, a good deal of disingenuousness was in evidence. HBO attached a disclaimer, acknowledging that the Mormon church had banned polygamy in the nineteenth century. But by situating the series in Salt Lake City, Mormonism's Vatican City, making the lead character and polygamist a Utah state senator, and depicting one of the sons as sexually attracted to his plural mother, HBO successfully equates polygamy with both modern Mormonism and sexual perversity. Plenty of murder, statutory rape, mental illness, and psychopathology helps round out the picture of this portrait of Mormon—but not really Mormon—culture. Beneath the trendy veil of appreciative diversity and difference lurk the familiar nineteenth-century slurs.

An appeal to diversity and tolerance generally requires an object of condescension if not contempt, and will create one where it does not find one. Consider a late twentieth-century study titled *Foundations of Religious Tolerance*. In the context of urging forbearance toward beliefs—and believers—we find especially repugnant, the author draws the following comparison: "We can trust Aristotle when he tells us that he loves truth and wisdom and is prepared to devote his life to them. But what about these young Mormons…who come proselytizing? We should be patient and rational in dealing with these…self-professed defender[s] of truth."[59] In other words, Mormons again serve, both rhetorically and ideologically, to affirm a value system predicated upon one's own ability to indulge even the most distasteful manifestations of difference.

THE MORMON COMPROMISE

One more major shift was in store for America's engagement with Mormonism, exemplified by two developments in the twenty-first century's second decade. Both developments served to illustrate the fraying of a century-old compromise, a tenuous accommodation that Mormonism and America reached in 1893. By that year, the church had done its utmost to qualify for full membership in the American polity. It had decreed an end to polygamy, abandoned its own political party, and was preparing for what would be the seventh and, finally, successful try for statehood.

Mormonism's participation in the 1893 World's Columbian Exposition, held in Chicago, served as a barometer of shifting American sentiments toward the faith. At the choral competition held on September 8, the Mormon Tabernacle Choir dazzled audience and judges alike, winning the silver medal. Greeted with rapturous acclaim, the choir had overnight become America's sweethearts. They were invited to provide patriotic music for the placement of the Liberty Bell at the Chicago Exposition. Their farewell concert was standing room only, journalists raved about the new singing sensation, and concert promoters lobbied the choir to tour the East. Suddenly, Mormons were not just legitimate—they were popular. And then, a funny thing happened on the way to the festivities. In conjunction with the great Columbian Exposition, organizers had planned a World's Parliament of Religion for September 11–22, 1893, to "promote and deepen the spirit of human brotherhood among religious men of diverse faiths." Over three thousand invitations had been sent worldwide, to bring together representatives of every world faith and Christian denomination in a momentous gesture of interfaith respect and dialogue. Many faiths were underrepresented—but only one group was deliberately and conspicuously left out altogether. And that was, not unpredictably, the Mormons. So even while the choir was singing its way into history and America's heart, the church was emphatically denied a voice in the nation's first attempt at a comprehensive interfaith dialogue. What seemed like a contradiction was actually a compromise, as has become clear in subsequent years.[60]

In the century since the Chicago fair, Mormons have been lauded for their many achievements. They are largely respected as good, decent, family-centered people, who are welcome to sing at presidential inaugurations (five times), provide a steady stream of recruits to the National Football League (Ty Detmer, Marc Wilson, and Steve Young, among others), as well as a basketball National Player of the Year (Jimmer Fredette), dance with the stars (*Time* lauded them as the "dancingest denomination"[61]— fifty years *before* they dominated reality dance shows), and gave the world David Archuleta on *American Idol*. In exchange, everyone agrees to downplay the theological side of the church. Charles Dickens's words still guide public discourse on the religion: "What the Mormons do, seems to be excellent; what they say, is mostly nonsense."[62]

This position was most emphatically exemplified in the phenomenally popular 2011 Broadway hit *The Book of Mormon*. This raucous and raunchy musical follows the exploits of two missionaries, the clueless Elder Cunningham and his supercilious mentor Elder Price, as their insular and naive backgrounds prove comically inadequate to the appalling realities of rural Uganda, with its brutal warlords, AIDS epidemic, famine, and poverty. Mormon reactions to the production were often confused and uncertain; some agreed with the critics who insisted the treatment was affectionate, even sweet, while other Mormons felt themselves again an object of mockery and scorn. They can be forgiven for their confusion, because the musical reenacts in dramatic form the complexities of the Chicago compromise. As J. B. Haws has noted, "what *The God Makers* had portrayed as sinister and ominous three decades earlier came across (like so many other religious beliefs over the years at the hands of [Matt] Stone and [Trey] Parker) as eccentric and laughable, but also, in this case, somehow innocent."[63] The musical equates Mormon theology with the most esoteric outliers of mainstream Mormonism: planets named Kolob, earning personal planets, and a Missouri Garden of Eden. And those beliefs, like Mormon doctrine in general, are not threatening because they are so ridiculously irrelevant to real world needs they don't *need* to be taken seriously. It was this key message church spokesman Michael Otterson correctly distilled from the play's reviews: "the idea that religion moves along oblivious to real-world problems in a kind of blissful naiveté."[64]

But like the judges who awarded the silver medal in Chicago to the Tabernacle Choir of a (discredited) faith tradition, the writers and their critics felt safe in bestowing plaudits upon Mormonism for *non*-faith-related attributes. As Haws noted,

> the credulity of the characters in *The Book of Mormon* did not feel threatening or dangerous, even if it did imply a Pollyanna sort of gullibility—and this because what was also inescapable was that the Mormon characters in *The Book of Mormon*, unlike the characters in so many other dramatic presentations of that faith, remained true to their beliefs in the face of increasing odds.... That persistence, even if ridiculously utopian (as in the song 'Sal Tlay Ka Siti' [Salt Lake City]), came across as determinedly genuine and even admirable.[65]

Whether naiveté or persistence won the day, it is clear that Mormon beliefs are made safe through caricature and ridicule. Any good the Mormons do, by implication, is in spite of their founding belief system. As at the Columbian Exposition, leaving behind their mythologies would seem to be the price Mormons must pay for admission to respectability and full participation in the larger world.

The tenuous compromise achieved in Chicago came flying apart when a Mormon threatened to bring his Mormonism, beliefs and all, to the highest office in the land.[66] As Mitt Romney appeared poised to capture the Republican nomination for president in 2008 and won the nomination in 2012, the rhetoric escalated to the point of mirroring the anti-Catholic paranoia of the nineteenth century. It may be true, as one scholar has noted, that the escalation results in part from the simple fact that Americans view individual Mormons one way, and institutional Mormonism another.[67] And a presidential candidate is more symbolic of the institution than is the Mormon living next door. But that no more makes the animus nonreligious than liking blacks in the particular but fearing them in the collective makes that animus nonracial. Assaults on a collectivity like an "institution" often *seem* less sinister because they seem less personal. But that does not mean the underlying motivations or causes are innocuous.

From the days of the Mormon Tabernacle Choir triumph, except for a small hiccup over the seating of Mormon senator Reed Smoot, elected in 1903,[68] Mormonism had moved in the direction of increasing harmony with American society. A Mormon, Harry Reid, became U.S. Senate majority leader in 2007, and four years earlier Mitt Romney had even been elected governor of a state far removed from the Mormon culture region. This is why the religious component to Romney's defeat in the 2008 Republican nominating contest came as such a shock to Mormon leadership and laity alike. The new direction twenty-first-century anti-Mormonism would take was signaled in 2006 by *Slate*'s Jacob Weisberg. Weisberg reversed a hundred years of strategy by making religion the explicit basis of his attack, shunning his predecessors' practice of reconstructing religious bias as ethnic, nativist, or ideological. "A Mormon President? No Way," his subtitle unabashedly proclaimed. Voters would be justified, he admonished, in dismissing as a candidate "someone who truly believed in the founding whoppers of Mormonism." To the obvious rejoinder that all religion is based in the supernatural, he could only weakly reply that the old faiths have had time to "turn their myths into metaphor." The fact that, contrary to his fantasy, none of the mainline churches have discarded "whoppers" like Christ's virgin birth and Resurrection, makes his singling out of Mormons look very much like the bigotry he weakly denies.[69]

What followed in the wake of Weisberg's piece was a feeding frenzy—renewed in 2011–2012—involving conflicted evangelicals, indignant Catholics, jubilant secularists, debating pundits, and stunned Mormons. Reminding us that heresy is more threatening than disbelief, prominent evangelicals publicly resorted to the pejorative "cult" word, and expressed fears that a Mormon presidency would legitimize the religion, even though Romney's positions aligned with evangelical views on virtually every political and moral question of the day.[70] Prominent Catholic intellectual Richard John Neuhaus, who himself doubted Mormonism's Christian status, but was perhaps mindful of Kennedy's campaign, criticized those who would "use religion to oppose a candidate for the presidency."[71] But the barrage only gathered momentum, as attackers resorted to language that could have come straight from nineteenth-century anti-Catholic Charlotte Tonna. Francis Boyle, a former Harvard law professor, asked with alarm if the American people wanted a president "taking orders from the Mormon pope and his college of cardinals... from Salt Lake Vatican City?"[72] Not to be outdone, author Jane Barnes, echoing the brazen bigotry of a Samuel

Morse, warned of Mormonism's "dark side," asking in the *New York Times*, which seemed to have proclaimed open season on Mormonism, "What if the church illegally used its money and influence to defeat Roe v. Wade or to pass the Federal Marriage Amendment while Romney was president?"[73] Such implications of criminality, dark designs, and governmental subversion went well beyond any antireligious vituperation that had been tolerated in the mainstream media for generations. It seemed but a step away from calling for the pogroms that accompanied nineteenth-century anti-Catholic hysteria. The paper's columnist Maureen Dowd joined in, applauding Bill Maher for having the courage, while others were "gingerly tiptoeing around," to dismiss Mormonism as "more ridiculous than any other religion."[74] Meanwhile, the conservative Jewish magazine *Commentary* decried anti-Mormonism as the "last socially acceptable hate" and noted that Dowd had gotten away with a level of religious invective that would never be tolerated against Jews or Muslims.[75] But the rhetorical Rubicon had been passed weeks earlier, when the most inflammatory charges imaginable had already been publicly aired. "An indoctrinated Mormon should never be elected as president of the United States of America," a guest told CNN. They have "experienced years of brainwashing." Then perhaps sensing the brainwashing charge was not spectacular enough, she quoted another source who alleged the Mormons were employing "the ritualized sexual abuse of children to ensure conformity" and "to subjugate the children involved and brainwash them into a satanic mindset."[76]

The openness and unabashed bigotry of these attacks suggest the possibility that the American taboo on religious intolerance may be eroding, and the clever manipulations of the past no longer necessary. Religious intolerance in the New World is as old as its earliest colonization, but a Jeffersonian ethic of religious toleration largely won out over open displays of bigotry and violence against religious minorities. As this survey of more than a century of popular fiction suggests, those undercurrents that remained were frequently hidden behind representational strategies that concealed the true nature of the animus. In the case of Catholics and Mormons, writers accomplished this feat by emphasizing—or constructing—an ethnicity that was at odds with American identity. Easier to attack Irish immigrants for covertly subverting American democratic ideals, or Mormon "Attilas" for their threat to womanhood and republican values, than either Catholicism or Mormonism as a system of religious belief.

In contemporary American politics, it is not only Jeffersonian tolerance but the Constitution's prohibition of a religious test that is invoked as a bulwark against lurking anti-Mormonism. But those bulwarks may be crumbling. William Clifford famously argued in 1877 that the decision to believe a religious proposition was fraught with moral implications (of a decidedly negative cast, in his view). The New Atheists (Sam Harris, Christopher Hitchens, Richard Dawkins, et al.) have extended that critique to argue that religious beliefs do not deserve the respect or room they have traditionally been accorded in the public sphere. In regard to the controversy over his own Catholicism, John F. Kennedy explicitly protested the imposition of "a religious test—even by indirection."[77] Damon Linker now suggests a radically new approach to this question. Scorning the strategies we have reviewed in this study, whereby religion is reconfigured to be condemned in another guise, he challenges the special protections traditionally afforded religious belief. "The constitutional right of every qualified citizen to run for office is not the same as saying that a candidate's religious views should be a matter of indifference."[78] And Linker finds in Mormonism his most compelling evidence for why we should reinterpret how we view—and implement—the constitutional prohibition of a religious test.

> Christianity in both the Catholic and Protestant traditions holds that direct revelation ended many centuries ago...but Mormonism is unique in the emphasis it places on prophetic utterances. Not only was the religion founded by a self-proclaimed prophet...but the man who holds the office of the president of the LDS Church is also considered to be a prophet—"the mouthpiece of God on Earth."[79]

Linker's argument is but a politicized version of the point raised a few years earlier by the best-selling book on Mormonism of the early twenty-first century, Jon Krakauer's sensationalistic exposé *Under the Banner of Heaven.*[80] Krakauer repeats the winning formula of nineteenth-century sensation novels, with only slightly more historical accuracy than his early counterparts. He brings journalistic flair to his account of Mormons, violence, and polygamy, linking a pair of deluded modern murderers with a skewed depiction of Mormonism's past and present. In 1984, two brothers belonging to a modern fundamentalist offshoot of early Mormonism brutally killed their brother's wife, Brenda Lafferty, and her infant daughter. Never mind that the murderers never had any connection to the Mormon church itself. Krakauer tells us that to understand how the ostensibly nice religion that produced Donny and Marie Osmond could also produce the perpetrators of brutal murder, we need to take a "clear-eyed journey into Mormonism's violent past." In court, one of these perpetrators, Ron Lafferty, had told a surprised judge that a homosexual angel was trying to invade his body through his rectum, hence the sign he wore on his posterior saying "exit only." But to understand this man, evaluated as a paranoid schizophrenic with "frontal lobe syndrome,"[81] Krakauer thinks we need to go deep into "this history of an American religion practiced by millions"?

He describes his project as an investigation into "the roots of brutality" and "the nature of faith." But the real lesson of religious history, he believes, is that the former is never further removed from us than the latter. "If Ron Lafferty were deemed mentally ill because he obeyed the voice of God," he queries, "isn't everyone who believes in God and seeks guidance through prayer mentally ill as well?"[82] The absurdity of the question reveals an astonishing simple-mindedness about very complex issues. Negotiating the right balance between the sanctity of conscience and public order has never been easy, except under the Inquisition and totalitarian despots. The Laffertys were not the first murderers to hear voices, and they won't be the last. Were the English who burned Joan of Arc at the stake just forward-thinking jurists? Should every Son of Sam provoke us to inquire into the sinister potential of Judeo-Christian religion?

For Krakauer, as for Linker, the safest version of religion would be the one that moves furthest away from Abrahamic foundations in the faith-filled response to a prophetic voice. The greatest surprise of all, in the early twenty-first century's engagement with Mormonism, is that the alarm raised by a concerned nineteenth-century Christian may prove prescient. John Russell, we saw, feared that attackers of Mormonism were implicitly, and perhaps deliberately, really attacking the foundations of Christianity itself. "The secret enemies of the Christian religion…were loud against the Mormons. In assailing their claims to working miracles and other professions, they leveled many a blow, safely, that bore equally hard upon the miracles of Scriptures."[83] In 2011, political satirist Stephen Colbert illustrated precisely how attacks on Mormonism can effect substantial collateral damage. Colbert mocked Mormons for claiming that "Joseph Smith received golden plates from an angel on a hill." Then he added with devastating sarcasm: "Everybody knows that Moses got stone tablets from a burning bush on a mountain."[84]

It would be ironic if Mormonism prompts a decisive step in the application of a religious test to participation in American politics not because it has moved so far from the mainstream that it shatters the limits of tolerance—but because it returns in so blatant a fashion to the mystery at the heart of all religious experience.

NOTES

INTRODUCTION

1. Artemus Ward, "A Mormon Romance: Reginald Gloverson," in *Artemus Ward: His Travels* (New York: Carleton, 1865), 84.
2. Edward Said, *The World, the Text, and the Critic* (Cambridge, Mass.: Harvard University Press, 1983), 12.
3. The most authoritative statistical analyses of plural marriage suggest that the percentage of Mormons in polygamous families fluctuated between about 25 percent and 45 percent between 1850 and 1880, declining sharply thereafter. See Kathryn M. Daynes, *More Wives Than One: Transformation of the Mormon Marriage System, 1840–1910* (Urbana: University of Chicago Press, 2001), 98–102.
4. Leonard J. Arrington and Jon Haupt, "The Missouri and Illinois Mormons in Ante-Bellum Fiction," *Dialogue: A Journal of Mormon Thought* 5.1 (Spring 1970): 37. No full-length treatment of the Mormon in fiction has been published. Several studies have contributed to both a bibliography of Mormon caricature and a summary of salient themes and character types. One of the first was the useful overview by Neil Lambert, "Saints, Sinners, and Scribes: A Look at Mormons in Fiction," *Utah Historical Quarterly* 36 (Winter 1968): 63–76. The same year, Arrington and Haupt published their study of four early anti-Mormon novels, "Intolerable Zion: The Image of Mormonism in Nineteenth-Century American Literature," *Western Humanities Review* 22 (Summer 1968): 243–60. The next year, they surveyed seven novels in the above-mentioned "Missouri and Illinois Mormons." Finally, Arrington returned to the theme with Rebecca Cornwall Foster in their article "Perpetuation of a Myth: Mormon Danites in Five Western Novels, 1840–90," *BYU Studies* 23.2 (Spring 1983): 147–65.
5. Dean L. May is paraphrasing Thomas O'Dea's claim. May, "Mormons," *Harvard Encyclopedia of American Ethnic Groups*, ed. Stephan Thernstrom (Cambridge, Mass.: Harvard University Press, 1980), 720. As early as 1954, O'Dea refers to the Mormons as a "near nation," an "incipient nationality," a "subculture with its own peculiar conceptions and values," and "a people." See "Mormonism and the Avoidance of Sectarian Stagnation: A Study of Church, Sect, and Incipient Nationality," *American Journal of Sociology* 60.3 (November 1954): 285–93. Later, he would say "the Mormon group *came closer* to evolving an ethnic identity on this continent than did any other comparable group" (my emphasis). O'Dea, *The Mormons* (Chicago: University of Chicago Press, 1957), 116.
6. Mauss's reference to Mormonism as a "subculture" appears to be common practice among sociologists. See his "Sociological Perspectives on the Mormon

Subculture," *Annual Review of Sociology* 10 (1984): 437–60. Mauss is, however, highly critical of endowing Mormonism with ethnic status: "If Mormons … can comprise an ethnic group, then who, one wonders, cannot?" At the same time, he is clear in imputing to Mormons "the self-interested *uses* of such terms." He also acknowledges that an "emergent ethnicity" may well be an accurate description of nineteenth-century Mormonism, which is the period of focus in this study. Jan Shipps, Mauss indicates, "has also revealed a tendency to continue thinking of even contemporary Mormons in ethnic terms." See Mauss, *The Angel and the Beehive: The Mormon Struggle with Assimilation* (Urbana: University of Illinois Press, 1994), 64–66 and 74n.

7. Joel Kotkin, *Tribes: How Race, Religion and Identity Determine Success in the New Global Economy* (New York: Random House, 1993), 246–49.

8. Harold Bloom, *The American Religion: The Emergence of the Post-Christian Nation* (New York: Simon & Schuster, 1992), 83. Martin Marty prefers the designation of Mormons as "a people," but has suggested that "ethnicity" may be appropriate as well. See Marty, "It Finally All Depends on God," *Sunstone* 11.2 (March 1987): 46.

9. Contrast this transformation of religion into quasi-ethnicity with Gerson Cohen's view of Jewishness. According to him, one of the legacies of Talmudic culture was that it "broke down forever the ethnic barriers to membership within the Jewish group. Conversion to the faith, submission to the yoke of the Torah—these were the keys to chosenness. For the first time in history a people nullified its ethnic status and reconstituted itself as a church." Cohen, "The Talmudic Age," in *Great Ages and Ideas of the Jewish People*, ed. Leo W. Schwarz (New York: Random House, 1956), 185.

10. "When the KGB Penetrated the FBI," *U.S. News and World Report*, October 15, 1984, 17.

11. Matthew Cooper, "The Bill-and-Newt Gurus," *U.S. News and World Report*, January 23, 1995, 19.

12. Scott Heller, "Getting It Right: Historian Shepherds Her 'Midwife's Tale' through Filming," *Chronicle of Higher Education*, January 13, 1995, A7.

CHAPTER 1

1. *Times and Seasons* 5.21 (November 15, 1844): 707.

2. Jan Shipps, *Mormonism: The Story of a New Religious Tradition* (Urbana: University of Illinois Press, 1985), 4.

3. Lewis Hanke was a pioneer in this area, writing in 1959 on how "conveniently applicable to the Indians" colonizers found Aristotle's theory of natural slavery. See his *Aristotle and the American Indians: A Study in Race and Prejudice in the Modern World* (Chicago: Henry Regnery, 1959), 11. Since then, an extensive body of work in the field of cultural studies and postcolonialism has explored how the discourses of colonialism construct an Other and through such construction a self as well. Important works include Peter Hulme's *Colonial Encounters: Europe and the Native Caribbean, 1492–1797* (New York: Methuen, 1986), Edward Said's *Orientalism* (New York: Pantheon, 1978), Mary Louise Pratt's *Imperial Eyes: Travel Writing and Transculturation* (New York: Routledge, 1992), and Stephen Greenblatt's *New World Encounters* (Berkeley and Los Angeles: University of California Press, 1993).

4. Hulme, *Colonial Encounters*, 14.

5. Sidney Z. Ehler and John B. Morall, eds. and trans., *Church and State through the Centuries: A Collection of Historic Documents with Commentaries* (New York: Biblo and Tannen, 1967), 199–200.

6. As Said himself describes the power relations of colonial discourse, "There is very little consent to be found...in the fact that Flaubert's encounter with an Egyptian courtesan produced a widely influential model of the Oriental woman." *Orientalism*, 6.
7. Pratt, *Imperial Eyes*, 7.
8. Cited by Dean L. May, "Mormons," in Thernstrom, *Harvard Encyclopedia of American Ethnic Groups*, 720. The tensions noted in Mormonism's unique status, and the literary representations they provoked, have been noted by Lydia Alix Fillingham. In her essay on Arthur Conan Doyle's *A Study in Scarlet*, she notes that "the liminal position of Mormonism means that their otherness always contains much sameness, that the horror directed against them would eventually be brought home." "'The Colorless Skein of Life': Threats to the Private Sphere in Conan Doyle's *A Study in Scarlet*," *English Literary History* 56.3 (1989): 674. I would have preferred to use the term "liminal" as well, to distinguish Mormonism's peculiar position from the merely marginal, had not Victor Turner endowed the term with other sociological significance.
9. R. Laurence Moore, for example, emphasizes Mormonism's situation as both marginal and typically American, though the deviance is, from his perspective, a cynical ruse on the Mormons' part. See "How to Become a People: The Mormon Scenario," in *Religious Outsiders and the Making of Americans* (New York: Oxford University Press, 1986), 25–47. For a slightly different take on the subject, see how Marvin S. Hill and James B. Allen trace the reversal of Mormon role from pariah to exemplum of American society in the 1940s and '50s, in Hill and Allen, eds., *Mormonism and American Culture* (New York: Harper & Row, 1972), 4–5.
10. Harold Bloom, *American Religion: The Emergence of the Post-Christian Nation* (New York: Simon & Schuster, 1992), 127. For the Tolstoy background see Leland A. Fetzer, "Tolstoy and Mormonism," *Dialogue: A Journal of Mormon Thought* 6.1 (Spring 1971): 13–29.
11. For a full-length treatment of this process of Utah's "Americanization" see Gustave O. Larson, *The "Americanization" of Utah for Statehood* (San Marino, Calif.: Huntington Library, 1971).
12. Thomas F. O'Dea and Janet O'Dea Aviad, *The Sociology of Religion*, 2nd ed. (Englewood Cliffs, N.J.: Prentice-Hall, 1983), 86.
13. Joel Kotkin, *Tribes: How Race, Religion and Identity Determine Success in the Global Economy* (New York: Random House, 1993), 4–5.
14. Gustave de Beaumont, "Religious Sects and Religious Freedom in America," in *Annals of America* (Chicago: Encyclopaedia Britannica, 1976), 6:151. (Originally an essay appended to *Marie ou l'esclavage aux États-Unis* [Paris, 1835], 2:183–225).
15. Michael Chevalier, *Society, Manners and Politics in the United States: Being a Series of Letters on North America*, trans. from 3rd Paris ed. (Boston: Weeks, Jordan, 1839; reprint, New York: Augustus Kelley, 1966), iii, 386.
16. Chevalier, *Society*, 390, 392.
17. Governor Daniel Dunklin, letter dated June 6, 1834, printed in *Missouri Intelligencer and Boon's Lick Advertiser* (July 5, 1834).
18. J. H. Beadle, "The Mormon Theocracy" (editorial), *Scribner's Monthly* 14.3 (July 1877): 391. Beadle's comments on intolerance of Mormons should not suggest for a moment that he was himself pained or genuinely bewildered about the situation. He had himself authored, in 1870, the inflammatory *Life in Utah; or, the Mysteries and Crimes of Mormonism, Being an Exposé of the Secret Rites and Ceremonies of the Latter-day Saints with a Full and Authentic History of Polygamy and the*

Mormon Sect from Its Origin to Its Present Time (Philadelphia: National Publishing Co., 1870). He was also a collaborator in the disaffected Mormon William A. Hickman's exposé, *Brigham Young's Destroying Angel: Being the Life, Confession, and Startling Disclosures of the Notorious Bill Hickman, the Danite Chief Himself* (Salt Lake City: Geo. A. Crofutt, 1872), and perhaps served as ghostwriter of Ann Eliza Young's *Wife No. 19, or, the Story of a Life in Bondage, Being a Complete Exposé of Mormonism....* (Hartford, Conn.: Dustin, Gilman and Co., 1875).

19. Beadle, "Mormon Theocracy," 392.
20. Sanford H. Cobb, *The Rise of Religious Liberty in America: A History* (1902; reprint, New York: Cooper Square, 1968), 2.
21. Cobb, *Rise of Religious Liberty*, 3.
22. [Morse, Samuel F. B.] "An American," Imminent Dangers to the Free Institutions of the United States through Foreign Immigration, and the Present State of the Naturalization Laws (New York: E. B. Clayton, 1835), 15–16.
23. Morse, *Imminent Dangers*, 26–28.

CHAPTER 2

1. Artemisia Foote, "Artemisia Sidnie Myers Foote's Experiences in the Persecuting of the Latter-day Saints in Missouri," undated typescript in LDSCA. The standard LDS account of the massacre is that of survivor Joseph Young, recounted in John P. Greene, *Facts Relative to the Expulsion of the Mormons or Latter Day Saints, from the State of Missouri, under the "Exterminating Order"* (Cincinnati. R. P. Brooks, 1839), 21–24.
2. Greene, *Facts Relative*, 26.
3. "I thank you for your suggestions with regard to writing a fuller sketch of my life for publication I have kept a journal of my life untill [sic] the present day in which I have recorded the most important events of my life, and the corespondence [sic] I have had...on the topics of Mormonism....As all these subjects are fully set forth and discussed in the Church works in book and pamphlet form...it would be superfluous for me to write them over again, for they are already written and published, better than I could do it." Warren Foote, *Autobiography of Warren Foote* (Mesa, Ariz.: Dale Arnold Foote, 1997), 3:152. Apparently, the "autobiography" is a three-volume condensation, in Foote's own hand, of journals he kept throughout his life.
4. Dean C. Jessee, ed., *The Papers of Joseph Smith*, vol. 1, *Autobiographical and Historical Writings* (Salt Lake City: Deseret, 1989), 269–70. Controversy exists over Smith's exact dating. No one doubts, however, that such an ambience characterizes some period or periods of his youth, since his area saw enough missionary activity to be named the "Burned-Over District." See Whitney R. Cross's classic study using that designation (Ithaca, N.Y.: Harper & Row, 1950).
5. Foote, *Autobiography*, 1:4. For a discussion of Mormonism in the context of contemporary seekerism see Dan Vogel, *Religious Seekers and the Advent of Mormonism* (Salt Lake City: Signature, 1988).
6. Jessee, *Papers*, 1:273.
7. Jessee, *Papers*, 1:277.
8. Daniel 2:34; Acts 3:21. Since Mormons have always used the King James Version of the Bible, citations are from that edition unless otherwise noted.
9. Book of Commandments (hereafter BC) 22:1, 4, 5, in *The Joseph Smith Papers: Revelations and Translations*, vol. 2, *Published Revelations*, ed. Robert Scott Jensen,

Richard E. Turley Jr., and Riley M. Lorimer (Salt Lake City: Church Historian's Press, 2011), 57.

10. Foote, *Autobiography*, 1:3–4.
11. Foote, *Autobiography*, 1:5.
12. BC 9:16 in *Revelations*, 39. The revelation was received in May 1829. Subsequent editions of the BC were published, with additional revelations, as the Doctrine and Covenants of the Church of Jesus Christ of Latter-day Saints (D&C). BC 9:16 is D&C 10:65 in the current version (Salt Lake City: Deseret, 1981).
13. Charles Dickens, "In the Name of the Prophet—Smith!" *Household Words*, July 19, 1851, 340.
14. BC 39:4 (D&C 37:3) and 43:37, 58 (D&C 45:43, 64) in *Revelations*, 92, 119, 121.
15. Parley P. Pratt, *Autobiography of Parley Parker Pratt*, 5th ed. (Salt Lake City: Deseret, 1961), 48.
16. Pratt, *Autobiography*, 48. Marvin S. Hill cites the *Journal History of the Church of Jesus Christ of Latter-day Saints* (Historical Department of the Church of Jesus Christ of Latter-day Saints) to the effect that by year's end, church membership in Ohio was 1,500. *Quest for Refuge: The Mormon Flight from American Pluralism* (Salt Lake City: Signature Books, 1989), 198.
17. BC 54.1 (D&C 52:2) and D&C 27:1 (D&C 57:1), in *Revelations*, 135, 464.
18. Foote, *Autobiography*, 1:7.
19. Foote, *Autobiography*, 1:7.
20. Foote, *Autobiography*, 1:8.
21. Foote, *Autobiography*, 1:8.
22. Foote, *Autobiography*, 1:28.
23. Foote, *Autobiography*, 1:28.
24. For details and additional sources see Stephen C. LeSueur, *The 1838 Mormon War in Missouri* (Columbia: University of Missouri Press, 1987).
25. The July speech was printed and distributed with Smith's blessing as a pamphlet and is reproduced in Peter Crawley, "Two Rare Missouri Documents," *BYU Studies* 14.4 (Summer 1974): 504.
26. Foote, *Autobiography*, 1:29.
27. *The Personal Writings of Joseph Smith*, ed. Dean C. Jessee (Salt Lake City: Deseret, 2002), 473.
28. Foote, *Autobiography*, 1:31.
29. Foote, *Autobiography*, 1:31.
30. Foote, *Autobiography*, 1:32.
31. Foote quotes a Missouri newspaper account of the "war" that gives the number of Mormons dead as fifty. No number is given for non-Mormons (1:42). Reliable figures on the Mormon persecutions are notoriously hard to come by.
32. Foote, *Autobiography*, 1:36.
33. For a discussion of the unique nature of the Nauvoo charter see James L. Kimball, "The Nauvoo Charter: A Reinterpretation," *Journal of the Illinois Historical Society* 64 (Spring 1971): 66–78.
34. *New York Herald*, June 17, 1842.
35. His candidacy was taken seriously by those who believed, as the *New York Herald* claimed, that since the Saints controlled the vote in Illinois, they controlled the West, and thus posed a threat to both candidates. See *Nauvoo Neighbor*, February 21, 1844, and Klaus J. Hansen, *Quest for Empire: The Political Kingdom of God and the Council of Fifty in Mormon History* (East Lansing: Michigan State University Press, 1967), 60–61.

36. In his study of the incident, a prominent legal scholar concludes that while certainly imprudent, the suppression of the press was not necessarily "entirely illegal." Dallin H. Oaks, "The Suppression of the *Nauvoo Expositor*," *Utah Law Review* 9 (Winter 1965): 862–903.

37. Merton L. Dillon, *Elijah P. Lovejoy, Abolitionist Editor* (Urbana: University of Illinois Press, 1964), 90, 161–77.

38. Oaks, "Suppression," 874.

39. Smith said, as he left Nauvoo, that he was going "like a lamb to the slaughter." *Times and Seasons* 5 (July 5, 1844): 585.

40. Foote, *Autobiography*, 1:73.

41. Foote, *Autobiography*, 1:74–75.

42. Richard L. Bushman, *Joseph Smith: Rough Stone Rolling* (New York: Knopf, 2005), 437.

43. Genuine free love communities (like Modern Times and Berlin Heights) were far more notorious than populous. But free love advocate Victoria Woodhull's run for president, the birth of the Free Love League, the Progressive Union, and other like-minded organizations, and a spate of celebrated trials of sexual reformers, all created an atmosphere in which any unconventional marital practice was likely to be seen as contributing to a headlong rush into societal decadence. Writing in 1841, for example, one D. R. Austin thought it "remarkable how these manias all tend to one point. Perfectionism, Unionism, and Mormonism, as they have been developed in this region, have all aimed directly at licentiousness. They feed and fatten upon one base passion." Letter to Rev. John A. Clark, in his *Gleanings by the Way* (Philadelphia: W. J. & J. K. Simon; New York: Robert Carter, 1842), 265. For a thorough treatment of free love communities see Taylor Stoehr, *Free Love in America: A Documentary History* (New York: AMS Press, 1979).

44. John C. Bennett, at one time Nauvoo's mayor and a close friend of Joseph Smith's, apparently used the prophet's teachings as a pretext for adultery. Excommunicated, he became an implacable enemy of the church, publishing in 1842 *The History of the Saints: Or an Exposé of Joe Smith and Mormonism.*

45. Foote, *Autobiography*, 1:82.

46. William Clayton, Diary, September 16, 1845. Cited in Hill, *Quest for Refuge*, 175.

47. *Warsaw Signal*, February 11, 1846.

48. Foote, *Autobiography*, 1:80.

49. Speaking in favor of the proposal, Parley P. Pratt "said that it would be the only chance for us to settle ourselves in that country peaceably. Our mails would then be caried [sic], and other public works done at the expence of the Government, and also the Government would be under obligation to protect us." The vote in John Taylor's camp took place July 12, 1846. Foote, *Autobiography*, 1:99.

50. Foote, *Autobiography*, 1:139.

51. Donald R. Moorman with Gene A. Sessions, *Camp Floyd and the Mormons: The Utah War* (Salt Lake City: University of Utah Press, 1992), 9. President Zachary Taylor's subsequent rejection of Utah's 1847 petition for statehood with the alleged remark "that Utah was the Sodom and Gomorrah of the West" does much to explain Mormon hostility toward Washington during this period (284). Regarding the Brocchus incident, the caustic explorer and Mormon observer Richard Burton felt the Mormons "behaved very well" in their restrained response to being "foully abused" at their own conference. See his *City of the Saints* (1861; ed. Fawn M. Brodie, New York: Knopf, 1963), 469–70.

52. Ray Allen Billington, *Westward Expansion* (New York: Macmillan, 1974), 466–67. See also Leonard J. Arrington and Davis Bitton, *The Mormon Experience* (New York: Random House, 1979), 164–65.

53. *New Orleans Courier*, April 3, 1857, quoted in Moorman, *Camp Floyd*, 12.

54. *Complete Discourses of Brigham Young*, 5 vols., ed. Richard S. Van Wagoner (Salt Lake City: Smith-Pettit Foundation, 2009), 2:982.

55. Foote, *Autobiography*, 1:147.

56. Such was the assessment of Brigham Young, at least: "Mr. Buchanan, with Messrs. Douglas, Cass, Thompson and others,...thought...by destroying or killing a hundred thousand innocent American citizens, to satisfy the pious, humane and patriotic feeling of their constituents, take the wind out of the sails of the Republicans and gain to themselves immortal honors" (*New York Times*, December 29, 1857, cited in Moorman, *Camp Floyd*, 15). This explanation has been offered by contemporary historians as well. Richard D. Poll, for example, asserts "there can be no doubt" that the Utah Expedition was undertaken "to clear the Democratic party of the charge that its political doctrines were contributing to Mormon delinquency." Poll, "The Mormon Question Enters National Politics, 1850–56," *Utah Historical Quarterly* 25 (1958): 131.

57. Moorman, *Camp Floyd*, 16.

58. This theory been used in a novelized account of the Utah War. See Leo Gordon and Richard Vetterli, *Powderkeg* (Novato, Calif.: Lyford, 1991).

59. Moorman, *Camp Floyd*, 28.

60. Foote, *Autobiography*, 1:150.

61. The Francher wagon train originated in Arkansas but was joined en route by a number of "Missouri Wildcats." This latter element apparently exacerbated local animosities by harassing settlers, vandalizing property, and taunting the Mormons. After they passed through Salt Lake, a number of Mormon settlements responded to their relentless provocations by refusing to sell them provisions, and tensions flared. Apprised of the looming crisis, Brigham Young on September 10 sent instructions to the Saints in the area not to meddle or interfere with the wagon train. The message arrived too late. On the morning of September 11, local militia, aided by a number of Paiutes, slaughtered most of the party. For the standard study of the Mountain Meadows massacre see Ronald W. Walker, Richard E. Turley, and Glen M. Leonard, *Massacre at Mountain Meadows* (New York: Oxford University Press, 2008).

62. Foote, *Autobiography*, 2:237.

CHAPTER 3

1. Thomas De Witt Talmage, "Were the Prayers for President Garfield a Failure?" *The Brooklyn Tabernacle, A Collection of 104 Sermons* (New York: Funk & Wagnalls, 1884), 37.

2. Paul Fussell, *Bad: Or, the Dumbing of America* (New York: Summit, 1991), 197.

3. The closest parallel to Governor Boggs's extermination/expulsion order may be the decree issued on October 25, 1862, by General Ulysses S. Grant. As "Commander of the Department of Tennessee," he ordered the expulsion of all Jews from the department within twenty-four hours. Unlike the Missouri edict, however, this order was never executed. It was repudiated by Washington and quickly withdrawn by Grant. See John A. Carpenter, *Ulysses S. Grant* (New York: Twayne, 1970), 29.

4. A sampling of standard accounts that address causes of friction with Mormons includes the following. For a general overview: Leonard J. Arrington and Davis Bitton, *The Mormon Experience: A History of the Latter-day Saints* (New York: Knopf,

1979) chapters 3–5 and 9, especially; for the early years: Richard L. Bushman, *Joseph Smith and the Beginnings of Mormonism* (Urbana: University of Illinois Press, 1984); for the Missouri years: Leland H. Gentry and Todd M. Compton, *Fire and Sword: A History of the Latter-day Saints in Northern Missouri, 1836–39* (Salt Lake City: Kofford, 2010) and Clark V. Johnson, ed., *Mormon Redress Petitions: Documents of the 1833–1838 Missouri Conflict* (Provo, Utah: Religious Studies Center, Brigham Young University, 1992); for the Nauvoo period: Annette P. Hampshire, *Mormonism in Conflict: The Nauvoo Years* (New York: Mellen Press, 1985); for the Utah period: Norman F. Furniss, *The Mormon Conflict, 1850–59* (New Haven, Conn.: Yale University Press, 1960); and for the American South: Patrick Mason, *The Mormon Menace: Violence and Anti-Mormonism in the Postbellum South* (New York: Oxford University Press, 2011).

5. Warren Foote, *Autobiography of Warren Foote* (Mesa, Ariz.: Dale Arnold Foote, 1997), 1:33. The relevant passage from General Clark's speech is probably as follows: "Oh! that I could…make you sufficiently intelligent to break that chain of superstition, and liberate you from those fetters of fanaticism with which you are bound—that you no longer worship a man." Clark did add, however, that "you have always been the aggressors" and have not been "subject to rule." The speech is recorded in *History of Caldwell and Livingston Counties, Missouri* (St. Louis National Historical Co., 1886). Cited in B. H. Roberts, *A Comprehensive History of the Church of Jesus Christ of Latter-day Saints* (Provo, Utah: Brigham Young University Press, 1965), 1.490–97.

6. Dean C. Jessee, ed., *The Papers of Joseph Smith*, vol. 1, *Autobiographical and Historical Writings* (Salt Lake City: Deseret, 1989), 273.

7. Roberts, *Comprehensive History*, 1:205.

8. BC 54:43 (D&C 52:42), in *Revelations*, 139.

9. "The Mormonites," *Religious Intelligencer*, September 7, 1833, 233.

10. "History of Joseph Smith," *Times and Seasons* 6.5 (March 15, 1845): 833.

11. Edward Strutt Abdy, *Journal of a Residence and Tour in the United States of North America, from April, 1833, to October, 1834* (London: Murray, 1835), 3:41.

12. Writing from his Missouri imprisonment during these conflicts, Pratt complained, "Do not the laws of Missouri provide abundantly for the removal from the state of all free negroes and mulattoes? (except certain privileged ones;) and also for the punishment of those who introduce or harbor them?" *History of the Late Persecution* (Detroit: Dawson and Bates, 1839), 10–11.

13. *Evening and Morning Star* 14 (June 1833): 109, 111.

14. Kenneth H. Winn, *Exiles in a Land of Liberty: Mormons in America, 1830–1846* (Chapel Hill: University of North Carolina Press, 1989), 89.

15. "History of Joseph Smith," *Times and Seasons* 6.5 (March 15, 1845): 833.

16. Orson F. Whitney, *Life of Heber C. Kimball* (Salt Lake City: Stevens and Wallace, 1945), 231.

17. "Letter to Isaac Galland," March 22, 1839, *The Personal Writings of Joseph Smith*, ed. Dean C. Jessee (Salt Lake City: Deseret, 2002), 456.

18. Johnson, *Mormon Redress Petitions*, xxxiv.

19. Johnson, *Mormon Redress Petitions*, 407.

20. Winn, *Exiles*, 89–90.

21. J. M. Peck, *A Gazetteer of Illinois* (Jacksonville, Ill.: Goudy, 1834), 92.

22. Gustave de Beaumont, "Religious Sects and Religious Freedom in America," in *Annals of America* (Chicago: Encyclopaedia Britannica, 1976), 6:152. (Originally an essay appended to *Marie ou l'esclavage aux États-Unis* [Paris, 1835], 2:183–225).

23. Abdy, *Residence and Tour*, 3:54.
24. Gary L. Bunker and Davis Bitton, *The Mormon Graphic Image, 1834–1914* (Salt Lake City: University of Utah Press, 1983), 82.
25. The original argument was put forward by David Brion Davis, "Some Themes of Counter-Subversion: An Analysis of Anti-Masonic, Anti-Catholic, and Anti-Mormon Literature," *Mississippi Valley Historical Review* 47 (September 1960): 205–24. Mark W. Cannon later addressed the issue in "The Crusades against the Masons, Catholics, and Mormons: Separate Waves of a Common Current," *BYU Studies* 3.1 (Winter 1961): 23. The limitations of Davis's argument have been pointed out by Leonard J. Arrington and Jon Haupt. "No doubt anti-Mormonism was in large part nativist," they write, "but Davis overlooks the international aspects of anti-Mormonism. [And] virtually all of Davis's anti-Mormon material is taken from sources dated *after* 1856." See their article, "The Missouri and Illinois Mormons in Ante-Bellum Fiction," *Dialogue: A Journal of Mormon Thought* 5.1 (Spring 1970): 45n.
26. Gustavus Myers, *History of Bigotry in the United States* (New York: Random House, 1943), 173–74. It is hard to resist commenting on a "history of bigotry" that unblushingly refers to early Utah Mormons as being "under the imperious leadership of a fanatical leader" (217).
27. Robert Richards [pseud.], *The Californian Crusoe; or, the Lost Treasure Found; a Tale of Mormonism* (London: Parker, 1854), 82.
28. John A. Clark, *Gleanings by the Way* (Philadelphia: W. J. & J. K. Simon; New York: Robert Carter, 1842), 259.
29. Orvilla S. Belisle, *The Arch Bishop; or, Romanism in the United States* (Philadelphia: William White Smith, 1854), dedication.
30. Gertrude Keene Major, *The Revelation in the Mountain* (New York: Cochrane Publishing, 1909), dedication.
31. Charles Pidgin, *House of Shame* (New York: Cosmopolitan, 1912), 89.
32. See the chapter "Troublesome Bedfellows: Mormons and other Minorities" in Bunker and Bitton, *Graphic Image*. Their book provides a thorough treatment of the Mormon stereotype as developed in illustrated magazines and periodicals. They address both the chronological development of the Mormon image in the media and recurrent themes.
33. The 1850s saw the earliest and most influential wave of anti-Mormon novels, including John Russell's *The Mormoness; or, the Trials of Mary Maverick* (Alton, Ill.: Courier Steam Press, 1853); Alfreda Eva Bell's *Boadicea, the Mormon Wife* (Baltimore: Arthur R. Orton, 1855); and Maria Ward's *Female Life among the Mormons* (London: Routledge, 1855).
34. Donald Bruce Johnson and Kirk H. Porter, *National Party Platforms, 1840–1972* (Urbana: University of Illinois Press, 1973), 27. The linking of slavery and polygamy was also effected by referring to both as that "peculiar institution." Army assistant surgeon Roberts Bartholow, for example, referred to Mormon children of plural marriages as "the progeny of the 'peculiar institution.'" See *Surgeon General's Office, Statistical Report on the Sickness and Mortality in the Army of the United States . . . from January, 1855 to January, 1860* (Washington, D.C.: George W. Bowman, 1860), 302.

    Although Emancipation made it impossible for later political platforms to link polygamy and slavery as campaign issues, both the Democrats and Republicans would continue to officially stand for the eradication of polygamy until 1904. See Edward W. Chester, *A Guide to Political Platforms* (Hamden, Conn.: Archon, 1977), 34–35. (The church officially suspended the practice in 1890.)

35. Johnson and Porter, *National Party Platforms*, 22.

36. Pratt, *Late Persecution*, 53.

37. See Klaus J. Hansen, *Quest for Empire: The Political Kingdom of God and the Council of Fifty in Mormon History* (East Lansing: Michigan State University Press, 1967).

38. Hansen, *Quest for Empire*, frontispiece.

39. See critiques of Hansen's "kingdom school" by D. Michael Quinn, "The Council of Fifty and Its Members, 1844 to 1955," *BYU Studies* 20.2 (Winter 1980): 163–97; and Marvin Hill, *Quest for Refuge: The Mormon Flight from American Pluralism* (Salt Lake City: Signature, 1989), xvi. Hill's assessment of the Mormon persecutions (and the thesis of his book) is succinctly stated: "Anti-pluralism was the main cause of persecution" (181).

40. Hugh Nibley, "Just Another Book," in *The Prophetic Book of* Mormon, ed. John W. Welch, vol. 8 of *The Collected Works of Hugh Nibley* (Salt Lake City and Provo: Deseret and Foundation for Ancient Research and Mormon Studies, 1989), 159. His studies of anti-Mormonism are collected in both that volume and in *Tinkling Cymbals and Sounding Brass: The Art of Telling Tales about Joseph Smith and Brigham Young*, ed. David J. Whitaker, vol. 2 of *Collected Works* (1991).

41. J. H. Beadle, "The Mormon Theocracy," *Scribner's Monthly* 14.3 (July 1877): 392.

42. Myers, *History of Bigotry*, 173.

43. *Latter Day Saints' Messenger and Advocate* 2.11 (August 1836): 355.

44. *Latter Day Saints' Messenger and Advocate* 2.11 (August 1836): 354.

45. Charles Dickens, *The Uncommercial Traveller* (1861; reprint, New York: Charles Scribner's, 1902), 262–63.

46. *New York Herald*, June 17, 1842.

47. James Silk Buckingham, *The Eastern and Western States of America* (London: Fisher, Sons, 1842), 194.

48. R. Carlyle Buley, *The Old Northwest: Pioneer Period, 1815–1840* (Indianapolis: Indiana Historical Society, 1950), 1:394.

49. "History of Joseph Smith," *Times and Seasons* 5.4 (February 15, 1844): 434.

50. William Walker Journal, April 7, 1851. Cited in Heman C. Smith, "Missouri Troubles," *Journal of History* 2.4 (October 1909): 440–41.

51. Ray Allen Billington, "Frontier Democracy: Social Aspects," in *The Turner Thesis: Concerning the Role of the Frontier in American History*, 3rd ed., ed. George Rogers Taylor (Lexington, Mass.: D. C. Heath, 1972), 178.

52. Edward Pessen, *Jacksonian America: Society, Personality and Politics* (Homewood, Ill.: Dorsey, 1978), 17.

53. Joel Kotkin, *Tribes: How Race, Religion and Identity Determine Success in the New Global Economy* (New York: Random House, 1993), 245.

54. Richard Burton, *City of the Saints* (1861; ed. Fawn M. Brodie, New York: Knopf, 1963), 224.

55. B. H. Roberts, *A Comprehensive History of the Church of Jesus Christ of Latter-day Saints* (Provo, Utah: Brigham Young University Press, 1965), 1:496–97.

56. "Letter to Isaac Galland," 424.

57. Foote, *Autobiography*, 1:96.

58. *Evening and Morning Star* 14 (June 1833): 111.

59. Book of Commandments 102:12, in *The Joseph Smith Papers: Revelations and Translations*, vol. 2, *Published Revelations*, ed. Robert Scott Jensen, Richard E. Turley Jr., and Riley M. Lorimer (Salt Lake City: Church Historian's Press, 2011), 564.

60. Abdy, *Residence and Tour*, 3:59, quoting Alma 27:9 from the Book of Mormon.

61. James Coates, *In Mormon Circles: Gentiles, Jack Mormons, and Latter-day Saints* (Reading, Mass.: Addison-Wesley, 1991), 29.

62. Ethan Smith, *View of the Hebrews* (Poultney, Vt.: Smith and Shure, 1825), 79.

63. James Adair, *The History of the American Indians* (London: E. and C. Dilly, 1775), cited in Smith, *View of the Hebrews*, 80.

64. Abdy, *Residence and Tour*, 3:59.

65. Foote, *Autobiography*, 1:96.

66. Catherine Lewis, *Narrative of Some of the Proceedings of the Mormons* (Lynn, Mass.: Catherine Lewis, 1848), 15.

67. *The Autobiography of Parley Parker Pratt, One of the Twelve Apostles of the Church of Jesus Christ of Latter-day Saints, Embracing His Life, Ministry, and Travels*, ed. Scot Facer Proctor and Maurine Jensen Proctor (Salt Lake City: Deseret, 2000), 218.

68. Jeffrey N. Walker, "Mormon Land Rights in Caldwell and Daviess Counties and the Mormon Conflict of 1838," *BYU Studies* 47.1 (2008): 5.

69. Contemporary but anonymous letter published in the *Boston Atlas*, and reprinted in the *Journal of History* [The Reorganized Church of Jesus Christ of Latter Day Saints] 2 (1909): 434.

70. Walker, "Mormon Land Rights," 41.

71. Daniel Walker Howe, *What Hath God Wrought* (New York: Oxford University Press, 2007), 491.

72. See Alexander L. Baugh, "A Call to Arms: The 1838 Defense of Northern Missouri" (PhD diss., Brigham Young University, 1996), 19–29. See also James B. Whisker, *The Rise and Decline of the American Militia System* (Selinsgrove, Penn.: Susquehanna University Press, 1999).

73. Howe, *What Hath God Wrought*, 430–32, 509.

74. David Grimsted, *American Mobbing, 1828–1861* (New York: Oxford University Press, 1998), 4.

75. Leonard Richards, *"Gentlemen of Property and Standing": Anti Abolition Mobs in Jacksonian America* (New York: Oxford University Press, 1971).

76. *Chardon Spectator*, October 30, 1835, in Edwin Brown Firmage and Richard Collin Mangrum, *Zion in the Courts: A Legal History of the Church of Jesus Christ of Latter-day Saints, 1830–1900* (Urbana: University of Illinois Press, 2001), 53.

77. Proctor and Proctor, *Autobiography of Parley Parker Pratt*, 247.

78. For an early but authoritative account of the system as practiced in the pre-Utah period see Leonard J. Arrington, "Early Mormon Communitarianism," in *Mormonism and American Culture*, ed. Marvin S. Hill and James B. Allen (New York: Harper & Row, 1972).

79. Myers, *History of Bigotry*, 173.

80. Beadle, "Mormon Theocracy," 392. Seven years later, when Beadle was a much harsher critic of Mormonism, he repeated the diagnosis. In his 1870 volume on "the Mysteries and Crimes of Mormonism," he stated that "the great cause of popular hostility, which finally led to the worst result, was the Mormon system of voting solidly, at the dictation of a few men." See his *Life in Utah or, the Mysteries and Crimes of Mormonism, Being an Exposé of the Secret Rites and Ceremonies....* (Philadelphia: National Publishing Co., 1870), 67.

81. Hill, *Quest for Refuge*, 399.

82. Hill, *Quest for Refuge*, 228.

83. Charles Dickens, "In the Name of the Prophet—Smith!" *Household Words*, July 19, 1851, 338.

84. D. Michael Quinn, trans. and ed., "The First Months of Mormonism: A Contemporary View by Rev. Diedrich Willers," *New York History* 54 (July 1973): 326.
85. Quinn, "First Months," 330.
86. Nibley, "Just Another Book," 161.
87. Dickens, "In the Name of the Prophet," 342.

CHAPTER 4

1. Laurence Moore, *Religious Outsiders and the Making of Americans* (New York: Oxford University Press, 1986), 38, 43.
2. *New York Herald*, June 14, 1842.
3. Dean C. Jessee, ed., *The Papers of Joseph Smith*, vol. 1, *Autobiographical and Historical Writings* (Salt Lake City: Deseret, 1989), 273.
4. First of the "Thirteen Articles of Faith," published originally in response to an inquiry by Charles Wentworth, editor of the *Chicago Democrat*, in the Mormon-owned *Times and Seasons* 3.9, March 1, 1842. Now canonized as part of LDS scriptures in *The Pearl of Great Price* (Salt Lake City: Deseret, 1981).
5. Henry Brown, *The History of Illinois, from Its First Discovery and Settlement to the Present Time* (New York: Winchester, 1844), 394.
6. James Silk Buckingham, The *Eastern and Western United States of America* (London: Fisher, Sons, 1842), 190–91.
7. See Paul Johnson, *The Birth of the Modern: 1815–1830* (New York: HarperCollins, 1991).
8. James Webb, *The Flight from Reason* (London: Macdonald, 1971), 7.
9. C. C. Goen, *Broken Churches, Broken Nation: Denominational Schisms and the Coming of the Civil War* (Macon, Ga.: Macon University Press, 1985), 187.
10. Milton V. Backman, *American Religions and the Rise of Mormonism* (Salt Lake City: Deseret, 1965), 309.
11. For references to the Osgoodites, Davidites, and numerous others see the useful study by Walter A. Norton, "Comparative Images: Mormonism and Contemporary Religions as seen by Village Newspapermen in Western New York and Northeastern Ohio, 1820–1833" (PhD diss., Brigham Young University, 1991).
12. Archibald Maxwell, *A Run through the United States during the Autumn of 1840* (London: H. Colburn, 1841), 1:24.
13. Maxwell, *Run through the United States*, 1:98, 246.
14. John Evans, *History of All Christian Sects and Denominations; Their Origin, Peculiar Tenets, and Present Condition*, 2nd ed. (New York: James Mowatt, 1844).
15. John Winebrenner, *History of All the Religious Denominations in the United States*, 2nd ed. (Harrisburg, Penn.: Winebrenner,1848), table of contents.
16. Robert Southey, *Letters from England* (1807; reprint, London: Cresset, 1951), 159.
17. Matthias's visit is important in Mormon history because it provided the context for the second of Smith's four principal recitations of the "First Vision" that are on record. For a contemporary account of Matthias, see William L. Stone, *Matthias and His Impostures: Or, the Progress of Fanaticism* (New York: Harper & Bros., 1835). The most thorough recent treatment, which includes an account of his audience with Joseph Smith, is Paul E. Johnson and Sean Wilentz, *The Kingdom of Matthias* (New York: Oxford University Press, 1994).
18. David Meredith Reese, *Humbugs of New York: Being a Remonstrance against Popular Delusion; Whether in Science, Philosophy, or Religion* (New York: Taylor, 1838), 265.

19. Edmund Flagg, *The Far West: Or, a Tour beyond the Mountains* (New York: Harper, 1838), 86–87.

20. John Greenleaf Whittier, *The Stranger in Lowell* (Boston: Waite, Peirce, 1845), 86.

21. Martin Marty, *Pilgrims in Their Own Land: 500 Years of Religion in America* (Boston: Little, Brown, 1984), 157, 161,

22. Thomas Jefferson, *The Writings*, ed. H. A. Washington (Washington, D.C.: Taylor & Maury, 1854), 7:257.

23. A thorough treatment of the movement is Robert Darnton's *Mesmerism and the End of the Enlightenment in France* (Cambridge, Mass.: Harvard University Press, 1968).

24. Charles Dickens, "In the Name of the Prophet—Smith!" *Household Words*, July 19, 1851, 338.

25. Ralph Waldo Emerson, *The Journals and Miscellaneous Notebooks*, vol. 13, ed. Ralph H. Orth and Alfred R. Ferguson (Cambridge, Mass.: Harvard University Press, 1978), 462.

26. R. Laurence Moore, *In Search of White Crows: Spiritualism, Parapsychology, and American Culture* (New York: Oxford University Press, 1977), 4.

27. Moore, *In Search of White Crows*, 4.

28. Howard Kerr, *Mediums and Spirit-Rappers and Roaring Radicals: Spiritualism in American Literature, 1850–1900* (Urbana: University of Illinois Press, 1972), 9.

29. Ruth A. McAdams, "The Shakers in American Fiction" (PhD diss., Texas Christian University, 1985), 33.

30. Marty, *Pilgrims*, 321.

31. Evans, *History of All Christian Sects*, 183.

32. Signe Toksvig, *Emanuel Swedenborg, Scientist and Mystic* (New Haven, Conn.: Yale University Press, 1948), 12–13.

33. Evans, *History of All Christian Sects*, 183–96.

34. Marty, *Pilgrims*, 323.

35. Mormonism's emphasis on personal revelation and the reality of spiritual phenomena led some Mormons to dabble in spiritualism, especially those disaffected intellectuals and businessmen who in 1869 formed the Godbeite movement. See Davis Bitton's study "Mormonism's Encounter with Spiritualism," *Journal of Mormon History* 1 (1974): 39–50; also, Ronald W. Walker, *Wayward Saints: The Godbeites and Brigham Young* (Urbana: University of Illinois Press, 1998).

36. See Alexander Campbell, "The Mormonites," *Millennial Harbinger* 2 (February 1831): 93.

37. J. H. Beadle, *Life in Utah; or, the Mysteries and Crimes of Mormonism, Being an Exposé of the Secret Rites and Ceremonies of the Latter-day Saints. . . .* (Philadelphia: National Publishing Co., 1870), 5–6.

38. McAdams, "Shakers," 11.

39. Daniel W. Patterson, *The Shaker Spiritual* (Princeton, N.J.: Princeton University Press, 1979), 102.

40. Greeley's account is published in "A Sabbath with the Shakers," *Knickerbocker, or New-York Monthly Magazine* 11 (June 1838): 532–37. Cited in Patterson, *Shaker Spiritual*, 100–101.

41. Edward Strutt Abdy, *Journal of a Residence and Tour in the United States of North America, from April, 1833, to October, 1834* (London: Murray, 1835), 1:262.

42. Evans, *History of All Christian Sects*, 211.

43. Cited in Leonard J. Arrington, "Early Mormon Communitarianism," in *Mormonism and American Culture*, ed. Marvin S. Hill and James B. Allen (New York: Harper & Row, 1972), 347.

44. Book of Commandments 44: 27, 29 in *The Joseph Smith Papers: Revelations and Translations*, vol. 2, *Published Revelations*, ed. Robert Scott Jensen, Richard E. Turley Jr., and Riley M. Lorimer (Salt Lake City: Church Historian's Press, 2011), 104.

45. McAdams, "Shakers," 21.

46. Kabbalistic tradition offers a precedent for such a belief, but neither Jewish nor Christian orthodoxy does. This is not to ignore the work that has been done by feminist theologians in locating female metaphors in the Hebrew scriptures or recuperating the femaleness associated with the figure of Sophia. But these attempts to "shape new speech about God" represent a radical challenge to what Elizabeth A. Johnson calls "classical theology" and "the restrictive inheritance of exclusive God-talk." See her *She Who Is: The Mystery of God in Feminist Theological Discourse* (New York: Crossroad, 1992), 5.

47. See articles 2, 3, 4, 7, 8, 9, and 10 of "The Articles of Faith," in *Pearl of Great Price*.

48. McAdams, "Shakers," 16.

49. The command to proselytize the Shakers came in a revelation recorded as Section 52 of the Book of Commandments. Parts of the revelation appear to be directed at refuting specific Shaker tenets: "whoso forbiddeth to marry is not ordained of God, for marriage is ordained of God unto man" (16), and "the Son of Man cometh not in the form of a woman" (21). At the same time, the communalism practiced by the Shakers and about to be implemented by the Saints is foreshadowed in verses 19–20: "But it is not given that one man should possess that which is above another, wherefore the world lieth in sin." In Jensen, Turley, and Lorimer, *Joseph Smith Papers*, vol. 2, *Published Revelations*, 129–30.

50. Thomas Colburn, letter in *St. Louis Luminary*, May 5, 1855, 2. Colburn wrote: "We had a lengthy interview with Martin Harris. . . . He confessed that he had lost confidence in Joseph Smith, consequently his mind became darkened, and he was left to himself; he tried the Shakers, but that would not do, then tried Gladden Bishop, but no satisfaction; had concluded he would wait until the Saints returned to Jackson Co., and then he would repair there."

51. McAdams, "Shakers," 11–12.

52. *Summary View of the Millennial Church, or United Society of Believers, Commonly Called Shakers*, 2nd ed. (1823; reprint, New York: AMS Press, 1973), 27.

53. *Summary View*, 27–28. A more detailed account is in *Testimonies of the Life, Character, Revelations and Doctrines of Mother Ann Lee*, 2nd ed. (1816; reprint of 1888 ed., New York: AMS Press, 1975), 93–99.

54. *Testimonies of the Life*, 75.

55. *Testimonies of the Life*, 98.

56. Abdy, *Residence and Tour*, 1:262.

57. Abdy, *Residence and Tour*, 1:262.

58. Robert Baird, *Religion in the United States of America* (Glasgow and Edinburgh: Blackie and Son, 1844), 284.

59. Ruth Alden Doan, *The Miller Heresy, Millennialism, and American Culture* (Philadelphia: Temple University Press, 1987), 191.

60. Doan, *Miller Heresy*, 4.

61. Doan, *Miller Heresy*, 45.

62. Webb, *Flight from Reason*, 3.

63. Moore, *In Search of White Crows*, 33.

64. Moore, *In Search of White Crows*, 43.

65. Kerr, *Mediums and Spirit Rappers*, 14.

66. Kerr, *Mediums and Spirit Rappers*, 14. See also Kenneth Andrews, *Nook Farm: Mark Twain's Hartford Circle* (Cambridge, Mass.: Harvard University Press, 1950), 33–34.
67. Moore, *In Search of White Crows*, 65.
68. Editorial, *New York Times*, June 12, 1852, and "Impostures and Delusions," *National Intelligencer*, April 25, 1853. Both reports are cited in Moore, *In Search of White Crows*, 27–28.
69. Webb, *Flight from Reason*, 2. Moore gives the number as 13,000 signatures (*In Search of White Crows*, 26).
70. Moore, *In Search of White Crows*, 99.
71. Moore, *In Search of White Crows*, 94.
72. Moore, *In Search of White Crows*, 44.
73. Ray Allen Billington, *The Protestant Crusade: 1800–1860* (New York: Macmillan, 1938), 20–21. His is still the standard treatment of anti-Catholicism in American history.
74. Billington, *Protestant Crusade*, 35.
75. Billington, *Protestant Crusade*, 70–71.

CHAPTER 5

1. The four were Marmaduke Stephenson, William Robinson, Mary Dyer, and William Leddra. Charles II put an end to such executions in 1661. See David S. Lovejoy, *Religious Enthusiasm in the New World: Heresy to Revolution* (Cambridge, Mass.: Harvard University Press, 1985), 127–29.
2. Ruth Alden Doan, *The Miller Heresy, Millennialism, and American Culture* (Philadelphia: Temple University Press, 1985), 127.
3. Isaac Haight, "Biographical [Autobiographical] Sketch of Isaac C. Haight" (Typescript in Special Collections, Brigham Young University Library, Provo, Utah), 3.
4. "A Singular Case of Heresy," *Times and Seasons* 4.2 (December 1, 1842): 26.
5. Robert W. Beers, *The Mormon Puzzle and How to Solve It* (New York: Funk & Wagnalls, 1887), 141.
6. It is true that from the perspective of religious sociology, the term "cult" can be meaningfully distinguished from other words like "sect," "denomination," etc. However, prominent religious scholar Martin Marty makes the case for the ease with which such labels carry the semblance of authority without real content. A cult, he said in an interview, has come to mean little more than "a religion I don't happen to like" (interview on *All Things Considered*, March 8, 1993, National Public Radio). This was precisely the case in Rev. Robert Jeffress's controversial relegation of Mormonism to "cult" status in his remarks at the Values Voters Summit (October 7, 2011) running up to the 2012 presidential election. His pretense of a theological determination was dismissed by virtually all commentators as transparent bigotry. See for example William C. Bennett, "Don't Judge Candidates by Their Faith," www.cnn.com/2011/10/11/opinion/bennett -jeffress-mormon-comments/index.html.
7. Rodney Stark and Charles Y. Glock, *American Piety: The Nature of Religious Commitment* (Berkeley and Los Angeles: University of California Press, 1968), 22.
8. Stark and Glock, *American Piety*, 58–59.
9. David Steinmetz, "Christian Unity: A Sermon by David Steinmetz," *News and Notes* 5.6 (April 1990), cited in Stephen Robinson, *Are Mormons Christian?* (Salt Lake City: Bookcraft, 1991), 36–37.

10. Robinson, *Are Mormons Christian?* viii–ix.
11. Lorenzo Snow Letters, quoted in Andrew F. Ehat and Lyndon W. Cook, eds., *The Words of Joseph Smith: The Contemporary Accounts of the Nauvoo Discourses of the Prophet Joseph Smith* (Orem, Utah: Grandin, 1994), 84.
12. Robinson, *Are Mormons Christian?* 60–61. It has been pointed out, correctly, that Mormon deification does not assert the racial ontological difference that characterizes other Christian treatments, like those of Eastern Orthodoxy.
13. See Terryl L. Givens, *When Souls Had Wings: Premortal Existence in Western Thought* (New York: Oxford University Press, 2009).
14. Truman G. Madsen, "Are Christians Mormon?" *BYU Studies* 15.1 (Autumn 1975): 259–80. David L. Paulsen, "Are Christians Mormon? Reassessing Joseph Smith's Theology in his Bi-centennial," *BYU Studies* 45.1 (2006): 35–128.
15. R. L. Richard, "Trinity, Holy," in *New Catholic Encyclopedia* (New York: McGraw-Hill, 1967), 14:299; and P. Achtemeier, ed., *Harper's Bible Dictionary* (San Francisco: Harper & Row, 1985), 1099. Both sources are cited in a fuller discussion of the subject by Robinson, *Are Mormons Christian?* 71–89.
16. Frederick Sontag, "New Minority Religions as Heresies," *International Journal for Philosophy of Religion* 14.3 (1983): 159.
17. Rodney Stark, "The Rise of a New World Faith," *Review of Religious Research* 26:1 (September 1984): 25.
18. Marty, interview, *All Things Considered.*
19. Peggy Fletcher Stack, "Some Keep a Close Eye on Mormonism," *Salt Lake Tribune* 10, June 1995. Another two hundred groups, Melton adds, target Mormons along with Jehovah's Witnesses. According to Keith E. Tolbert and Eric Pement, 174 agencies and individuals were targeting Latter-day Saints as of 1993. See their 1993 *Directory of Cult Research Organizations: A Worldwide Listing of 729 Agencies and Individuals* (Trenton, Mich.: American Religious Center, 1993), 51–53.
20. James Coates, *In Mormon Circles: Gentiles, Jack Mormons, and Latter-day Saints* (Reading, Mass.: Addison-Wesley, 1991), 198.
21. Stark, "New World Faith," 27.
22. Stark, "New World Faith," 19.
23. *Journal of Discourses*, G. D. Watt, reporter (Liverpool and London: F. D. and S. W. Richards et al., 1854–1886; reprint, Salt Lake City: n.p., 1967), 16:346.
24. *Journal of Discourses*, 14:169.
25. In Harold Bloom's formulation, "Mormons, if they are at all faithful to the most crucial teachings of Joseph Smith and Brigham Young, no more believe in American democracy than they do in historical Christianity." I take his second point, but not his first. Bloom, *American Religion: The Emergence of the Post-Christian Nation* (New York: Simon & Schuster, 1992), 91.
26. Rudolf Otto, *The Idea of the Holy*, 2nd ed., trans. J. W. Harvey (London: Oxford University Press, 1950), 12, 13, 28, 146.
27. Emil Brunner, *Our Faith* (New York: Scribner's Sons, 1954), 11–12.
28. Elizabeth A. Johnson, *She Who Is: The Mystery of God in Feminist Theological Discourse* (New York: Crossroad, 1992), 7. Her citations are Augustine, *Sermo* 52, c. 6, n. 16 (*PL* 38.360); Anselm, *Proslogium*, chaps. 2–3, *Saint Anselm: Basic Writings*, trans. S. N. Deane (LaSalle, Ill.: Open Court, 1974); Hildegard of Bingen, *Scivias*, trans. Mother Columbia Hart and Jane Bishop (New York: Paulist, 1990), bk. 1, vision 1 *ST* I, q. 3, preface; Luther, theses 19 and 20, "The Heidelberg Disputation," *Luther: Early Theological Works*, trans. and ed. James Atkinson (Philadelphia: Westminster, 1962); Simone Weil, *Waiting for God*, trans. Emma Craufurd (New

York: Harper & Row, 1973), 32; and Sallie McFague, *Models of God: Theology for an Ecological, Nuclear Age* (Philadelphia: Fortress, 1987), 35.

29. Mary Bednarowski, for one, notes that both Mormonism and the Unification Church "maintain that special revelation did not end with the Bible." *New Religions and the Theological Imagination in America* (Bloomington: Indiana University Press, 1989), 7.

30. This is the name of a popular book that discusses several "cults," Mormonism among others. Written by Walter Martin, *Kingdom of the Cults* is used as a text at some fundamentalist colleges (Minneapolis: Bethany House, 1985).

31. Thomas O'Dea and Janet O'Dea Aviad, *The Sociology of Religion*, 2nd ed. (Englewood Cliffs, N.J.: Prentice-Hall, 1983), 86.

32. John Russell, *The Mormoness; or, the Trials of Mary Maverick* (Alton, Ill.: Courier Steam Press, 1853), 44.

33. Charles Pidgin, *House of Shame* (New York: Cosmopolitan, 1912), 90.

34. Robert Richards [pseud.], *The Californian Crusoe; or, the Lost Treasure Found; a Tale of Mormonism* (London: Parker, 1854), 60–61.

35. Henry Brown, *The History of Illinois, from Its First Discovery and Settlement to the Present Time* (New York: Winchester, 1844), 403.

36. Josiah Quincy, *Figures of the Past* (Boston: Little, Brown, 1926), 326.

37. C. S. Lewis, *Perelandra* (New York: Macmillan, 1965), 11.

38. Hugh Nibley, "Unrolling the Scrolls," in *Old Testament and Related Studies*, ed. John W. Welch, Gary P. Gillum, and Don E. Norton, in vol. 1 of *The Collected Works of Hugh Nibley* (Salt Lake City and Provo, Utah: Deseret Book and Foundation for Ancient Research and Mormon Studies, 1989), 122–23. Nibley attributes the term "cosmism" to the nineteenth-century scholar Carl Schmidt (122).

39. Hugh Nibley, "Treasures in the Heavens," *Old Testament*, 171. Nibley discusses the cosmist heresy in several of his works, but especially pages 122–24, 187–88, and 212 of the above volume.

40. Sterling McMurrin, *The Theological Foundations of the Mormon Religion* (Salt Lake City: University of Utah Press, 1965), 2. Again, Truman Madsen notes the irony of a shift on the part of contemporary theologians toward this same position that "the old dualism must go." He quotes the Quaker Rufus Jones, to give one example, as insisting that "the two world theory has become impossible to those who think in the terms of this generation." See Jones, *The Radiant Life* (New York: Macmillan, 1944), 150 cited in Madsen, "Are Christians Mormon?" 262.

41. Harold Bloom, *The Western Canon* (New York: Harcourt Brace, 1994), 6.

42. Orson Pratt, *Divine Authenticity of the Book of Mormon* 1 (1850): 4.

43. *Latter Day Saints' Messenger and Advocate* 1.6 (March 1835): 95.

44. Francis W. Kirkham, *A New Witness for Christ in America* (Independence, Mo.: Zion's, 1942), 1:267.

45. "Brother Curtis and the Trial for Blasphemy," *Latter-day Saints' Millennial Star* 2.4 (August 1841): 63.

46. *Religious Herald* 59.1 (April 9, 1840).

47. Thomas O'Dea, *The Mormons* (Chicago: University of Chicago Press, 1957), 26.

48. Stark, "New World Faith," 19.

49. *Religious Herald* 83.2 (May 31,1840).

50. *Religious Herald* 59.1 (April 9, 1840).

51. D. Griffiths Jr., *Two Years in the New Settlements of Ohio* (London, 1835; reprint, Ann Arbor: University Microfilms, 1966), 132–40.

52. The term "has come to be too easily applied to anybody whose religion we don't like." Martin Marty, interview, *All Things Considered*.

53. From *Dictionary of Bible and Religion*, cited in Ed Briggs, "Traits Are Listed That Make Religious Cults Destructive," *Richmond Times Dispatch*, March 5, 1993, A8.

54. John Henry Cardinal Newman, *An Essay on the Development of Christian Doctrine* (London: Longmans, Green, 1909), 20. Cardinal Newman's book added momentum to a vigorous and ongoing debate. As an example of a more contemporary examination of "the problem of whether Christian doctrine has changed, and if it has why it has, and which changes are legitimate, if any are, and which are not," see R. P. C. Hanson, *The Continuity of Christian Doctrine* (New York: Seabury, 1981), 22. Hanson critiques Newman's work and outlines alternative models of development.

55. The new edition of the gospels produced by the seminar was published as *The Five Gospels: The Search for the Authentic Words of Jesus* (New York: Macmillan, 1993). Their version casts large doses of skepticism upon the material traditionally attributed to Jesus and adds Thomas to the canon. The seminar's contempt for canonical ossification is shown by their provocative dedication to "Thomas Jefferson, who took scissors and paste to the gospels" (v).

56. Quoted in Jeffery L. Sheler, "Cutting Loose the Holy Canon," *U.S. News and World Report*, November 8, 1993, 75.

57. Paul Tillich, *Christianity and the Encounter of the World Religions* (New York: Columbia University Press, 1961), 71.

58. William Mulder, "'Essential Gestures': Craft and Calling in Contemporary Mormon Letters," *Weber Studies* 10.3 (Fall 1993): 7.

59. William Blake, "A Vision of the Last Judgment," in *The Poetry and Prose of William Blake*, ed. David V. Erdman (Garden City, N.Y.: Doubleday, 1965), 555.

60. Dean C. Jessee, ed., *The Papers of Joseph Smith*, vol. 1, *Autobiographical and Historical Writings* (Salt Lake City: Deseret, 1989), 276.

61. Otto, *Idea of the Holy*, 27n.

62. Book of Commandments 24.2, in *The Joseph Smith Papers: Revelations and Translations*, vol. 2. *Published Revelations*, ed. Robert Scott Jensen, Richard E. Turley Jr., and Riley M. Lorimer (Salt Lake City: Church Historian's Press, 2011), 60. The prophecy is from Daniel 2.

63. Doctrine and Covenants (1835) 27:4, in Jensen, Turley, and Lorimer, *Smith Papers*, vol. 2, *Published Revelations*, 464.

64. Quincy, *Figures of the Past*, 326.

65. *New York Herald*, August 4, 1842.

66. J. M. Peck, *Gazetteer of Illinois* (Jacksonville, Ill.: Goudy, 1834), 53–54.

67. John Ruskin, letter to Henry Acland, May 24, 1851, in John Ruskin, *Works*, 39 vols., ed. E. T. Cook and Alexander Wedderburn (London: George Allen, 1903–1912), 36:115.

68. Paul Johnson, *The Birth of the Modern, 1815–1830* (New York: HarperCollins, 1991), 562.

69. Thomas Carlyle, *Sartor Resartus: The Life and Opinions of Herr Teufelsdröckh* (London: Walter Scott, 1873), 237, 233.

70. Carlyle, *Sartor Resartus*, 238.

71. Carlyle, *Sartor Resartus*, 237.

72. Andrew F. Ehat and Lyndon W. Cook, eds., *The Words of Joseph Smith: The Contemporary Accounts of the Nauvoo Discourses of the Prophet Joseph Smith* (Orem, Utah: Grandin, 1994), 169.

73. Stan Larson, "The King Follett Discourse: A Newly Amalgamated Text," *BYU Studies* 18.2 (Winter 1978): 200.
74. M. H. Abrams, *Natural Supernaturalism: Tradition and Revolution in Romantic Literature* (New York: Norton, 1971), 384.
75. D&C 131:7–8.
76. Gotthold Lessing, "On the Proof the Spirit and of Power," in *Lessing's Theological Writings*, trans. Henry Chadwick (Stanford, Calif.: Stanford University Press, 1957), 53.
77. *Journal of Discourses*, 18:231.
78. Stark, "New World Faith," 18.

CHAPTER 6

1. Fawn Brodie, *No Man Knows My History: The Life of Joseph Smith the Mormon Prophet* (New York: Knopf, 1977), vii.
2. Nathan Hatch, *The Democratization of American Christianity* (New Haven, Conn.: Yale University Press, 1989), 127.
3. See Thomas C. Leonard, "News for a Revolution: The Exposé in America, 1768–1773," *Journal of American History* 67 (1980): 26–40. Cited with discussion in Hatch, *Democratization*, 24ff.
4. George Givens, *In Old Nauvoo: Everyday Life in the City of Joseph* (Salt Lake City: Deseret, 1990), 263.
5. Cited in Hatch, *Democratization*, 142.
6. Isaac Clark Pray, *Memoirs of James Gordon Bennett and His Times* (New York: Stringer and Townsend, 1855), 416.
7. Pray, *Memoirs*, 465.
8. Manuscript History of the Church, C-1, 1265. LDS Archives.
9. *New York Herald*, May 21 and June 14, 1842.
10. *New York Herald*, August 13, 1842.
11. Pray, *Memoirs*, 311.
12. *New York Herald*, September 9, 1842.
13. *New York Herald*, April 3, 1842.
14. *New York Herald*, January 19, 1842.
15. *New York Herald*, May 25, 1842.
16. Smith mentioned this practice with particular gratitude. See *New York Herald*, January 19, 1842. The same issue contained the text of his revelation in which Christ testified to the calling of Joseph Smith as the Latter-day Prophet (published in the Book of Commandments, "A Preface").
17. Pray, *Memoirs*, 355.
18. Joseph Smith, "Journal, 1842–43," in Scott H. Faulring, ed., *An American Prophet's Record: The Diaries and Journals of Joseph Smith*, 2nd ed. (Salt Lake City: Signature, 1989), 311.
19. Pray, *Memoirs*, 311.
20. *Warsaw (Ill.) Signal*, June 19, 1844. Quoted in Dallin H. Oaks and Marvin S. Hill, *Carthage Conspiracy: The Trial of the Accused Assassins of Joseph Smith* (Urbana: University of Illinois Press, 1975).
21. Gary L. Bunker and Davis Bitton, "Illustrated Periodical Images of Mormons, 1850–1860," *Dialogue: A Journal of Mormon Thought* 10.3 (Spring 1977): 84. For a thorough treatment of the Mormon stereotype as developed in illustrated magazines and newspapers see their *The Mormon Graphic Image, 1834–1914* (Salt Lake City: University of Utah Press, 1983).

22. William J. Gilmore, *Reading Becomes a Necessity of Life: Material and Cultural Life in Rural New England, 1780–1835* (Knoxville: University of Tennessee Press, 1989), 19–20.

23. Gilmore, *Reading Becomes a Necessity*, 20. Lending support to Gilmore's claim of a virtually universal interest in reading are the literacy rates of that period. Russel Blaine Nye gives an estimate of 90 percent by the year 1820 in *The Cultural Life of the New Nation, 1776–1830* (New York: Harper & Row, 1960), 250. The figure for 1840 (the earliest census data available) is only 9 percent illiteracy for the white adult population and 22 percent for the total adult population. See Bureau of the Census, *Historical Statistics of the United States, Colonial Times to 1957* (Washington, D.C.: Government Printing Office, 1961), 206.

24. Morse Peckham, *Beyond the Tragic Vision: The Quest for Identity in the Nineteenth Century* (New York: George Braziller, 1962), 28.

25. William Wordsworth, *Lyrical Ballads, and Other Poems, 1797–1800*, ed. James Butler and Karen Green (Ithaca, N.Y.: Cornell University Press, 1992), 15, 22, 32.

26. Wordsworth, *Lyrical Ballads*, 31.

27. Paul G. Trueblood, *Lord Byron* (Boston: Twayne, 1977), 61.

28. Frank Luther Mott, *Golden Multitudes: The Story of Best Sellers in the United States* (New York: Macmillan, 1947), 304–5. His study of best sellers in America includes a year-by-year appendix, based on sales as a percentage of total population.

29. Mott, *Golden Multitudes*, 76–79.

30. *Brother Jonathan*, April 1843, cited in Mott, *Golden Multitudes*, 78.

31. Quoted in Jerome McGann, "The Text, the Poem, and the Problem of Historical Method," *New Literary History* 12.2 (Winter 1981): 273.

32. Charlotte Elizabeth [Tonna], *The Works of Charlotte Elizabeth* (New York: M. W. Dodd, 1849), 1:ii.

33. Mary Martha Sherwood, *The Nun* (Princeton, N.J.: Moore Baker, 1834), 175. (1st ed., London: Seeley and Sons, 1833.)

34. Sherwood, *Nun*, 125.

35. Sherwood, *Nun*, 141–42, 145.

36. Sherwood, *Nun*, 208.

37. Sherwood, *Nun*, 209.

38. Sherwood, *Nun*, 212.

39. Sherwood, *Nun*, 211.

40. Maria Monk, *Awful Disclosures of the Hotel Dieu Nunnery of Montreal* (New York: Maria Monk, 1836).

41. Mrs. A. G. Paddock, *The Fate of Madame La Tour; a Tale of Great Salt Lake* (New York: Fords, Howard, & Hulbert, 1881), 349–50; A New York Detective, "The Bradys among the Mormons—or—Secret Work in Salt Lake City," *Secret Service; Old and Young King Brady, Detectives*, no. 964 (July 13, 1917), 14.

42. See the survey of the genre by Richard VanDerBeets, *The Indian Captivity Narrative: An American Genre* (Lanham, Md.: University Press of America, 1984).

43. VanDerBeets, *Captivity Narrative*, 35.

44. The gothic novel did find an American home in altered form, of course. As early as 1798 Charles Brockden Brown had published *Wieland*, a novel combining physical terror with psychological horror. In this adapted genre, the medieval trappings of European gothic are replaced by the natural labyrinths and caves of an American wilderness.

45. Jane Tompkins, *Sensational Designs: The Cultural Work of American Fiction, 1790–1860* (New York: Oxford University Press, 1985), xii.

46. Tompkins, *Sensational Designs*, xi.
47. Tompkins, *Sensational Designs*, 45.
48. Tompkins, *Sensational Designs*, 46.
49. Welford D. Taylor, "Journalism and the Popular Press in Nineteenth-Century Fiction," unpublished ms, n.p., in author's possession.
50. David S. Reynolds, *Beneath the American Renaissance: The Subversive Imagination in the Age of Emerson and Melville* (New York: Knopf, 1988), 59, 323.
51. Taylor, "Popular Press," n.p.
52. Hatch, *Democratization*, 126.
53. According to Wordsworth's subjectivist poetics, identical texts would embody different values if their originary "passions" or "causes" were different. Meter, figures of speech, phraseology, even the emotion elicited by a work are all irrelevant to its value if the forms result from "mechanical adoption" rather than "passion excited by real events." Wordsworth, "Appendix," *Lyrical Ballads*, 761.
54. Orestes Brownson, *The Spirit Rapper* (Boston: Little, Brown, 1854), v.
55. David S. Reynolds, *Faith in Fiction: The Emergence of Religious Literature in America* (Cambridge, Mass.: Harvard University Press, 1981), 188.
56. George Lippard, *Memoirs of a Preacher* (1849; reprint, Philadelphia: Peterson, 1864), 63.
57. Lippard, *Memoirs*, 167.
58. Lippard, *Memoirs*, 166.
59. Lippard, *Memoirs*, 82.
60. Minnie M. Brashear, *Mark Twain, Son of Missouri* (Chapel Hill: University of North Carolina Press. 1934), 131–33.
61. See the numerous references in Howard Kerr, *Mediums and Spirit Rappers and Roaring Radicals: Spiritualism in American Literature, 1850–1900* (Urbana: University of Illinois Press, 1972).
62. Ruth A. McAdams, "The Shakers in American Fiction" (PhD diss., Texas Christian University, 1985), 58.
63. McAdams, "Shakers," 138. As McAdams points out, Hawthorne's change of heart has been discussed by a number of scholars.
64. Ray Allen Billington, *The Protestant Crusade: 1800–1860* (New York: Macmillan, 1938), 118.
65. From Luther's introduction to Robert Barnes's *History of the Popes*, written in 1536, cited in Billington, *Protestant Crusade*, 2–3.
66. Tonna, *Works*, 1:i.
67. Tonna, *Works*, 1:ii.
68. Tonna, *Works*, 1:ii.
69. Sherwood, *Nun*, 1.
70. Sherwood, *Nun*, 2.
71. See the aftermath described by Billington, *Protestant Crusade*, 99–108.
72. Sherwood, *Nun*, 3.
73. Sherwood, *Nun*, 326.
74. Sherwood, *Nun*, 2.
75. Monk, *Awful Disclosures*, 3, 5.
76. Orvilla S. Belisle, *The Arch Bishop; or, Romanism in the United States* (Philadelphia: William White Smith, 1854), xiii.
77. Belisle, *Arch Bishop*, 20.
78. De Los Lull, *Father Solon; or, the Helper Helped* (New York: Wilbur B. Ketcham, 1888), 3–4.

79. M. Quad [Charles Bertrand Lewis], *Bessie Baine: Or, the Mormon's Victim* (1876), in the *Novelette* no. 5 (Boston: G. W. Studley, 1898), 20.

80. Senator Aaron Harrison Cragin (N.H.), debate on the Cummins Bill, Cong. Globe, 41st Cong., 2nd Sess. (May 18, 1870), 3576–77.

81. Cragin, Cummins Bill, 3581.

82. Thomas Estes Noell (Mo.), "Equality of Suffrage," appendix to Cong. Globe, 39th Cong., 2nd Sess. (February 11 and 18, 1867), 111.

83. Paddock, *Madame La Tour*, 349–50.

84. "Against the Admission of Utah as a State. Memorial of Citizens of Utah, against the Admission of That Territory as a State," Cong. Globe, 42nd Cong., 2nd Sess. (May 6, 1872), 70.

85. "Against the Admission of Utah," 61.

86. "Against the Admission of Utah," 72.

87. "Against the Admission of Utah," 79.

CHAPTER 7

1. Rudolf Otto, *Idea of the Holy*, trans. J. W. Harvey, 2nd. ed. (London: Oxford University Press, 1950), 72.

2. All of Frothingham's books were published in 1854. According to the fifth-edition preface, his *Convent's Doom*, published with *The Haunted Convent*, sold "more than 40,000 copies...within ten days after publication in their original form"; they were "two of the most successful Convent stories of the day." Charles W. Frothingham, *The Convent's Doom: A Tale of Charlestown in 1834; and the Haunted Convent*, 5th ed. (Boston: Graves & Weston, 1854).

3. Frothingham, *Convent's Doom*, 7.

4. Frothingham, *Haunted Convent*, 22.

5. Frothingham, *Convent's Doom*, 6–7.

6. Orvilla S. Belisle, *The Arch Bishop; or, Romanism in the United States* (Philadelphia: William White Smith, 1854), xiii.

7. These figures can be derived from the tables on "Latter-day Saint Emigrants Sailing to America," *Deseret News 1989–90 Church Almanac* (Salt Lake City: Deseret, 1989), 166–68.

8. John Russell, *The Mormoness; or, the Trials of Mary Maverick* (Alton, Ill.: Courier Steam Press, 1853), 44.

9. Most of these can be found in Chad Flake's comprehensive *Mormon Bibliography, 1830–1930* (Salt Lake City: University of Utah, 1978).

10. This is the number given by Rebecca Cornwall Foster and Leonard J. Arrington in their article "Perpetuation of a Myth: Mormon Danites in Five Western Novels, 1840–90," *BYU Studies* 23.2 (Spring 1983): 147–65. Arrington lists fifty of them in his study co-authored with Jon Haupt, "Intolerable Zion: The Image of Mormonism in Nineteenth Century American Literature," *Western Humanities Review* 22 (Summer 1968): 243–60.

11. The Danites, or Avenging Angels, was the name of a Mormon self-defense group formed during the Missouri War. Sampson Avard, an officer in the organization, grew exasperated at the depredations of the anti-Mormons and began to reply with equal aggression, whereupon Joseph Smith withdrew support and disavowed Avard. Once captured, Avard defected and turned state's evidence against the Saints, providing fodder for many novelistic accounts of Mormon violence. See Foster and Arrington, "Perpetuation of a Myth."

12. *Illustrated Christian Weekly*, June 17, 1876, 299.

13. I use the term "Oriental" deliberately because it is the term that recurs in the period literature I am citing, and reflects the stereotypical nature of nineteenth- and early twentieth-century categories of understanding imposed upon both Asian culture and Mormons. Arrington and Haupt allude briefly to this stereotype as "the lustful Turk," one of seven stereotypes they discuss in "Intolerable Zion."

14. Russell, *Mormoness*, 38.

15. As Russell's son recorded, "Father heard from them the heartrending stories and barbarity of the cut-throat Missourians. Hence came the story of 'Mary Maverick, the Mormoness.'" S. G. Russell, "Prof. John Russell," in *Transactions of the Illinois State Historical Society for the Year 1901* (Springfield, Ill.: Phillips Bros., 1901), 103.

16. Russell, *Mormoness*, 55.

17. Russell, *Mormoness*, 39.

18. Russell, Mormoness, 42.

19. Russell, *Mormoness*, 42.

20. Russell, *Mormoness*, 53.

21. Russell, *Mormoness*, 49.

22. [Burt L. Standish], "Frank Merriwell among the Mormons: Or, the Lost Tribes of Israel," *Tip Top Weekly,* June19, 1897, 2.

23. Standish, "Frank Merriwell," 9.

24. Standish, "Frank Merriwell," 24.

25. Standish, "Frank Merriwell," 26.

26. Russell, *Mormoness*, 55, 69, 71.

27. Russell, *Mormoness*, 68–69.

28. Russell, *Mormoness*, 69.

29. Charles Heber Clark [Max Adeler], *The Tragedy of Thompson Dunbar, a Tale of Salt Lake City* (Philadelphia: Stoddart, 1879), 11, 16.

30. Mary Wollstonecraft, *A Vindication of the Rights of Women* (London, 1792; New York: Norton, 1988), 19.

31. Senator Aaron Harrison Cragin (N.H.), debate on the Cummins Bill, Cong. Globe, 41st Cong., 2nd Sess. (May 18, 1870), 3576–77.

32. Cragin, Cummins Bill, 3577.

33. Sir Arthur Conan Doyle, *A Study in Scarlet* (London 1888; New York: Burt, n.d.), 129; James Oliver Curwood, *The Courage of Captain Plum* (Indianapolis: Bobbs-Merrill, 1908), 261.

34. Sydney Bell, *Wives of the Prophet* (New York: Macaulay, 1935), iv; E. D. Howe, *History of Mormonism* (Painesville, N.Y.: E. D. Howe, 1834), 12.

35. Jennie Switzer [Bartlett], *Elder Northfield's Home: Or, Sacrificed on the Mormon Altar* (New York: J. Howard Brown, 1882), 115.

36. Clark, *Thompson Dunbar*, 10.

37. Clark, *Thompson Dunbar*, 11.

38. For a comprehensive study—and critique—of the Mormonism/Islam analogy see Arnold H. Green and Lawrence P. Goldrup, "Joseph Smith, an American Muhammad? An Essay on the Perils of Historical Analogy," *Dialogue: A Journal of Mormon Thought* 6.1 (1971): 46–58.

39. Edward Said, *Orientalism* (New York: Pantheon, 1978), 150.

40. Doyle, *Study in Scarlet*, 128. Some years after this rather unfavorable portrait of the Mormons, he visited Salt Lake on a lecture tour. The novel, he remarked, "could have been easily brought up to prejudice opinion against me, but as a matter of fact no allusion was made to it save by one Gentile doctor, who wrote and

urged me to make some public apology. This of course I could not do, as the facts
were true enough." *Our Second American Adventure* (Boston: Little, Brown, 1924),
86–87.
41. Doyle, *Study in Scarlet*, 148.
42. Standish, "Frank Merriwell," 15.
43. Curwood, *Captain Plum*, 70.
44. Switzer, *Elder Northfield's*, 42.
45. Switzer, *Elder Northfield's*, 85–86.
46. Zane Grey, *Riders of the Purple Sage* (New York: Harper, 1912), 13.
47. Curwood, *Captain Plum*, 97.
48. "History of Joseph Smith," *Times and Seasons* 6.5 (March 15, 1845): 832–33.
49. Dane Coolidge, *The Fighting Danites* (New York: Dutton, 1934), 37–38.
50. Jack London, *Star Rover* (1914; New York: Arcadia House, 1950), 135.
51. Standish, "Frank Merriwell," 9.
52. Coolidge, *Fighting Danites*, 101. Indeed, the Native Americans did see Mormons
and "Americans" differently. The former enjoyed generally amicable relations with
Native Americans. This history of their "sympathies for, and kindness to, the poor
Indians around [them]," combined with a kinship born of shared persecution,
even led the artist George Catlin to advise Brigham Young to unite with the Indian nations in a "grand fraternity" to defy the power of the federal government.
Letter, May 8, 1870, cited in Larry C. Coates, "George Catlin, Brigham Young, and
the Plains Indians," *BYU Studies* 17.1 (Winter 1976): 115–16.
53. Warren Foote, *Autobiography of Warren Foote* (Mesa, Ariz.: Dale Arnold Foote,
1997), 1:96–97.
54. Manuscript History of the Church, D-1, 1431–32, LDS Archives.
55. Stanley Ivins, "Notes on Mormon Polygamy," *Western Humanities Review* 10 (Summer 1956): 238–39.
56. *Surgeon General's Office, Statistical Report on the Sickness and Mortality in the Army
of the United States...from January, 1855 to January, 1860* (Washington, D.C.:
George W. Bowman, 1860), 301–2.
57. *Harvard Encyclopedia of American Ethnic Groups*, ed. Stephan Thernstrom (Cambridge, Mass.: Harvard University Press, 1980), 720.
58. "The Mormons: Who and What They Are," *Phrenological Journal* 52.1 (1871): 38.
59. "Mormons: Who and What They Are," 38, 44.
60. *How to Read Character: A New Illustrated Hand-Book of Phrenology and Physiognomy*
(New York: Samuel R. Wells, 1874), 31. For an interesting survey of the reciprocal interest of Mormons and phrenologists see Davis Bitton and Gary L. Bunker,
"Phrenology among the Mormons," *Dialogue: A Journal of Mormon Thought* 9.1
(Spring 1974): 43–61.
61. John C. Bennett, *The History of the Saints; or an Exposé of Joe Smith and Mormonism*, 3rd ed. (Boston: Leland and Whiting, 1842), 180–86.
62. Mark Twain, *Roughing It* (Hartford: American Publishing, 1872), 101.
63. *The Portable Oscar Wilde*, ed. Richard Aldington and Stanley Weintraub (New York:
Penguin, 1981), 705.
64. Russell, *Mormoness*, 38.
65. *Deseret News 1995–96 Church Almanac* (Salt Lake City: Deseret News, 1994),
418.
66. The linking of Mesmerism and Mormonism has been pointed out by Gary L. Bunker and Davis Bitton. They found the connection alleged, in one form or another,
by writers of popular fiction, a medical consultant for the *New York Weekly Herald*,

a Mormon phrenologist, and even Smith's biographer, Fawn Brodie. Their explanation of motive is twofold: the connection "offered a naturalistic explanation of Joseph Smith's success" and had the advantage of discrediting two "delusions" simultaneously by bringing them into contact with one another. See "Mesmerism and Mormonism," *BYU Studies* 15.2 (Spring 1975): 146–70.

67. Switzer, *Elder Northfield's*, 230.
68. Grey, *Riders*, 274.
69. Maria Ward, *Female Life among the Mormons: A Narrative of Many Years' Experience among the Mormons....* (London: Routledge, 1855), 38.
70. Ward, *Female Life*, 9.
71. Ward, *Female Life*, 230.
72. *New York Herald*, May 10, 1842 (extra ed.).
73. *New York Herald*, April 3, 1842.
74. Curwood, *Captain Plum*, 129.
75. Curwood, *Captain Plum*, 165.
76. Coolidge, *Fighting Danites*, 182.
77. Standish, "Frank Merriwell," 12.
78. Coolidge, *Fighting Danites*, 131–32.
79. Curwood, *Captain Plum*, 80.
80. Theodore Winthrop, *John Brent* (New York: Lovell, 1862), 92.
81. Grey, *Riders*, 159.
82. Switzer, *Elder Northfield's*, 64.
83. [Prentiss Ingraham], "Buffalo Bill and the Danite Kidnappers; or, the Green River Massacre," *Buffalo Bill Stories: A Weekly Devoted to Border History,* February 1, 1902, 2.
84. Ingraham, "Buffalo Bill," 9.
85. Coolidge, *Fighting Danites*, 142
86. Grey, *Riders*, 277.
87. Grey, *Riders*, 277–78.
88. Stevenson's treatment is perhaps unique in that he is treating the stereotype with the levity he thought it deserved. Though not known as a Mormon sympathizer, he at least found more that was mockworthy in the caricature than in the subject. Robert Louis Stevenson, *The Dynamiter* (New York: Scribner, 1925).
89. Mrs. W. A. King, *Duncan Davidson; a Story of Polygamy* (Philadelphia: Dorrance, 1928), 27.
90. Young recounts this initial sentiment in a speech delivered in the Salt Lake Tabernacle. *Journal of Discourses*, G. D. Watt, reporter (Liverpool and London: F. D. and S. W. Richards et al., 1854–1886; reprint, Salt Lake City: n.p., 1967), 3:266. See Louis Kern, for example, who refers to the "burden of Celestial marriage" under which "Mormon males chafed" and which for women "was even more trying." *An Ordered Love: Sex Roles and Sexuality in Victorian Utopias—the Shakers, the Mormons, and the Oneida Community* (Chapel Hill: University of North Carolina Press, 1981), 174–75.
91. Richard S. Van Wagoner, *Mormon Polygamy: A History* (Salt Lake City: Signature, 1989), 92–93.
92. Kern, *Ordered Love*, 191.
93. Van Wagoner, *Mormon Polygamy*, 92–93.
94. Van Wagoner, *Mormon Polygamy*, 92. For more on the subject of polygamous divorces see Eugene E. Campbell and Bruce L. Campbell, "Divorce among Mormon Polygamists: Extent and Explanations," *Utah Historical Quarterly* 46 (Winter 1978): 4–23.

95. Kern, *Ordered Love*, 203.
96. Ralph Waldo Emerson, *The Journals and Miscellaneous Notebooks*, ed. Susan Sutton Smith and Harrison Hayford (Cambridge, Mass.: Harvard University Press, 1978), 14:204–5.
97. M. Quad [Charles Bertrand Lewis], *Bessie Baine: Or, the Mormon's Victim* (1876), in the *Novelette* no. 5 (Boston: G. W. Studley, 1898), 13.
98. [William Loring Spencer], *Salt-Lake Fruit: A Latter-Day Romance* (Boston: Rand, Avery, 1884), iii, v.
99. Standish, "Frank Merriwell," 8.
100. Curwood, *Captain Plum*, 104–5.
101. Mrs. T. B. H. Stenhouse, *"Tell It All": The Story of a Life's Experience in Mormonism* (Hartford, Conn.: Worthington, 1874), vi.
102. Curwood, *Captain Plum*, 279–80.
103. Switzer, *Elder Northfield's*, 261–62.
104. B. H. Roberts, *A Comprehensive History of the Church of Jesus Christ of Latter-day Saints* (Provo, Utah: Brigham Young University Press, 1965), 6:185.
105. Roberts, *History*, 6:186n. This number was cited by a congressman from Iowa in the House of Representatives on October 4, 1888.
106. Philip S. Robinson, *Sinners and Saints* (Boston, 1883; reprint, New York: AMS Press, 1971), 98, 103–4.
107. Robinson, *Sinners and Saints*, 69.
108. Louis Sherwin, "The Morals of Mormons" (June 1917), in *The Smart Set Anthology of World Famous Authors*, ed. Burton Rascoe and Groff Conklin (New York: Halcyon, 1934), 167.
109. Switzer, *Elder Northfield's*, 72.
110. Switzer, *Elder Northfield's*, 3.
111. Church membership by 1882 had reached 146,000 (*Deseret 1989–90 Church News Almanac*, 204). Obviously, the vast majority of this influx was by way of conversion, not birth. Therefore, in the early years of Mormonism especially, most members would have been reared in other religious and cultural settings.
112. As early as 1842 in the Mormon capital of Nauvoo, a Lyceum debate was held on the question "Should Females be educated to the same extent of Males?" Minutes are not available, but evidence of the consensus reached is pretty strong. According to county records, over half the students enrolled in Nauvoo's schools were female. Brigham Young was on record as saying "We believe that women…should…study law or physics or become good bookkeepers and be able to do the business in any counting house." Slightly earlier, a witness to the migration of Mormons into Illinois had observed that "the women were generally well educated and as a rule were quite intelligent." In fact, it has been suggested that the Mormons' liberal views on the equality of the sexes were in part responsible for hostility to the church in Illinois. For a fuller discussion of the subject see George Givens, *In Old Nauvoo: Everyday Life in the City of Joseph* (Salt Lake City: Deseret, 1990), 227–36.
113. Switzer, *Elder Northfield's*, 3–4.
114. Winthrop, *John Brent*, 177, 164.
115. Winthrop, *John Brent*, 185.
116. Winthrop, *John Brent*, 313.
117. Stephen Greenblatt, *Renaissance Self-Fashioning: From More to Shakespeare* (Chicago: University of Chicago Press, 1980), 9.

CHAPTER 8

1. "Intimidation, Wizardry Marked Tiny Cult's Rule," *Richmond Times-Dispatch*, March 3, 1993, A8.
2. *Molko v. Holy Spirit Association for the Unification of World Christianity*, 252 California Reporter (Supreme Court of California, 1989), 122–56. That case cites numerous precedents as well.
3. *Meroni v. Holy Spirit Association for the Unification of World Christianity*, 480 New York Supplement, 2nd Series (Supreme Court of New York, 1984), 707.
4. See, for instance, Dick Anthony, "Pseudoscience and Minority Religions: An Evaluation of the Brainwashing Theories of Jean-Marie," *Social Justice Research* 12.4 (1999): 421–56.
5. *Molko v. Holy Spirit*, 146–47.
6. Meredith B. McGuire, *Religion: The Social Context* (Belmont, Calif.: Wadsworth, 1987), 68. The study cited in David Bromley and Anson D. Shupe, "The Tnevnoc Cult," *Sociological Analysis* 40.4 (Winter 1979): 361–66.
7. Harold Bloom, *The American Religion: The Emergence of a Post-Christian Nation* (New York: Simon & Schuster, 1992), 116. There is some irony here in Bloom's echo of the surgeon general's 1858 report that alluded to "the Mormon expression of countenance," cited in the previous chapter.
8. Bloom, *American Religion*, 108.
9. Bloom, *American Religion*, 94.
10. Bloom, *American Religion*, 270.
11. Rodney Stark, "The Rise of a New World Faith," *Review of Religious Research* 26.1 (September 1984): 18–19.
12. A recent example is the full-length, exposé-style treatment *The Mormon Corporate Empire* by John Heinerman and Anson Shupe (Boston: Beacon Press, 1985).
13. Heinerman and Shupe, *Corporate Empire*, 154.
14. Klaus J. Hansen, *Quest for Empire: The Political Kingdom of God and the Council of Fifty in Mormon History* (East Lansing: Michigan State University Press, 1967), 247.
15. Brent Scowcroft was President Bush's national security adviser, and Roger Blaine Porter his chief assistant for economic and domestic policy.
16. Merlin B. Brinkerhoff, Jeffrey C. Jacob, and Marlene M. Mackie, "Mormonism and the Moral Majority Make Strange Bedfellows? An Exploratory Critique," *Review of Religious Research* 28.3 (March 1987): 236, 240.
17. These comments were part of a letter intended for public distribution, written by Rhonda Abrams, regional director of the ADL to Dr. Richard Lindsay, director of public communications of the Church of Jesus Christ of Latter-day Saints, May 25, 1984.
18. The analysis was included as an "Advisory Report to the Religious Executives of Arizona," published in the NCCJ's newsletter, *Programs in Pluralism* 2 (March–April 1984): 2.
19. Michael Austin, "Mormons in Popular Literature Bibliography, 1979–2000," www.adherents.com/lit/austin_biblio.html, February 10, 2012.
20. Jennifer Blake, *Golden Fancy* (New York: Fawcett, 1980), cover blurb.
21. Tony Hillerman, *The Thief of Time* (New York: Harper & Row, 1988), 196.
22. Martin E. Marty, "Explaining the Rise of Fundamentalism," *Chronicle of Higher Education*, October 28,1992, A56.

23. Terry J. Christlieb, letter to the editor, *Chronicle of Higher Education*, December 2, 1992, B5. The criticism was a response to Marty's October essay on fundamentalism.
24. Gerald Petievich and anonymous critic describing Irvine's work, cited in blurb to Robert Irvine's *Called Home* (New York, St. Martin's, 1991).
25. Robert Irvine, *The Angel's Share* (New York: St. Martin's, 1989), 105, 107.
26. Robert Irvine, *Gone to Glory* (New York: St. Martin's, 1990), 135.
27. Irvine, *Called Home*, 134.
28. Irvine, *Called Home*, 14.
29. Cleo Jones, *Prophet Motive* (New York: St. Martin's, 1984), 73.
30. Jones, *Prophet Motive*, 195.
31. Jones, *Prophet Motive*, 164.
32. Irvine, *Called Home*, 134.
33. Jones, *Prophet Motive*, 73.
34. Jones, *Prophet Motive*, 192.
35. Irvine, *Gone to Glory*, 25.
36. Irvine, *Angel's Share*, 187.
37. Jones, *Prophet Motive*, 26.
38. Jones, *Prophet Motive*, 41.
39. Jones, *Prophet Motive*, 185–86.
40. Jones, *Prophet Motive*, jacket blurb.
41. Dan Amira, "Newt Gingrich Says Affairs Make Him 'More Normal' Than Mitt 'Only Has Sex with His Wife' Romney," *New York*, January 24, 2012, http://nymag.com/daily/intel/2012/01/gingrich-normal-affairs-romney.html.
42. L. E. Modesitt Jr., *The Parafaith War* (New York: Tor, 1996), 6.
43. Bloom, *American Religion*, 80–81, 88.
44. Jones, *Prophet Motive*, 73.
45. Tom Clancy, *The Hunt for Red October* (Annapolis: Naval Institute Press, 1984), 200.
46. Tom Clancy, *Clear and Present Danger* (New York: Putnam's Sons, 1989), 480.
47. In October 1995, LDS president Gordon B. Hinckley announced that "our statisticians tell me that some time in February of 1996, just a few months from now, there will be more members of the Church outside the United States than in the United States." *Deseret News Archives*, October 7, 1995.
48. According to a report by the Population Reference Bureau, "The 'Ozzie and Harriet' model of 1950's television fame—a breadwinning husband and a wife who stayed home with the children—once was the dominant pattern in America. Now, one in five married couples with children fits in." *Lynchburg News and Daily Advance*, August 28, 1992.
49. Frances Lang, "The Mormon Empire," *Ramparts* 10 (September 1971): 40.
50. John le Carré, *The Russia House* (New York: Bantam, 1990), 211.
51. David Savran, "Tony Kushner Considers the Longstanding Problems of Virtue and Happiness," *American Theatre*, October 1994, 102–3.
52. Tony Kushner, *Angels in America*. In part two, "Perestroika," there is even a parodic reenactment of an episode from Joseph Smith's history, in which he hid the golden plates under a hearthstone in the family residence.
53. Cristine Hutchison-Jones, "Center and Periphery: Mormons and American Culture in Tony Kushner's *Angels in America*," in *Peculiar Portrayals: Mormons on the Page, Stage, and Screen*, ed. Mark T. Decker and Michael Austin (Logan: Utah State University Press, 2010), 6.
54. The characterization of the play's moral comes from Hutchison-Jones but is pointedly evident to any viewer (11).

55. These and other examples are given by David Gates, "White Male Paranoia," *Newsweek*, March 29, 1993, 49.
56. A *Time* editorial made this same point a few decades ago: "The assimilation of Hispanics is news because two allied groups of political operators are trying to pretend that it isn't happening. Leaders of ethnic communities fear the success of their communities because it makes special favors unnecessary and deprives leaders of their status as favor brokers." Richard Brookhiser, "The Melting Pot Is Still Simmering," *Time*, March 1, 1993, 72.
57. John Russell, *The Mormoness; or, the Trials of Mary Maverick* (Alton, Ill.: Courier Steam Press, 1853), 55, 69, 71.
58. "Nuclear Meltdown," *Picket Fences*, CBS, January 22, 1993.
59. Jay Newman, *Foundations of Religious Tolerance* (Toronto: University of Toronto Press, 1982), 12.
60. Reid Neilson provides a comprehensive overview of the week, and its contradictory outcomes, in *Exhibiting Mormonism: The Latter-day Saints and the Chicago World's Fair* (New York: Oxford University Press, 2011).
61. *Time*, June 22, 1959.
62. Charles Dickens, "In the Name of the Prophet—Smith!" *Household Words*, July 19, 1851, 385.
63. John Ben Haws, "The Mormon Image in the American Mind: Shaping Perception of Latter-day Saints, 1968–2008" (PhD diss., University of Utah, 2010), 559.
64. Michael Otterson, "A Latter-day Saint View of Book of Mormon Musical," *Washington Post* blog *On Faith*, April 14, 2011. Cited in Haws, "Mormon Image," 559.
65. Haws, "Mormon Image," 559.
66. Presidential politics is not the only arena where a Mormon candidate can panic the electorate. In the 1994 elections both Senator Ted Kennedy of Massachusetts, in his reelection contest against Mitt Romney, and Representative L. F. Payne of Virginia, in his race against challenger George Landrith, publicly exploited the Mormon affiliation of their opponent. The *Boston Globe*, the Catholic Archdiocese of Boston, and other organizations protested the Kennedy tactics. See Daniel Allott, "Ted Kennedy's Anti-Mormon Moment," *American Spectator*, May 23, 2012, http://spectator.org/archives/2012/05/23/ted-kennedys-anti-mormon-momen/1. In the Virginia race, Payne's polling firm went so far as to circulate campaign literature that said, "George Landrith is a Mormon" and then proceeded to ask voters if his background raised any doubts—"serious doubts, minor doubts, or no doubts." See "Payne Survey Angers Landrith," *Lynchburg News and Daily Advance*, September 28, 1994.
67. Haws, "Mormon Image," 547.
68. Kathleen Flake argues that the important enduring compromise made at the turn of the century was not Mormonism's acquiescence to cultural rather than religious status, but its agreement to conform to Protestant religious forms. See her *Politics of Religious Identity: The Seating of Senator Reed Smoot, Mormon Apostle* (Chapel Hill: University of North Carolina Press, 2004).
69. Jacob Weisberg, "Romney's Religion: A Mormon President? No Way," *Slate*, December 20, 2006, www.slate.com/articles/news_and_politics/the_big_idea/2006/12/romneys_religion.html.
70. Most prominent in this labeling was Robert Jeffress, who made the charge at the Values Voter Summit in Washington, D.C., in October 2011.
71. Quoted in Haws, "Mormon Image," 496.
72. Background Briefing Broadcast, http://ianmasters.com/content/january-19-real-winners-election-mitts-first-amendment-problems-end-christian-right.

73. "There Is a Dark Side to Mormonism," *New York Times*, February 1, 2012, www.nytimes.com/roomfordebate/2012/01/30/what-is-it-about-mormons/there-is-a-dark-side-to-mormonism.

74. Maureen Down, "Anne Frank, a Mormon?" *New York Times*, October 18, 2011.

75. Jonathan S. Tobin, "Mormon PR Campaign Fights Last Socially Acceptable Hate," *Commentary*, November 18, 2011, www.commentarymagazine.com/2011/11/18/mormon-pr-campaign-religious-hatred/.

76. Tricia Erickson made these charges on CNN's *In the Arena*, August 3, 2011. She cited Ed Decker for the allegations of child sexual abuse. Reported by Kevin D. Williamson, "An American Gospel," *National Review Online*, April 9, 2012, www.nationalreview.com/articles/295305/american-gospel-kevin-d-williamson?pg=2.

77. "Transcript: JFK's Speech on His Religion," www.npr.org/templates/story/story.php?storyId=16920600.

78. Damon Linker, "The Big Test," *New Republic*, December 21, 2006.

79. Linker, "Big Test."

80. Jon Krakauer, *Under the Banner of Heaven: A Story of Violent Faith* (New York: Doubleday, 2003).

81. Lafferty was so evaluated by Xavier Amador, a clinical psychologist. Pamela Manson, "Lawyers Request Mental Competency Hearing for Ron Lafferty," *Salt Lake Tribune*, December 11, 2009, www.sltrib.com/news/ci_13979951.

82. Krakauer, *Under the Banner*, xxiii, 294.

83. Russell, *Mormoness*, 44.

84. *The Colbert Report*, August 10, 2011, www.colbertnation.com/the-colbert-report-videos/394360/august-10–2011/yaweh-or-no-way – – mormons – -god-s-poll-numbers.

INDEX

CPSIA information can be obtained
at www.ICGtesting.com
Printed in the USA
LVHW010746090119
603223LV00002B/74/P

9 780199 933808